# Law's Metaphors:
# Interrogating Languages of
# Law, Justice, and Legitimacy

T0355426

*Edited by*

**David Gurnham**

**WILEY** Blackwell

This edition first published 2016
Editorial organization © 2016 Cardiff University Law School
Chapters © 2016 by the chapter author

Blackwell Publishing was acquired by John Wiley & Sons in February 2007. Blackwell's
publishing programme has been merged with Wiley's global Scientific, Technical, and Medical
business to form Wiley-Blackwell.

*Editorial Offices*
350 Main Street, Malden, MA 02148-5020, USA
9600 Garsington Road, Oxford OX4 2DQ, UK

For details of our global editorial offices, for customer services, and for information about how to
apply for permission to reuse the copyright material in this book please see our website at
www.wiley.com/wiley-blackwell

*Registered Office*
John Wiley & Sons Ltd, The Atrium, Southern Gate, Chichester, West Sussex PO19 8SQ.

*Library of Congress Cataloging-in-Publication Data*
Names: Law's metaphors (2015 : Southampton, England) | Gurnham, David,
    editor. | Socio-Legal Studies Association, sponsoring body.
Title: Law's metaphors : interrogating languages of law, justice, and
    legitimacy / edited by David Gurnham.
Description: Oxford, UK ; Malden, MA, USA : Wiley Blackwell, 2016. | Includes
    papers presented as the seminar "Law's methaphors" held in September 25,
    2015 at the School of Law, University of Southampton.–ECIP Introduction.
    | Includes bibliographical references and index.
Identifiers: LCCN 2016003723 | ISBN 9781119266822 (pbk. : alk. paper)
Subjects: LCSH: Law–Language–Congresses.
Classification: LCC K487.L36 L39 2016 | DDC 340/.14–dc23
LC record available at http://lccn.loc.gov/2016003723

A catalogue record for this title is available from the British Library.

ISBN: 978-1-119-26682-2

Set in the United Kingdom by Godiva Publishing Services Ltd
Printed in Singapore by C.O.S. Printers Pte Ltd

# Contents

JOURNAL OF LAW AND SOCIETY
VOLUME 43, NUMBER 1, MARCH 2016
ISSN: 0263-323X, pp. 1–7

# Law's Metaphors: Introduction

## David Gurnham*

Having only recently begun to address the subject of metaphor directly in my own work,[1] it struck me that a collection of new essays exploring how metaphors shape notions of law and justice would be a timely contribution to interdisciplinary legal studies. For me, part of the mysterious appeal of metaphor is that, while technically understood to be a description that is figurative rather than literal (and hence a description of one thing in terms of something else), it also exceeds this definition, operating somewhere *between* the literal and the figurative. This has to do with its etymological roots in the Greek *metaphora* (a transfer, or a carrying over) and from *meta-pherein* (over, across + to carry, bear).[2] In attempting to define metaphor in literal terms therefore, we are immediately surrounded by images that evoke a sense of meaning in motion, slippery, and on the move. Metaphor *is* ... a boat, a ferry, a bridge, carrying a freight of meaning between one conceptual shore and another.

It should be no surprise to find that these mental images come to mind readily, since as has been observed elsewhere, metaphors disguise themselves as such and embed themselves deeply within language by substituting something else rather than merely offering a comparison. We might say that language is thus inherently metaphorical, or to put it another way, the literal and the metaphoric are not separate from each other, since what we might

* School of Law, University of Southampton, University Road, Southampton SO17 1BJ, England
d.gurnham@soton.ac.uk

Grateful thanks to the Journal for financially supporting the 'Law's Metaphors' seminar at Southampton in September 2015 and to the SLSA for supplying the larger part of the funds for that event; also, to the many friends and colleagues who assisted in reviewing the articles; finally, to the scholars who contributed the articles.

 1 D. Gurnham, *Crime, Desire and Law's Unconscious: Law, Literature and Culture* (2014) ch. 4.
 2 R.K. Barnhart (ed.), *Chambers Dictionary of Etymology* (1999).

1

ordinarily think of as a literal meaning might turn out to be a result of some forgotten metaphoric substitution. Embracing this view of (legal) language as a sea of metaphors, this issue presents eight articles that in different and divergent ways calls attention to metaphors used *in* law (for example, causation conceived in terms of a *chain*), metaphors *for* law (the failings of the court of chancery imagined by Dickens in terms of *fog everywhere*), as well as to law itself as metaphor for other things (collected anxieties about race, religion, and national identity represented in French law banning the wearing of the niqab).[3]

Metaphors constitute what one of the contributors to this collection calls a 'hidden grammar of being', often able to evade notice due to having become 'conventional or idiomatic', and hence quite different from other linguistic devices that may be used to confer meaning much more conspicuously.[4] **Angela Condello** sets out to interrogate this quality of metaphor, and investigates the relationship between metaphor and analogy. The latter is usually considered a near-relative of metaphor (working on the basis of resemblance rather than substitution), but Condello uses Aristotle's *Rhetoric* to show how the development of the common law generates metaphors on the basis of analogizing to existing metaphors. To take one of Condello's examples, an individual owning land under which oil is discovered to be flowing may not be said to own that oil because it is analogous to a stream: in both cases the metaphor of a wild animal – which cannot be owned unless and until it is reduced to captivity – serves to demonstrate the relevant legal relationship and status. This nesting of analogy and metaphor is a theme also developed by **Nicola Lacey**, arguing that the metaphor of proportionality – which in legal discourse evokes a sense of natural order, reason, and inherent fairness – demonstrates how analogy (the comparison of two different things) is central to metaphorical construction. We can find this method of construction in legal scholarship more widely, for example, Gary Watt's reading of legal maxims such as 'equity follows law', situating equity to law as a shepherd is to his sheep, not passively trailing them but helpfully 'steering' them.[5]

If metaphor is primarily thought of as a poetic device then we might suppose that placing it at the centre of attention in a law journal necessitates a 'law and literature' approach. However, something that I think is borne out by the articles collected in this issue is that such a supposition would be mistaken, and that in fact *any* attempt to understand law in terms of its language must contend with metaphor at some level. If (as Aristotle puts it) metaphor means 'the application of a word that belongs to another thing',[6]

---

3 Please note that these examples are given to illustrate the ways in which metaphor and law intersect and do not represent the themes of the articles in this issue.
4 M. LeBaron in this collection, pp. 146–7.
5 G. Watt, *Equity Stirring: the story of justice beyond law* (2009) 102–3.
6 Aristotle, *Poetics*, trans. D.A. Russell and ed. S. Halliwell (1995) 21.7.

2

then the skill of using metaphor lies in being able to perceive 'the similarity in dissimilars'.[7] Perhaps because our attention as lawyers is focused otherwise than on the language itself, the ubiquity of law's metaphors may be less immediately apparent than those to be found in poetry. But this arguably only underlines the importance of our being aware of how the meaning of things in law gets 'carried over' by its metaphors: *from* where meaning gets carried and *to* where it ends up. We need to be aware, for example, of how this works at the level of the foundations of law: for example, the 'social contract' imagines society under the law in terms of an actual agreement in which parties make specific compromises; the 'body politic' imagines the authority of the state as the non-mortal body of the monarch – 'that cannot be seen or handled' – representing the people as a whole.[8] Moreover we need similarly to attend to the way that metaphors populate common legal terminologies:

> the *sources* of law, ... legal *grounds* in argumentation, ... its disciplinary *boundaries*, ... the legal *corpus*, with its *long arm*, its equity *conscience*, its *blind* justice, even its fully developed, organismic *constitution*.[9]

The reasons why such awareness is important may be obvious to those used to working within legal language, but it is worth spelling out here. Hegel argued that the task of constructing and making practical use of metaphor is not so much one of *perception* as *invention*, since it is thanks to the 'wit' of the poet, that his or her chosen substitute seems natural when in fact no necessary connection exists.[10] Why should we be so drawn to the metaphor of the contract as a means for conceiving of the origins of a society of people governed by law, when other metaphors might as usefully do? It is in exposing and exploiting this cultural contingency that the opportunity for critical reflection on law's metaphors will very often lie, as Nicola Lacey points out with respect to the metaphor of proportionality being realized not in some divine natural order but in particular events and in the development of particular institutions interested in affirming their power, legitimacy, and necessity. How are we even to begin to comprehend the idea that law has 'authority' and that it may 'rule', if not by translating or substituting those things in our minds for 'symbols, allegories, metaphors'[11] that we can relate to in physical terms? And what interests govern the precise translations and substitutions that this leads to? This is an insight of general importance for legal theory and for how we conceive the relationship between law and society.

---

7 id., 23.5.
8 E.H. Kantorowicz, *The King's Two Bodies: A Study in Mediaeval Political Theology* (1957) 7–9 (quoting Plowden).
9 A. Philippopoulos-Mihalopoulos in this collection, p. 49, original emphasis.
10 G.W.F. Hegel, *Aesthetics, Lectures on Fine Art, Vol. 1*, tr. T.M. Knox (1975) 407.
11 P. Goodrich, *Law in the Courts of Love: Literature and Other Minor Jurisprudences* (1996) 143.

If metaphors are comparisons in which the comparison itself (or the fact that a comparison was ever made) is in some way obscured, replaced or even *supressed* by the substitutive character of metaphor, then it follows that becoming skilled at using metaphors means learning to manipulate how people understand things, framing concepts according to a particular point of reference, and muting other possible ways of making sense of them. This method for supressing one meaning in favour of another is precisely the point of metaphors that presents law as *enclosed* within particular spaces and processes such as courtrooms, the trial, lawyers' offices, and parliament, argues **Andreas Philippopoulos-Mihalopoulos**. In his article, Philippopoulos-Mihalopoulos suggests that law's claim to be abstract, objective, rational, and detached from the material bodies that make up its operations and effects, is central to the way it justifies itself and its special status for us (its subjects). He argues that law's sometimes clumsy enclosing and legitimizing metaphors (for example, the words 'Dieu et Mon Droit' strategically displayed in courtrooms) are deployed in legal rhetoric in order to draw our attention away from its 'materiality': that is to say, from the reality that 'life is thick with law', and that, in fact, law spills over and beyond its enclosures. If this is to imply (as Philippopoulos-Mihalopoulos claims) that law in general is itself a metaphor for some kind of failure, then this idea is developed from a literary jurisprudential perspective by **Ian Ward**. Ward considers law's treatment in the English 'sensation' novel of the nineteenth century, finding law as such to be curiously both present and absent. Sensation novels such as Anthony Trollope's *The Eustace Diamonds* channelled the public's thirst for tales of crime and sexual scandal but also its anxiety about the governing institutions' impotence in bringing offenders and transgressors to justice. Instead, argues Ward, the novel seemed to take up the role of 'regulatory surrogate'. Law therefore metaphorizes a broader social malaise and loss of confidence in the natural durability and permanence of an ordered society.

The opportunity for law's metaphors to affect perceptions and beliefs without being noticed has very real consequences for its subjects. Esther Peeren sounds a note of caution when she warns that: 'If repeated and con-ventionalized, metaphors can define certain individuals or groups as superior and dispossess others by establishing or reinforcing negative stereotypes.'[12] The potential for law's metaphors to be violent and constraining (both symbolically and also by legitimizing actual violence) is represented for some legal scholars in the very image of Lady Justice herself. Goodrich has suggested that, rather than upholding the highest values of truth and justice, 'the blindfold on the face of justice seems plausibly to have also benefitted men through the limitation, mutilation ... or sensory deprivation of

---

12 E. Peeren, *The Spectral Metaphor: Living Ghosts and the Agency of Invisibility* (2014) 5.

4

women.'[13] Legal measures to variously identify, segregate, and punish those considered most dangerous or undesirable are made plausible by metaphors evoking vermin ('crime-*infested* neighbourhoods'), disease ('crime *spreading*'), and crawling insects ('migrants *swarming*'), though the third of these at least is for now arguably too conspicuous to be particularly effective as a framing device, as David Cameron discovered last summer.[14]

Riffing on Lakoff and Johnson's famous description of 'metaphors we live *by*',[15] Peeren refers to metaphors that 'certain people (are made to) live *as*, ... through which they are made sense of and come to make sense of themselves.'[16] For Peeren, the *spectral* metaphor accounts for what she describes as the living death endured by illegal migrants – persons that must make themselves invisible to the authorities and occupying the lowliest of jobs are very often rendered invisible to people they serve as well. In this vein, **Anne Quéma**'s article poses a question with profound implications that echo through two and a quarter centuries of legal history, namely: how could it be that the case of *Gregson* v. *Gilbert* (1783), at the centre of which was a decision by a ship's captain to have 130 African slaves thrown into the Caribbean Sea in order to conserve supplies, concerned the question of compensation for the loss of insured goods rather than murder? The answer is that the court (and eighteenth-century maritime law more generally) conceived of African slaves through the metaphor of the human-thing, and as such legitimized the status of slaves as categorized alongside all of the rest of the goods traded across the Atlantic. Quéma reads the legacy of this metaphorical displacement of the humanity of certain people into modern law: in prisons, in chain-gangs, and in executions. Rather than analysing the legal process and judgment directly, Quéma rereads it through M.N. Philip's poem *Zong!* in which the text of *Gregson* v. *Gilbert* is fragmented and reassembled so as to displace the human-thing metaphor in favour of new metaphors that remember the slaves as people who were murdered, and that seeks to speak to and with the dead people rather than merely about them.

An important aspect of critical work on legal metaphors explored by many of these articles is its usefulness in enabling new avenues of thought to emerge from hitherto apparently stable or solid theoretical and normative positions. By reimagining legal metaphors in positive ways – by recognizing their potential to frame a subject and for the latter to be altogether *re*framed by imagining new sorts of metaphors – important conceptual change may

---

13 P. Goodrich, 'Gynaetopia: Feminine Genealogies of Common Law' (1993) 20 *J. of Law and Society* 296.

14 F. Boyle, 'David Cameron used "swarm" instead of "plague" in case it implied that God had sent the migrants' *Guardian*, 3 August 2015, at <http://www.theguardian.com/uk-news/commentisfree/2015/aug/03/cameron-swarm-plague-god-migrants-calais>.

15 G. Lakoff and M. Johnson, *Metaphors We Live By* (2003), emphasis added.

16 Peeren, op. cit., n. 12, p. 6.

become possible.[17] **Adam Gearey** offers an account of what he identifies in Hegelian terms as the underlying legal traditions and doctrines – namely, that sense of mutual recognition in the social world that constitutes a living 'spirit'. Agreeing with F.W. Maitland that the appropriateness of the metaphor of the 'body' of law comes from law being 'a living thing', Gearey finds its animating spirit in 'the complex of metaphorical substitutions where a set of institutions and doctrines "stand in for" or represent our under-standing of ourselves as rational subjects rooted in our "own" traditions and mores.' Gearey's subtle narrative interlaces Hegel's *sittlichkeit* with Maitland's writings in praise of the mechanism of the peculiarly English invention that is the trust. Maitland conceived the trust as a 'shell', pro-tecting individuals without any formal entitlement in law against uncon-scionable reliance on legal title, and in this way 'hiding' them from the power of the state and commercial interests.

If Gearey's article focuses its energy and attention on the metaphoric substitutions in the ethical *life* of law and legal discourse, then my own article (**David Gurnham**) may be read as doing the opposite, focusing instead on uses of metaphor in legal scholarship that evoke a sense of the supernatural, ghostly, and discomforting. My article examines uses of the 'myth' metaphor: first in feminist-informed scholarship on beliefs and attitudes about rape, and then also in work that is critical of that scholarship and its theoretical foundations. The article argues that the struggle between these two broadly conceived groups to control the myth metaphor has an *uncanny* effect, the evidence of which can be found in references to the product of (allegedly mythical) beliefs and attitudes in terms of spectral apparitions or 'doubles'. The article goes on to draw on Janet Halley's influential but contentious critique of feminist theory to suggest that, while this uncanny effect may on the one hand account for the fraught nature of debates about rape and sexual assault, it may also prove to be politically enabling and productive in moving them forward.

Finally, **Michelle LeBaron** is similarly motivated by a desire to effect a sense of movement towards new critical and discursive terrains in her article on recent developments in contemporary legal education in the United States. A combination of social, economic, and political forces are bringing about potentially radical changes to the nature, delivery, and capacity of law as a profession; legal education must respond to these developments, of course, but how? LeBaron argues that for too long the debate about legal education has been dominated by metaphors that frame the issue com-batively as one of crisis and competition for law schools and their graduates and lineally in terms of learning technical skills. Her article thoughtfully and passionately advocates for law schools to move away from such frames of reference and towards instead metaphors that emphasize the importance of a

17 See Watt, op. cit., n. 5, p. 79.

legal education in much broader (and hence more adaptive) terms: for fomenting a professional identity, creativity and innovation, morality and ethics. LeBaron's article reminds us that metaphors may be 'marked' or 'unmarked' – that is to say, conspicuous and consciously chosen or subtle and unconscious. Like many of the other contributions to this collection, her argument is a call to uncover the contingency of apparently natural or inevitable meanings that 'unmarked' metaphors in particular guide us towards, and to effect the sorts of changes we want with new deployments of metaphor.

I hope that the articles in this collection, which demonstrate a broad range of legal topics as well as critical perspectives, convince you that attention to law's metaphors – while not in itself a novel idea by any means – is, and remains, crucially important for addressing the interface between law and society. To refer once more to a metaphor that runs through this collection: the study of law in its context *is* (like law itself) a life, and a life that is lived through discovering and uncovering new ways to understand the constitutive, disciplinary, and persuasive powers of language.

JOURNAL OF LAW AND SOCIETY
VOLUME 43, NUMBER 1, MARCH 2016
ISSN: 0263-323X, pp. 8–26

# Metaphor as Analogy: Reproduction and Production of Legal Concepts

ANGELA CONDELLO*

*Metaphor can be compared to analogy because they both have, additionally to their rhetorical competence, an epistemic force. Through analogy legal concepts are reproduced according to similarity; reproduction is always a new production and thus analogy and metaphor in law have a poietic force. The reproduction and production (poiesis) of legal concepts through metaphor by analogy concerns the interference between classificatory operations in law and legal epistemology: in every categorization of the unknown by means of the known, legal ontology and legal epistemology intersect.*

## INTRODUCTION: ANALOGICAL AND METAPHORICAL PROCESSES IN LEGAL DISCOURSE

By arguing that metaphor – from the legal perspective – is like analogy, in this article I advance a diachronic idea of the connection between law and language. The main thesis I discuss is that *every ontology entails an epistemology* and therefore every process of classification through analogy in legal discourse shows the interaction between two dimensions that philosophy tends to separate (ontology – 'what is there', and epistemology – 'what we know about what is there'). Because of this interaction, categorization is not a simple semantic operation, but through the structural alignment preliminary to the comparison from which analogical inference derives, categorization entails imagination and it thus also (re)produces knowledge.

Analogical and metaphorical processes are crucial in legal discourse since law is permanently adapting to the changes in reality and, therefore, is permanently facing the challenge of classifying new objects and concepts:

* Department of Law, Università di Roma TRE, Via Ostiense, 161, 00154 Roma, Italy
angela.condello@uniroma3.it

We are temporal creatures, and the situations we find ourselves in, the situations that make up the fabric of our lives, are always evolving and developing. The omnipresence of change throughout all human experience thus creates a fundamental problem for law, namely, how can law preserve its integrity over time, while managing to address the newly emerging circumstances that continually arise throughout our history? (. . .) Our problem is how law can be both stable and capable of growth (. . .).[1]

Like ordinary language, legal language connects the general and the particular through classificatory operations. For instance, the classification of a term in a contract as a 'condition' will depend on various aspects, among which are:

(i) the general and abstract characterization of a 'condition' conventionally accepted;

(ii) the cases where the classification of that term has been in issue;

(iii) the role that 'conditions' play within the contract and within contractual liability;

(iv) the interrelation with other concepts and with other aspects of contract law.

In order to give a general and abstract definition of a term, one has to refer to the term's prototypical relation of reference.

Yet deciding whether one aspect or another of the characterization of the semantic frame of a term is prevalent is obviously complex. The problem for the interpreter is to decide whether a case falls within the frame of a particular norm and, more specifically, whether an object falls into a particular category. As Charnock points out,[2] in his presentation of open texture Hart used the term 'penumbra' to refer to what in prototype theory is called the 'periphery'. He followed a tradition found in American jurisprudence.[3] He thus presented roller skates – among other things – as penumbral instances of vehicles. Even more unlikely examples have been envisaged in both English and American cases. In *Garner* v. *Burr*,[4] a poultry shed was accepted as a vehicle, while in *McBoyle* v. *US*[5] an aircraft was not. In the case of *Garner*, a farmer had added iron wheels to a poultry shed and pulled it with his tractor on the highway. He was prosecuted, and finally acquitted of violating the British Road Traffic Act 1930, which stipulated that any 'vehicle' travelling on a public highway must be fitted with pneumatic tyres. The reason that motivated this decision was that a 'vehicle' was understood as a means of transportation on wheels or runners and used for the carriage of persons or

---

1 M. Johnson, 'Mind, metaphor, law' (2006–2007) 58 *Mercer Law Rev.* 845.

2 R. Charnock, 'Hart as Contextualist? Theories of Interpretation in Language and the Law' in *Law and Language: Current Legal Issues Vol. 15*, eds. M. Freeman and F. Smith (2013) 128.

3 See *Olmstead* v. *US* 381 U.S. 479 (1965) and *Griswold* v. *Connecticut* 277 U.S. 438 (1928).

4 *Garner* v. *Burr* [1951] 1 K.B. 31.

5 *McBoyle* v. *US* 283 U.S. 25 (1931).

goods. However, the farmer was not carrying anything at the time. So the feature that was primarily used to judge membership of the category of 'vehicles' in the context of the British Traffic Act was that of transportation of goods or people.

While *McBoyle* was also judged on the basis of what could be classified as a vehicle, this involved a different contextual criterion for similarity. In the United States, the National Motor Vehicle Theft Act, punishing whoever transports, or caused to be transported – in inter-state or foreign commerce – a motor vehicle, knowing it to have been stolen, defined 'motor vehicle' as including 'an automobile, automobile truck, automobile wagon, motorcycle, or any other self-propelled vehicle not designed for running on rails'. In 1931 the Supreme Court of the United States of America had to decide whether to apply this Act in the case of *McBoyle* v. *United States*. According to the Supreme Court, the definition 'an automobile, automobile truck, automobile wagon, motorcycle or any other self-propelled vehicle' should not apply to aircraft. The problem was the meaning of the word 'vehicle' in the phrase 'any other self-propelled vehicle not designed for running on rails'. The phrase under discussion recalled the popular concept related to the term 'vehicle'. As the definition explicitly mentioned automobile truck, automobile wagon, and motorcycle, the words 'any other self-propelled vehicle not designed for running on rails' meant a 'vehicle' in the popular sense, that is, in the interpretation of the Supreme Court, a vehicle running on land. While the relevant similarities differ in the two cases, they nevertheless seem to share the same prototypical example to which all other members of the category are compared, namely, that automobiles are considered as prototypical vehicles in both cases.

In *Thrifty-Tel* v. *Bezenek*[6] and *CompuServe* v. *Cyber Promotions*,[7] courts applied the Common Law action of trespass to chattels in order to decide cases where the plaintiff had received undesired emails. Chattels are material goods and the trespass to chattels is a type of tort whereby the infringing party has intentionally or negligently interfered with another person's lawful possession of a chattel (some kind of movable personal property). The interference can be any physical contact with the chattel in a quantifiable way, or any dispossession of the chattel (whether by taking it, destroying it, or barring the owner's access to it). So the material interference is necessary for the application of the trespass to chattels. In order to apply it, the judges had to use analogical arguments. The action of trespass requires an intentional contact and a concrete interference with the mobile good, the chattel. The problem was that an email account is much less concrete an object than a physical space. In order for it to be as a mobile, material good (which is the necessary condition for the application of the trespass to chattels), an

---

6 *Thrifty-Tel* v. *Bezenek* 46 Cal. App. 4th 1559 (1996).
7 *CompuServe Inc.* v. *Cyber Promotions Inc.* 962 F. Supp. 1015 (1997) U.S. Dist.

analogy had to be drawn. The trespass to chattels was used for the first time to decide an internet law case in *Thrifty-Tel* v. *Bezenek*, decided by the Court of Appeals of California. In this case there had been an intrusion (provoked by the action of sending spam continuously) into the email account of the plaintiff. The telephone service provider (plaintiff) made a complaint of illicit appropriation against the parents of some children that had hacked (through an action called 'phreaking') their domains. The children had entered Thrifty-Tel's informatic system by manually creating authorization codes; then they had used the software to search for new codes of access. The Court of Appeal decided to apply the trespass to chattels because of the 'tangible' materiality of the electronic particles of which the electronic signals were made. The Court, in order to justify the analogical inference, pointed out that there was a clear similarity between the electronic particles and other types of interference, like that produced by electromagnetic waves (that could also cause damage). *Thrifty-Tel* opened the path to the application of trespass to chattels to the internet. The next leading case was *CompuServe* v. *Cyber Promotions*: the latter, offering commercial services online, transmitted huge volumes of emails to the net that were the property of CompuServe (in spite of CompuServe's spam filters). The Court of Ohio, recalling *Thrifty-Tel*, held that the electronic signals received by CompuServe were sufficiently tangible to justify an action of trespass. The contact was in fact intentional, since the spam email had been sent intentionally.[8]

These examples prove that many of the most basic concepts in ordinary and in legal language have complicated internal structures and exhibit what are known as 'prototypicality effects' and, most importantly, that the proper application of concepts is an imaginative activity through and through because concepts are complexly structured. According to propotype theory (Rosch), people build their categories around *prototypical models*. Prototype characterization applies also to our most important abstract (thus, also, to legal) concepts, and not just to concrete physical objects. Legal concepts have complex structures and the principles for extending them presuppose some cognitive flexibility in the face of changing situations.

Through the analogical (and metaphorical) extension of a concept from one field to another, knowledge grows. Property law can be taken as an example:

> at the center of the category are prototypical instances of property, such as a house, hand-tool, or land. These cognitive prototypes are what are activated

---

8 Later on, in *Intel Corp* v. *Hamidi* 71 P.3d 296 (Cal. 2003), the California Supreme Court distinguished (and implicitly questioned) *CompuServe* on the basis that there was no evidence that the spam emails of a disgruntled former employee, Hamidi, caused any physical harm to Intel's servers. In any case, the use made of analogy in *CompuServe* remains an interesting example of the application of metaphor by analogy in law.

first for us when we read, hear, or think about the term 'property'. These prototypical instances satisfy a common idealized cognitive model in which property is: a discrete physical object or spatial expanse; that persists through time; is subject to exclusion from use by others; is alienable; and is useful. Extending out from the central prototypes are many noncentral members that do not possess all of the features specified by the central idealized cognitive model. Thus water is, in American culture, though not in certain Native American cultures, conceived of as potential property even though it is not a discrete object.[9]

Further from the centre (the prototypical idea of property) are other types of property that are not physical entities; the principle of extension for most of these cases is conceptual metaphor. For instance, we speak of intellectual property (ideas that can be copyrighted or patented or excluded from use by others). The concept of property is a vast, radially structured category with a small number of central members or prototypical cases surrounded at various distances by non-central members, according to principles of extension.


## COMMON ROOTS: METAPHOR *BY* ANALOGY

According to Aristotle, 'metaphor is the application of a strange term either transferred from the genus and applied to the species or from the species and applied to the genus, or from one species to another or else by analogy'.[10] The third type of metaphor (by analogy), the transfer from species to species, can be regarded as including all metaphors, in the sense that all metaphors involve a mental transfer from one type of object to another, from one domain of thought to another. Aristotle's larger purpose was to explain how metaphor promotes a consciousness and awareness of 'revolutionary' relations that subsist between objects and concepts that constitute reality. For Aristotle, the main function of metaphor is the acquisition and transmission of knowledge. Aristotle's overriding concern in the treatment of metaphor is expressed in the *Rhetoric*:

> easy learning is naturally pleasant to all, and words mean something, so that all words which make us learn something are most pleasant. Now we do not know the meanings for strange (i.e. unknown) words, and proper terms we know already. It is metaphor, therefore, that above all produces this effect; for when Homer calls old age stubble, he teaches and informs us through the genus; for both have lost their bloom.

Aristotle says that proverbs illustrate metaphors of the third type, that is to say, from species to species (metaphor by analogy). For instance, in the connection 'the acorn falls near the tree', the metaphoric meaning is 'the son resembles his father'; the proportion on the background is:

---

9 Johnson, op. cit., n. 1.
10 Aristotle, *Poetics* (1457b.7), at <http://www.perseus.tufts.edu/hopper/text?doc= Perseus%3Atext%3A1999.01.0056%3Asection%3D1457b>.

$$\text{acorn : tree = son : father}$$

'Acorn' and 'son' are species of progeny and 'tree' and 'father' species of progenitor. The major exhibit in Aristotle's theory of metaphor is where the construal proceeds on the basis of analogy. It is only in the *Poetics* that he describes his first three types at all. Elsewhere, when he talks about metaphor it is exclusively in terms of the type by analogy:

$$\text{Dionysus : cup = Ares : shield}$$

From these examples, it is now clear that for Aristotle analogy is a type of metaphor, but logically not all metaphors correspond to an analogy.[11] All metaphors, though, are based on a proportion and on a structural alignment that allows the 'jump' from one semantic field to another. According to this idea of metaphor, poetic metaphors too, since they involve an alignment that then allows the assimilation and the predication of an attribute in the new field, have an epistemic potential. In the following section I argue that metaphors work through structural alignment, relational commonalities, and then projection. Exactly like analogies. Even though there are metaphors that work by imagining previously unthought connections, that link dimensions otherwise not connected, alignment is central for analogical as much as for metaphorical predication.

### COMMON DYNAMICS: STRUCTURAL ALIGNMENT AND COMPARISON

According to Gentner, metaphor is like analogy in that they both convey chiefly relational commonalities: for example, *encyclopedias are gold mines, job is a jail*.[12] The capacity to convey relational commonalities is based on structure-mapping theory: metaphors convey that a system of relations holding among the base objects also holds among the target objects, regardless of whether or not the objects themselves are intrinsically similar.

The process of conveying common traits is based on the fact that both metaphor and analogy involve structural mapping processes. According to structure-mapping theory,[13] analogical and metaphorical mapping are processes of establishing a *structural alignment* between different represented situations and then projecting inferences. The alignment is determined according to *structural consistency* constraints:

---

11 Aristotle, *Rhetoric*, book III, at <http://www.perseus.tufts.edu/hopper/text?doc= Perseus%3Atext%3A1999.01.0060%3Abook%3D3>.
12 D. Genter and A.B. Markman, 'Structure Mapping in Analogy and Similarity' (1997) 52 *Am. Psychologist* 45.
13 id.

(i) one-to-one correspondence between the mapped elements in the base and target, and

(ii) parallel connectivity, in which the arguments of corresponding predicates also correspond.

In addition, the selection of an alignment is guided by the *systematicity principle*: a system of relations connected by higher-order constraining relations such as causal relations.

Conceptual metaphors in cognitive linguistics allow to understand an idea and a conceptual domain in terms of another idea or of another conceptual domain. Conceptual metaphors are seen in language in our everyday lives; they shape not just our communication, but also the way we think and act. In George Lakoff and Mark Johnson's work,[14] we see how everyday language is filled with metaphors we may not always notice. An example of one of the commonly used conceptual metaphors is 'argument is war'. The way argument is thought of is shaped by this metaphor of arguments being war and battles that must be won. Argument can be seen in ways other than as a battle, but we use this concept in order to shape the way we think of argument and the way we go about arguing. According to Lakoff and Johnson, conceptual metaphors are used very often to understand theories and models. A conceptual metaphor uses one idea and links it to another to better understand something. These metaphors are prevalent in communication and we do not just use them in language; we actually perceive and act in accordance with the metaphors. The presence of systems of metaphors between domains suggests that such metaphors are processed as systematic analogies.

One of the first theories aimed at large-scale domain mappings was the 'domain-interaction' hypothesis: Tourangeau and Sternberg proposed that a good metaphor is one that, first, involves two very different domains and thus has high between-domain distance; and, second, shows low within-space distance between the base and target items in their very distant respective spaces.[15]

Most importantly, metaphors can promote alignment across domains. Metaphorically (thus analogically, according to Aristotle), linking two domains alters one's view of one or both domains and this restructuring of domain(s) makes inferences about the target domain possible. This point usefully contradicts the assertion that the (common) law grows *only* incrementally or 'interstitially'. This theory of metaphor as analogy shows instead that relevant (albeit constrained) cognitive leaps are sometimes needed for the law to grow.

Conceptual metaphors (like, for instance, property – that can be applied to both physical and non-physical space) can be extended to new occurrences

14 G. Lakoff and M. Johnson, *Metaphors We Live By* (1980).
15 R. Tourangeau and R. Sternberg, 'Understanding and Appreciating Metaphors' (1982) 11 *Cognition* 203.

14

of existing domain mappings: metaphors do not (only) draw on existing similarities but, rather, *create* similarities by providing structural alignments for the target domain. Structure-mapping theory suggests that metaphors are processed as structural alignments, based on some initial relational commonalties. Then further inferences are projected from the more concrete or familiar base to target. Thus, alignment highlights parallel structure, and inference-projection creates new knowledge in the target. This last fits with Lakoff's emphasis on new knowledge: abstract domains are not structured *de novo* by concrete domains but, rather, begin with some structure of their own and accept further structure from a commensurable concrete domain. Alignment serves to provide the needed constraint on possible conceptual metaphors and the space for a comparison between non-homogeneous semantic fields. Processing extended metaphors involves alignment and mapping. I claim that metaphor is like analogy in legal discourse in that it starts with an alignment:

- metaphorical understanding begins with a symmetric (non-directional) alignment process;
- if an alignment is found, then further inferences are directionally projected from base to target;
- directionality in metaphor comprehension arises *after* the initial stage of structural alignment.

The process of structural alignment allows for the induction of metaphorical categories, which may come to be lexicalized as secondary senses of metaphor base terms. Novel metaphors involve base terms that refer to a domain-specific concept, but are not yet associated with a domain-general category. They are interpreted as comparisons: direct structural alignments between the literal base and target concepts. Novel metaphors are processed by aligning the literal senses of the terms involved. The comparison leads to a new categorization (the novel metaphor becomes a conventional metaphor).

As metaphors become conventional there is a shift *from comparison to categorization* (from reproduction to production): the interpretation of novel metaphors involves sense creation, but the interpretation of conventional metaphors involves sense retrieval. Through metaphorical thinking, lexical and semantic extensions are comprehended via a mapping from a (typically 'embodied' and concrete) domain of experience to another (typically abstract) domain of experience; the concrete domain is invoked to explain phenomena in the abstract or in a less familiar domain of experience (this is what happens with property, for instance).

Thus metaphor is also a species of categorization: metaphors are processed as class inclusions since the base concept is used to access or derive an abstract metaphorical category to which the target concept is assigned.

In the structural alignment which is fundamental for both analogy and metaphor, *comparison* is the central process. Novel metaphors are understood only by comparison. Conventional metaphors can be understood by accessing stored abstractions, yet these metaphoric abstractions are the

15

product of past comparisons. Comparison is central because it is central to alignment in both metaphor and analogy – both metaphors and analogy are alignment-based.

Structural alignment, inference projection, and progressive abstraction and generalization are employed in the processing of metaphor. Individual metaphors evolve over the course of their lives from alignment-based processing in the early stages to projection-based processing as they become conventionalized. Conventionalization of legal conceptual metaphors (property is both physical and non-physical) can also take the form of large-scale conventional systems of metaphors.

Legal objects and concepts are categorized in terms of prototypes and family resemblances. Prototypical concepts (for example, prototypical property) can be extended metaphorically: metaphorical concepts allow one to structure an experience partially in terms of another experience.[16] In order to prepare the metaphorical transfer, a coherent structuring of the purpose of the proposition and of the communicative action in general has to be provided. Understanding takes place in terms of entire domains of experience and not in terms of isolated concepts.

The metaphor highlights other experiences since it gives the concept a new meaning. The fact that it gives new meaning is relative, personal, and contextual. For the same reasons (structural and semantic alignment), new metaphors create new realities and open new systems and new structural alignments. New metaphors structure and restructure the cognitive system. New similarities can be created by new metaphors: structural metaphors can induce similarities (can create new patterns of similarity). Lakoff and Johnson claimed that: 'most of our conceptual system is metaphorically structured: that is, most concepts are partially understood in terms of other concepts. This raises an important question about the grounding of our conceptual system.'[17] By establishing new connections, we make progress and we achieve knowledge.[18]

Knowledge and understanding take place in terms of entire domains of experience and not in terms of isolated concepts. Knowledge and under-standing, through metaphorical thinking, grow and are enlarged since metaphors give concepts new meanings. New metaphors have the power to create new realities. The reproduction (the application of an existing category to a new object), when it comes to similarity (thus when it comes to

16 Lakoff and Johnson, op. cit., n. 14, p. 77.
17 id., p. 56.
18 Discussing the fundamental function of metaphor and analogy in human and legal thought, of course, does not imply logically that there is no literal meaning. Words still have a sense in themselves. Here I am discussing the implications of meta-phorical processes in legal argument and epistemology without addressing the possibility/impossibility of a stable literal sense of legal terms (which I think is outside this discussion).

16

metaphor and analogy) is a new production. The structural alignment based on already existing similarities creates other similarities (that would have not been perceived otherwise). Repetition of structural equilibria of concepts in legal discourse is thus a poietic process.

## ANALOGY, METAPHOR, AND PROTOTYPE

The reproduction (and production) of legal concepts through analogical processes is related to the possibility of extending an original meaning to new fields of knowledge, a dynamic analysed in prototype theory, as developed in psycholinguistics under the impulse of Eleanor Rosch's work.[19] According to this theory, analogy is the motor of our general common-sense ability to classify things under concepts, and the best explanation of linguistic meaning, pretty much in the way metaphor has been shown to operate in legal classification and inference. This view of categorization is indeed supported by developmental studies of the way children master new categories based on examples, as well as language acquisition and understanding. Based on psycho-developmental and ethnological studies, prototype theory argues that, contrary to a widely shared view, linguistic concepts and general categories are not definable in terms of necessary and sufficient satisfaction conditions. In other words, there is no fixed set of conditions that can possibly determine what belongs to a concept or a category, and what does not.

More precisely, two main theses distinguish prototype theory of categories from the standard theory:

(i) categories are not conceived in terms of definitions encompassing necessary and sufficient conditions but, rather, in terms of prototypes (most representative exemplars of the category), or of combinations of traits, attributes, and properties that are typical of a category;

(ii) categorization is not an activity of verification of satisfaction conditions but, rather, a measure of degrees of similarity of an object to the prototype of the category. The flexibility of the prototypical conception allows it to account for the fuzziness of its referential applicability, the non homogeneity of categories, and the adaptability to the changing conditions of reality (allowing the incorporation of new instances in the existing categories), while preserving its structural stability.

For instance, there is no fixed set of traits (for example, having feathers, having a beak, being able to fly, and so on) that defines what is a bird. Rather, each community (legal, linguistic or cultural) retains certain exemplars as prototypical of a category (best exemplars) and others as more

---

19 E. Rosch, 'Natural categories' (1973) 4 *Cognitive Psychology* 328.

peripheral instances, depending on their degree of proximity with the exemplary instances, that is, on their similarity. So while a robin might be considered as a prototypical example of bird, most people would consider that an ostrich or a penguin is less representative of this category. Categories are thus not well delimited sets of instances with clear-cut boundaries and determinate tests for deciding what falls in or out. Rather, they have an internal gradient structure and fuzzy boundaries. And the features that we commonsensically use to characterize instances of a certain class are prototypical but in no way necessary nor sufficient.

This relates to the fact that what constitutes a *relevant similarity* and thus what can produce a relevant analogy (by driving the inclusion under a given category) is context dependent – depending on the linguistic and/or cultural community. In discussions on the role of similarity in the prototype model of categorization, it has been pointed out that while bats share many features with birds, they nevertheless fall out of this category. For example, in the Australian language Nunggubuyy, the category that comes closer to our category of bird does include bats as well. So the dimensions along which degrees of similarity are measured to judge category membership might vary among groups, even in cases where the traits that are considered prototypical are the same. Indeed, even for us, prototypical birds do fly.

Classificatory analogies assist in deciding whether or not to allocate a legal case to an existing category. The use of analogies in classification makes sense of the common idea that analogies are based on relevant similarities between the facts of cases. In the classification, the similarities that matter are those related to the characterizations and functions of the concept in the existing cases, and are a matter of degree. It is a particular feature of the legal decision-making process that the *classification* should also be *consistent* with previous cases, that is, with existing decisions (for common law systems) or with existing norms (for civil law systems), even when these earlier cases could have been decided otherwise. The point is that even if the line being drawn between cases is, in a significant sense, arbitrary, it is being drawn in a systematic way (consistent and coherent with the system), rather than leaving arguable cases to be decided on an ad hoc basis by individual courts: the aspiration, at least, to systemic coherence in law is fundamental.

In order to decide if two legal cases are similar, one has to look at classifications. Classifications are in fact fundamental in order to decide if two cases fall in the same category and, thus, if the same *rationale* applies. Classification is also the premise for metaphorical and analogical thinking and inference in law. Let us consider, for instance, the developments in United States legislation concerning rights over oil and gas. The general common law rule is that owners of land have property rights to everything which is on or below their land. But people do not have property rights over otherwise unowned things that move over their land – such as wild animals – unless and until they reduce them into their possession. This leads to the question whether the owner of land under whose property lies part of a reservoir of oil or gas has property rights on the oil and gas. It was decided that he or she does not, drawing in part on the analogy of English case law on rights over groundwater. These previous cases had held that there was a right to extract water, but no ownership in the water until it was reduced into the possession of the landowner. The question of property rights on oil and gas could be analogized to groundwater rights (through an operation of structural alignment, because, of course, the two types of rights are relevantly different) – and could be used metaphorically, for the same reason – because both involve fluids that circulate beneath more than one property and whose extent is uncertain.

All forms of analogical and metaphorical reasoning draw on the fact that legal doctrines are not simply a body of standards with a particular structure but are, instead, a body of standards with an intelligible *rationale* nestling within wider bodies of law. The operation of analogical and metaphorical reasoning relies both on the structure and the *rationale* of legal doctrines. Its importance lies in the way that it serves the court's adjudicative functions: it enables courts to develop the law in ways that are both faithful to existing legal doctrine and sensitive to the novel context in which the law is to be applied.

For analogical reasoning to operate properly, we have to know that case A and case B are *relevantly* similar and that there are no *relevant* differences between them. It means that there should not be any differences between the two cases either that (i) do not make a difference in light of the relevant precedents, which foreclose certain possible grounds for distinction, or (ii) cannot be fashioned into the basis for a distinction that is genuinely principled.

In order to appreciate the relevance of the similarities (in order to proceed according to metaphor) and the differences between two or more cases, a priori or a posteriori classification is central: as a matter of fact, only classificatory operations make it possible to decide whether a case falls in the frame of reference of a general or of a substantive principle or not. For instance, when someone says that the term 'liberty' includes (and can refer to) the right to seek an abortion, she is resorting to substantive principles and not to mere semantics. In law, reasoning devoted to classification involves some value judgement that is not always disclosed. Substantive principles and the consequent classifications play a crucial role for the evaluation of the similarities: as Cass Sunstein points out, analogical reasoning can go wrong when one case is said to be analogous to another on the basis of a unifying principle that is accepted without its having been tested against other possibilities, or when some similarities between two cases are deemed decisive with insufficient investigation of relevant differences.[20] An example

---

20 C.R. Sunstein, 'On Analogical Reasoning (1993) 106 *Harvard Law Rev.* 741.

could be the case of cross burning in which the Court had to distinguish a case about flag burning.[21]

This case shows how analogies provide constraints on reasoning in a way that makes the correct legal outcome different from the correct moral outcome. The First Amendment of the Bill of Rights states that:

> Congress shall make no law respecting an establishment of religion, or prohibiting the free exercise thereof; or abridging the freedom of speech, or of the press; or the right of the people peaceably to assemble, and to petition the government for a redress of grievances.

The law of free speech is an especially good area for investigating the power of analogies in legal discourse: most of the reasoning in that area is in fact analogical in nature.

Does cross burning fall under the category of 'action' or of 'speech' under the First Amendment? Cross burning could be considered as an action, and not as speech, and this would mean it was outside of the First Amendment (action is unprotected by the First Amendment). In order to claim constitutional protection under the First Amendment, a person must be saying or writing words. In the past, though, flag burning was qualified as speech; thus, how could cross burning not qualify as free speech under the current interpretation of the First Amendment? A general criterion for classifying actions that fall into the category protected by the First Amendment is the fact that they produce some kind of anger or resentment: the classification, from this perspective, would be based more on the effects produced than on the action itself. The practice of law constrains the scope of analogical reasoning, even if analogical reasoning in ethics is not similarly constrained. But acts that qualify as speech can be regulated only if they produce some kind of anger or resentment.

In order to establish whether an action falls into a class of actions protected by a law, we should delve deeper into the concept involved: what does 'freedom of speech' mean in a specific society? As the *R.A.V.* majority emphasized, the hypothetical ordinance is not a general proscription against fighting words: it reflects a decision to single out a certain category of fighting words, defined in terms of audience reactions to speech about certain topics. The question is then whether a subject-matter restriction of this kind is acceptable. If the court is to accept the subject-matter restriction in the cross-burning case, it must be persuaded that the state is not discriminating against particular viewpoints but is genuinely concerned about severe and distinctive harms. This effort to compare cases with one another usually operates when no unitary general theory is available against which individual instances can be simply measured. The question is: according to which criteria can we judge whether two actions are *actually* similar and (most importantly in legal interpretation) *relevantly* similar? Are

---

21  *R.A.V.* v. *City of St. Paul* II2 S. Ct. 2538 (1992).

the criteria for evaluating the similarity given a priori? If we are asking what sorts of speech are protected by the First Amendment, we might ask some questions about the purposes of that Amendment, or the scope of its coverage, and then apply our answers to various cases (writing, speaking, acting as in the cases of the cross burning and the flag burning) – rather than refusing to specify the general theory in advance and spending time examining the endless cases that are the staple of free speech law: perjury, misleading commercial speech, conspiracies, false cries of 'fire!' in a crowded theatre, and so forth. Sometimes there may be no criteria for truth in law except for our considered judgements about particular cases, once those judgements have been made to cohere with each other. In order to judge on the similarity between two cases, one should consider the consistency (which is like a structural mapping) among particular judgements and principles.

The extended version of the prototype theory (there are in fact many versions but they share a common core) operates two related revisions on the standard version. First, it entails the hypothesis that there is one central exemplar situated at the centre of each category, and a set of non-prototypical exemplars at the periphery is abandoned. With this prototypical organization of categories, the idea that the prototypes are those against which all other instances are compared, and with which they necessarily share a set of features, is also abandoned. Prototypicality is no longer con-sidered a driving categorization, but as an effect of categorization according to a more general Wittgensteinian principle of family resemblance. That is, 'the idea that members of a category may be related to one another without all members having any properties in common that define the category'.[22] Note that this extended version is not incompatible with the standard prototype theory, as similarity with respect to a prototype becomes a particular case of family resemblance. So the extended prototype theory makes space for all the members of category, but does not require that they have any trait in common.

## LAW *AS* LANGUAGE

Analogy entails a theory of interpretation in an intersubjective dimension. Through analogical thinking, legal argumentation is linked to a theory of knowledge. In order to understand the function of analogy in law we should first of all understand law as a system of verbal signs (words) whose meaning is fixed contextually and diachronically. I claimed that analogy concerns proportionality of relationships – when something is repeated, it is

---

22 G. Lakoff, 'Cognitive Models and Prototype Theory' in *Concepts and Conceptual Development: Ecological and Intellectual Factors in Categorization*, ed. U. Neiser (1987) 63.

given again and it is also reconceptualized. Every symmetry is a repetition: analogy thus entails a contamination between a priori and a posteriori.

What is repeated in law? What is the *new* trait, the *new* aspect in the repetition on which analogical thinking is based? The same questions could be asked about metaphor: what is repeated and what is new in metaphor? Through metaphor, language multiplies concepts, categories, and definitions. When a concept (like 'property') is extended to non-physical objects, something is repeated through a symmetry. Repetition multiplies concepts and categories in law, therefore, we can say that repetition is *creative* because in repetitive seriality there is always a moment in which a new trait, a new aspect emerges. The creative potential lies in the power of the contamination between different objects or concepts, in the process of the transferring of some traits that becomes a way through which a new sense is acquired. Repetition is like a rewriting: an object is the same in that it is like another. Analogies and metaphors help us to cross the boundaries of knowledge by the creation of new symmetries.

Neither metaphor nor analogy are neutral. There is an evaluative and substantive aspect of the use and acceptance of metaphors: their use as either weapons (where a given metaphor is mobilized in the legal/political stage), or as battlefields (where different groups fight over the control over the signification of a metaphor). This is true especially if we accept the idea that in legal discourse, analogy and metaphor show new aspects of reality. It is because of their epistemic value that they can (and do) constitute battlefields. Through them, legal systems create their regularities by connecting a *logos* with an *episteme*. The potential politicization of metaphor and analogy mirrors the nature of law as a language that functions contextually. Already White had noted that:

> law is not merely a system of rules (or rules and principles), or reducible to policy choices or class interests, but that it is rather what I call a language, by which I do not mean just a set of terms and locutions, but habits of mind and expectations – what might also be called a culture. It is an enormously rich and complex system of thought and expression, of social definitions and practices, which can be learned and mastered, modified or preserved, by the individual mind. The law makes the world. And the law in another sense (…) is a kind of cultural competence: an art of reading the special literature of the law and an art of speaking and writing – or making compositions of one's own in this language. It is a branch of rhetoric. Of course the law is not just a language, for it is in part about the exercise of political power. But I think the greatest power of law lies not in particular rules or decisions but in its language, in the coercive aspect of its rhetoric – in the way it structures sensibility and vision.[23]

The idea of law as language that I present here is against the possibility of a 'neutral language' and thus against the possibility of a neutral epistemology. The use of language is crucial to any legal system — not only in the

23  J.B. White, *The Legal Imagination* (1973).

same way that it is crucial to politics in general, but particularly in respect to the fact that law makers typically use language to make law, and courts typically use language to state the grounds of their decision. Philosophy of law shares a tension that affects philosophy of mind and metaphysics, and perhaps all the central areas of philosophy: it is often unclear which problems are problems of language, and which are not.

Goodrich notes that:

> lawyers and legal theorists have successfully maintained a superb oblivion to the historical and social features of legal language and, rather than studying the actual development of legal linguistic practice, have asserted deductive models of law application in which language is the neutral instrument of purposes peculiar to the internal development of legal regulation and legal discipline.

From this perspective, the possibility of analysing law as a specific stratification of an existent language system has been excluded. Together with this possibility has been excluded 'the denial of the heuristic value of analysing legal texts themselves as historical products organised according to rhetorical criteria.'[24]

Analogy and metaphor show that legal language, like any other language usage, is a social practice. Legal discourse is responsible for its place and role within the political commitments of its times. Legal utterance is a social discourse. Already in classical thought (Aristotle), legal meaning was linked not only to truth (and thus to the verisimilitude/probability dichotomy) but also, and just as directly, to the collective actions of the political assembly, therefore to some kind of system of truth production (and reproduction).

Structuralism showed how the most striking and significant features common to linguistic analysis and legal science are their diachronic nature and their historicity. For structuralism, what a sign (a term) signifies in itself is largely irrelevant: its combination (syntagmatization) is rule-governed and context-dependent, and certain combinations are impossible or nonsensical within a given code and context.[25]

A thorough analysis of metaphor and analogy contributes to criticism of the dominant view within both linguistics and jurisprudence, holding that language and legal communication are to be understood best as structurally determined activities, as specialized normative enterprises that can be studied scientifically according to internal laws, or grammar, of a static, governing, code. The objection to such accounts is that they privilege the concept of a system and the desire for order over and against the history of the system and the possibility of accounting for the actual relationships and usages that determine its realization.

---

24 P. Goodrich, 'Law and Language: An Historical and Critical Introduction' (1984) 11 *J. of Law and Society* 173, at 173.
25 F. de Saussure, *Cours de Linguistique Générale* (1916/1995).

This analysis invites us to turn back to legal structuralism as a style (Barthes, White, Duncan Kennedy), as Desautels-Stein noted recently.[26] Legal structuralism is worth reawakening; it is a 'style back in style', involving the use of semiotic theory and the view that a given period of legal thought should be analysed as a contextual language system.

The sense or meaning the legal verbal signs refer to is fixed contextually according to a balance of interests and values (influenced by the state of the world and the state of affairs). Linguistically, names, signs, and expressions can be equal in designation, but not in sense and meaning. There are many possible *states of affairs* among which is the actual one: the real world. Carnap suggested that the intensional potential of a verbal sign is an assignment of an extension given to the verbal sign by a specific *state of affairs*: intensions can be given a precise mathematical embodiment as functions of states, while extensions are relative to a single state.

For instance, the term 'property' acquires the meaning that is functional in a determined context because of the necessity of attributing a sense to the verbal sign 'privacy'. We can therefore take for granted that no legal system consists only of verbal signs and of linguistic acts: only circumstances (contexts, states of the world, states of affairs) give meanings to signs. In Bentham's legal theory, language is pictured as the basis of an innovative account of law as the expression of the will of a sovereign in a political community:

> a law may be defined as an assemblage of signs declarative of a volition conceived or adopted by the sovereign in a state, concerning the conduct to be observed in a certain case by a certain person or class of persons, who in the case in question are or are supposed to be subject to his power.[27]

Any good account of the meaning and interpretation of legal discourse needs to deal with the way in which its application depends on the context of its use and on evaluative considerations (of the interpretive community and/or authority). The dependence of the effect of legal language on context is an instance of a general problem about communication, which philosophers of language have approached by distinguishing semantics from pragmatics.

Legal language has one special feature that distinguishes it from ordinary language: legal *systems are based on institutions and processes for adjudication of disputes* about the application of language that arise (partly) as a result of their context dependence. Evaluative reasoning and intuition about the contingent context is central. For instance, we can decide whether an action is a 'search' or not for the purpose of the Fourth Amendment by understanding the amendment as pursuing a value, and by making an evaluative judgement as to whether the word 'privacy' can be interpreted as applying to the search in respect of the requirement of certainty in criminal

---

26 J. Desautels-Stein, 'Back in Style' (2014) 25 *Law and Critique* 141.
27 J. Bentham, *Of the Limits of the Penal Branch of Jurisprudence* (2010) 24.

liability. The content of the law cannot be identified without resort to evaluative reasoning. Evaluative considerations justify the use of a word in a specific context and thus support its analogical or metaphorical application.

Like every other system of signs, law is to be interpreted diachronically and for the application and realization of the law, the function of the interpretant is central: verbal signs exist only in time, and therefore temporality is a determinant factor in the process of the realization and 'coming into being' of legal concepts. Sense (or meaning) is produced by the articulation of the signs and by the differences between them. Verbal signs are meaningful only inside a broader system of other signs and because of their differences with them. The meaning is not in the signs, but *between* the signs. A subject perceives a shape only among other shapes and among many profiles: similarly, it is possible for a subject to perceive the sense to which a sign refers only where there is *discontinuous multiplicity of signifiers* since it is the temporal synthesis that fixes the sense of each signifier in a specific semantic context. By looking at it from the perspective of metaphor and analogy, legal discourse appears as a temporal process: legal concepts originate from the interpretive activities of the concrete acting agents, more specifically, from the intersubjective communicative experience. From such a perspective, legal discourse can be conceived as an organ of the spirit and concepts as products of intersubjective experience.

The meaning of legal terms is fixed conceptually by an intentional temporal process that relates the verbal signs with the context of reference and the subjects (the 'intepretant'). In ordinary language, naming and meaning are the result of necessity and therefore of power. In law, naming and meaning are also fixed by an intepretive process influenced by the necessity of the decision-making process. Meaning is thus functional in legal discourse more than in ordinary language.

## METAPHORS AND ANALOGIES IN LAW AS ARGUMENT AND COGNITION THROUGH IMAGINATION

*Metaphor as analogy*: this statement in the title suggests connecting metaphor and analogy through their common processes of argumentation and cognition through imagination.[28] In conclusion, it is on this shared aspect that I want to focus in order to assess the thesis of a common ground of metaphor and analogy. Aristotle had noted that figures of speech constitute devices of what he defined as *lexis* – diction, elocution, style. It is the *lexis* that makes the *logos* appear. It is through the forms of the argument that a discourse is developed; through figures of speech (metaphor) and

---

28 P. Ricoeur, 'The Metaphorical Process as Cognition, Imagination and Feeling' (1978) 5 *Critical Inquiry* 143.

thought (analogy), the *logos* is embodied by displaying and illustrating forms and traits of what is behind and 'under' the forms and traits (the epistemic '*sub-stantia*'). Figures of speech and of thought allow the visibility of discourse.

The argumentative-classificatory operations and the cognitive operations intersect in metaphor and analogy; while we categorize, we discover. The coincidence of the ontological and the epistemic level is made possible by imagination: in the *process* of building resemblance, alignments and iconic moments are implied, since making metaphors and drawing analogies are consequences of a contemplation of similarities and of possibilities of likeness.

The transfer of predicates that is made possibile by metaphor and analogies in law can be either an attempt to fill up a lexical lacuna or an additional argument functional to validate a thesis. In both cases, the statement produced through the reproduction and production 'cycle' works on reducing conceptual gaps in legal systems by the establishment of a new semantic pertinence that corresponds to the generation of a semantic innovation (the 'production' that follows the 'reproduction'). The mode of functioning of similarity, as consequent to structural alignment, is immanent (non-extrinsic) to the predicative process. The alignment (which is processed at an imaginative level) entails the new predication: things or concepts that were remote appear as close, since resemblance reveals generic kinship between heterogeneous semantic fields.

The structural alignment prior to metaphor and analogy involves a tension between semantic incongruence (space on the internet, space outside the internet) and semantic congruence (property on the internet, property outside the internet). The likeness is based on sameness and difference and the assimilation is the product of an evaluation of identical and different predicates (through imagination).

*Metaphor as analogy* invites us to reflect on the well-established distinction between sense and representation in law: these processes compel us to explore the thresholds between the verbal and the non-verbal, and, as Nelson Goodman had it, to 'make' and 'remake' reality.

26

JOURNAL OF LAW AND SOCIETY
VOLUME 43, NUMBER 1, MARCH 2016
ISSN: 0263-323X, pp. 27–44

# The Metaphor of Proportionality

Nicola Lacey*

*The idea of proportionality has figured prominently in moral, legal, and political theory. It has been central to the articulation of an ideal of limited punishment in modern legal orders, and to judicial and academic efforts to lay down standards for legitimate state conduct in a range of areas. Setting out from a broad view of the role of metaphor, I map histories of proportionality in different spheres (law, politics, culture), spaces (nation states and regions), and legal areas (criminal, public, international, and private law), before moving on to consider the conditions under which abstract ideas like proportionality assume a salience within particular spheres of legal or political discourse. Focusing on the case of appeals to proportionality in criminal justice, I develop an argument about the conditions under which they enjoy some capacity to coordinate expectations or beliefs, and consider how far this thesis might be generalizable to other fields.*

## INTRODUCTION

The idea of proportionality has figured prominently in modern moral, legal, and political theory. It has been central to the articulation of an ideal of limited punishment in modern legal orders. And, particularly in recent years, it has assumed a central place in the judicial and academic efforts to lay down standards for legitimate state conduct, and for judicial oversight of the exercise of power in a range of areas within human rights, administrative, public, international, and private law. But what role is this pervasive metaphor playing in law and legal discourse, and what explains the extraordinary recent upswing in its fortunes?

* *Law Department, London School of Economics, Houghton Street, London WC2A 2AE, England*
*n.m.lacey@lse.ac.uk*

I am grateful to Hanna Pickard, Thomas Poole, David Gurnham, and two JLS referees for helpful comments on a previous draft of this article, and to Victoria McGeer and Philip Pettit for discussion of its argument. I would also like to thank colleagues at an LSE Law Department research seminar for helpful feedback.

In this article, I aim to tackle these questions. Setting out from a broad view of the role of metaphor in legal and other social discourses, I map out histories of proportionality in different spheres (law, politics, culture), spaces (nation states and regions), and legal areas (criminal, public and private law), before moving on to consider the conditions under which abstract ideas like proportionality assume a salience within particular spheres of legal or political discourse. Focusing on the case of appeals to proportionality in criminal justice, I then go on to develop an argument about the conditions under which they enjoy some capacity to coordinate expectations or beliefs, and consider how far this thesis might be generalizable to other fields. In doing so, I clarify the relationship between my argument in this article and that in a recent paper co-authored with Hanna Pickard, in which we argued that scholars of criminal justice have been apt to be misled by the apparently determinate power of an idea whose force in fact ultimately depends on a surrounding infrastructure of attitudes and institutions.[1]

THREE PRELIMINARY QUESTIONS

Before embarking on this project, three preliminary matters must be addressed. First, we need to resolve the question of how we should under-stand the idea of metaphor in and beyond law, and, in particular, the degree to which metaphor is distinct within language. Second, we need to give an account of why the appeal to metaphor in law and legal discourse might be thought to be of distinctive importance to law and society scholarship – an issue which immediately invites reflection on the roles or functions of metaphor within the production of legal meaning and the exercise of legal power. And third, we need some account of the history, contours, and role of proportionality, understood as one of the foundational metaphors of modern law. I shall take each of these questions in turn.

Starting, then, with our first question, we can set out from the standard dictionary definition of metaphor as a figure of speech in which one thing stands in for or represents – etymologically, carries over, transfers, carries across – something else to which it does not directly refer. As such, metaphor has much in common with similes, analogies, symbols such as images, parables.[2] In each case, meaning is conveyed by the drawing of a connection

---

1 N. Lacey and H. Pickard, 'The Chimera of Proportionality: Institutionalising Limits on Punishment in Contemporary Social and Political Systems' (2015) 78 *Modern Law Rev.* 216.
2 Hence the role of metaphor in lending authority and persuasiveness to law is com-parable to that of images: C. Douzinas and L. Nead (eds.), *Law and the Image: The Authority of Art and the Aesthetics of Law* (1999); A. Gearey, *Law and Aesthetics* (2001); L. Mulcahy, *Legal Architecture: Justice, due process and the place of law* (2011).

28

between ostensibly different phenomena. And the centrality of both imagery and metaphorical language to law – to both its operations in language and our view of it and its significance – is immediately apparent: scales of justice; the image of justice as blind; 'chains' of causation are just three obvious examples mentioned at various points in this collection.

But there is nonetheless a puzzle here, and though we should not allow it to paralyse the important enterprise of analysing the role of metaphor in law, we must nonetheless pause to acknowledge it. This puzzle lies in the argument – familiar in influential post-structuralist work, but also a matter of common sense[3] – that in some sense language is inevitably metaphorical, in that words stand in for things – objects, ideas, situations – which they are not. This complicates the idea of a 'literal' correspondence between word and phenomenon to which metaphor purportedly stands in contrast, and hence suggests that the metaphoricity of language may occupy a spectrum rather than presenting a discrete category of linguistic usage. Moreover, this complication seems particularly apposite to legal language, in which so many concepts – 'contract' would be a good example – constitute at once discrete legal entities identified by and with a particular term, and broader social arrangements and ideas which are implicitly invoked in the deployment of that legal term.

While acknowledging this inevitably metaphorical tinge to legal language, I propose in what follows to handle the complication which it implies by simply stipulating that my focus will be on instances of metaphor in and around law in which the appeal to an idea, object or situation, which is not literally that referred to, is playing a certain role in transmitting meaning. The distinctive force of metaphor, in my account, lies in the way it assists in the legitimation of the relevant legal arrangement and/or in the coordination of social expectations around that arrangement.[4] This it achieves by implicitly making reference to a web of connections reaching well beyond its ostensible point or points of reference. (Note that, on this approach, the metaphoricity of a particular instance of legal language is contingent and may change over time: for example, while the terms 'contract' and 'crime' are undoubtedly metaphorical in this sense, the term 'tort' is arguably no longer so to a vast number of English law's subjects.) In taking this stipulative route out of the potential dilemma posed by my first question, I am of course also suggesting an answer to my second question about the distinctive role of metaphor in law. If law's metaphors are playing an important role in legitimating and coordinating legal arrangements, then they are central to both the significance of law and the stability of law's place in the constitution of social relations.

---

3 This argument is taken up in more detail in N. Lacey, 'Community in Legal Theory: Idea, Ideal or Ideology?' (1995) 15 *Studies in Law, Politics and Society* 105.
4 Compare the account of the power of metaphor presented in G. Lakoff's and M. Johnson's classic, *Metaphors We Live By* (1980).

Third and finally, then, what do I mean by 'proportionality', and what justifies my particular focus on appeals to proportionality among the myriad metaphors which populate legal discourse and social, cultural, and political discourse about law? On the face of it, this focus may seem odd, given proportionality's origins in ancient mathematics, from which it travelled into aesthetics.[5] But proportionality also has a long history in legal and political realms, where it featured in the ancient worlds of Greece, India, and Rome, notably as a part of just war theory: the proposition that the anticipated benefits of waging a war must be proportionate to the harm risked, just as the treatment of those caught up in war must be governed by norms of proportionality.[6] And, I shall argue, this fascinating blend of political, logical, and aesthetic meaning assumed a particular salience in the construction of modern ideas of the rule of law in Europe from the seventeenth century on.

It is useful to set out from a clear formal meaning to proportionality. An appeal to proportionality indicates a claim about the existence of a broad moral or practical equivalence or comparability between two different phenomena: a wrongful act and a punishment; an assault and a reaction in self-defence; a piece of negligent conduct and an award of damages; a prima facie discriminatory impact and a compensating legitimate purpose; a perceived social problem or danger and a governmental response which imposes certain social costs or impinges upon certain rights. As such, proportionality is an essentially analogical concept, and hence, while not a metaphor in the strict sense of the term, nonetheless presents a paradigm of what we might call the method of metaphor: in other words, it conveys meaning by evoking

---

5 The mathematics of proportion are sometimes argued to have been used in an aesthetic context by the Greek sculptor Polykleitos as early as the fifth century BC; better established is the role of proportion in the work of Plato and of Euclid in the first century BC, from which it found its way, via Roman thought (see n. 6 below), to the work of artists such as Piero della Francesca and Leonardo da Vinci, in fifteenth- and sixteenth-century Italy. Da Vinci, in particular, provided illustrations for Lucia Pacioli's *De Divina Proportione* in 1509, and is often credited with inventing the term 'sectio aurea', or the 'golden section', 'golden mean' or 'golden ratio', widely used in Renaissance art and still exerting influence in modern times – the most spectacular instance perhaps being Le Corbusier's Modulor system of architectural proportion.

6 The appeal to proportionality in just war theory may be found in Cicero's *De Officiis* Book 1, as in his *Treatise on the Commonwealth* and *Treatise on the Laws,* and in the Sanskrit epic the *Mahabharata*; it also features in the just war theories of Augustine, Aquinas, Grotius, Hobbes, and Locke, among many others. A number of recent articles have set recent appeals to proportionality in the context of this much longer intellectual history: see, for example, E. Engle, 'The History of the General Principle of Proportionality: An Overview' (2012) 10 *Dartmouth Law J.* 1, which traces the origins of the concept of proportionality in political morality back to Aristotle; and T. Poole, 'Proportionality in Perspective' (2010) *New Zealand Law Rev.* 369, which traces the concept back to the ideas of cosmic order in Plato and republican balance or harmony in Cicero, emphasizing its metaphysical or even 'celestial' inflection, as well as its role in identifying the political community to which its requirements apply.

a relationship between two different phenomena.[7] And precisely because of this method of claiming equivalence or comparability between two different things, the upshot of an appeal to proportionality depends either on surrounding social consensus about that comparability or on institutional mechanisms or arrangements which can produce, stabilize, and legitimate a particular judgement of 'proportional' equivalence – an issue to which I will return.

Note, however, that the very word, or concept, of proportionality arguably at least begins this work of legitimation or justification, because of the way in which an appeal to proportionality evokes an ideal of harmony, natural (quasi-geometric) order or coherence founded on reason and issuing in fairness, social justice, and limits on power. And, notwithstanding its ancient origins, proportionality has assumed a distinctive importance in the self-conception of modern social orders, contributing to what Charles Taylor has called a 'modern social imaginary'.[8] This is why, for example, appeals to proportionality loom so large in the foundational texts of modern political philosophy. Proportionality stands as a key concept in the long history of efforts not only to modernize and temper punishment or to rationalize and civilize the retributive approach which dominated pre-modern punishment, but also more generally as a source of the discursive legitimation of power. This it achieves by purporting to bring discretionary power within limits by establishing a criterion of appropriateness for its exercise, in the form of a normative relationship between an exercise of power and that (the wrong-doing or harm inherent in or proceeding from the relevant conduct) in relation to which the power is being exercised. Hence the concept of proportionality occupies a central place in the work of Enlightenment thinkers and reformers across many nations: Montesquieu, Beccaria, Jefferson, and Bentham, to name just four of the most important.[9]

The centrality of appeals to proportionality in underpinning the evolution of modern criminal justice systems and in evoking the notion of rationally limited and appropriately exercised power which characterizes modern ideas of legality or the rule of law, which form the main object of my inter-pretation in this article, would arguably in itself be sufficient to justify

---

7 The closely related concept of 'balancing' is of course a more central case of metaphor. I have chosen to focus on proportionality because of both its longer history in legal-political discourse and its yet wider reach across different systems and doctrinal areas.

8 C. Taylor, *Modern Social Imaginaries* (2004).

9 C.L. de Montesquieu, *De l'esprit des loix* (1748); C. Beccaria, *On Crimes and Punishments* (1764/2009); T.A. Jefferson, 'A Bill for Proportioning Crimes and Punishments in Cases Heretofore Capital' in *The Papers of Thomas Jefferson*, ed. J.P. Boyd (1950); J. Bentham, *An Introduction to the Principles of Morals and Legislation*, eds. H.L.A. Hart and J.H. Burns (1781/1996). For discussion, see J.Q. Whitman, 'The Transition to Modernity' in *The Oxford Handbook of Criminal Law*, eds. M. Dubber and T. Hörnle (2014) ch. 5.

selecting proportionality as my focus in this analysis of law's metaphors. But the role of proportionality in discourse within and about law is, of course, not exhausted by the criminal law and, particularly in the legal systems of the continent of Europe,[10] proportionality has long occupied a central position in the construction of legal mechanisms for checking public power, and hence in the articulation of principles of judicial review. Moreover, in recent years, appeals to proportionality both in judicial discourse and in political and cultural discourse about law and about law reform have experienced a huge growth, with proportionality tests in public law travelling via European legal institutions and via international human rights norms into the common law; and with proportionality in the United States travelling from its Eighth Amendment origins and alternating with the familiar concept of balancing in various areas of constitutional and private law.[11] Alongside the continuing renaissance of neoclassical ideas of penal justification, represented in sentencing guideline systems and the espousal of justice- or just desert-based sentencing reform in many jurisdictions,[12] proportionality can therefore claim to be one of the central metaphors underpinning the persuasiveness, legitimacy, and coordinating power of modern law.

10 I. Porat and M. Cohen-Eliya, *Proportionality and Constitutional Culture* (2013) ch. 1.
11 For key examples amid an extensive literature indicating the salience of appeals to proportionality in the penal theory literature and its analogous recent deployment in other areas such as human rights, and public, international, and private law across many jurisdictions, see R. Alexy, *A Theory of Constitutional Rights*, tr. J. Rivers (2002); A. Barak, *Proportionality: Constitutional Rights and their Limitations* (2012); J. Bomhoff, *Balancing Constitutional Rights* (2013) 10–30; R.S. Frase, 'Excessive Prison Sentences, Punishment Goals, and the Eighth Amendment: "Proportionality" Relative to What?' (2004) 89 *Minnesota Law Rev.* 571; A. Ristroph, 'Proportionality as a Principle of Limited Government' (2005) 55 *Duke Law J.* 263; G. Letsas, 'Rescuing Proportionality' in *Philosophical Foundations of Human Rights*, eds. R. Cruft, M. Liao, and M. Renzo (2014); Porat and Cohen-Eliya, id.; E.T. Sullivan and R.S. Frase, *Proportionality Principles in American Law: Controlling Excessive Government Actions* (2008). Also G. Webber, *The Negotiable Constitution: On the Limitation of Rights* (2009); C. Steiker, 'Prevention as a Limit on the Preventive Justice' in *Prevention and the Limits of the Criminal Law*, eds. A. Ashworth and L. Zedner (2013) 194; G. Huscroft, B. Miller, and G. Webber (eds.), *Proportionality and the Rule of Law: Rights, Justification, Reasoning* (2014); K. Moller, *The Global Model of Constitutional* Rights (2015) ch. 7; V.C. Jackson, 'Constitutional Law in an Age of Proportionality' (2015) 124 *Yale Law J.* 2680.
12 A. Ashworth, *Sentencing and Criminal Justice* (2010, 5th edn.); A. Ashworth and A. von Hirsch, *Proportionate Sentencing: Exploring the Principles* (2005); and A. von Hirsch and N. Jareborg, 'Sweden's Sentencing Statute Enacted' (1989) *Criminal Law Rev.* 275.

To engage in any really thorough project of mapping these various histories of proportionality across time, space, and subject matter would be a massive task, well beyond the scope of a single article. It is worth noting that such a project would be a hugely valuable contribution to historicized socio-legal enquiries, and a very useful complement to existing work tracking the genealogy of other social, legal, and political concepts of central importance to the trajectory of modern social orders: the individual self and person-hood;[13] human rights;[14] responsible agency.[15] For my purposes in this article, however, it will be sufficient to draw out of the rationale for a focus on proportionality provided in the previous section a schematic account of the trajectory of metaphors of proportionality across three dimensions. This account will allow us to map the differences of emphasis, meaning, and inflection which can arise within the umbrella of a single metaphor, depending on the context in which and purposes for which it is invoked.

### 1. Appeals to proportionality in different sites: law, politics, culture

The appeal to proportionality as part of the project of constructing specifically modern legal orders finds its most prominent history in the criminal law, notably as part of an effort to build a modern equivalent to the premodern retributive ethic captured by the *lex talionis* and forms of dis-cretionary, often monarchical, power.[16] Indeed, Thomas Jefferson's 1778 Bill for Proportioning Crimes and Punishments in the early formation of the United States combines the appeal to proportionality with a continuing commitment to talionic punishments in a striking way:

---

13 C. Taylor, *Sources of the Self: The Making of Modern Identity* (1989); D. Wahrman, *The Making of the Modern Self* (2004); R. Porter (ed.), *Rewriting the Self: Histories from the Renaissance to the Present* (1997); L. Siedentop, *Inventing the Individual: The Origins of Western Liberalism* (2014). Underlying notions of the subject and its relation to power are, of course, also fundamental to much of Michel Foucault's work, notably, in this context, *Discipline and Punish: The Birth of the Prison*, tr. A. Sheridan (1977).

14 L. Hunt, *Inventing Human Rights: A History* (2007); C. Douzinas, *The End of Human Rights* (2000); C. Douzinas and C. Gearty (eds.), *The Meanings of Rights: The Philosophy and Social Theory of Human Rights* (2014).

15 N. Lacey, *Women, Crime and Character: From Moll Flanders to Tess of the d'Urbervilles* (2008); L. Farmer, *Making the Modern Criminal Law: Criminalization and Civil Order* (2016). Engle and Poole (both op. cit., n. 6) have made important contributions to the project of mapping proportionality, as has D. Kennedy: see his 'A Transnational Genealogy of Proportionality in Private Law' in *The Foundations of European Private Law*, eds. R. Brownsword et al. (2011) 185.

16 The much longer history of appeals to proportionality in just war theory in both classical and natural law traditions presents a fascinating precursor to modern, rationalist approaches to proportionality in penal theory – as indeed do the graduated fines of ecclesiastical law: see Whitman, op. cit., n. 9, p. 84.

33

> Whosoever on purpose and of malice forethought shall maim another, or shall disfigure him, by cutting out or disabling the tongue, slitting or cutting off a nose, lip or ear, branding, or otherwise, shall be maimed or disfigured in like sort: or if that cannot be for want of the same part, then as nearly as may be in some other part of at least equal value and estimation in the opinion of a jury...[17]

In the 'neoclassical' revival of retributivism, repackaged in the sanitized form of 'just deserts' in the 1970s, the appeal to proportionality takes a very different institutional form, realized through the technical mode of procedural mechanisms such as sentencing guideline systems or presumptive sentence statutes. In each case, however, the work being done by the metaphor of proportionality is similar: it evokes the sorts of limits on power emblematic of a modern commitment to legality or the rule of law, and does so by implicit appeal to some natural order of rational relationship between one thing – a crime – and another – a penalty.

A similar mechanism is at work in the appeal to proportionality in public law, which is often traced back to Prussian administrative law of the nineteenth century,[18] though it undoubtedly has deeper roots in the liberal political thought and ancient sources already reviewed. In the specific context of adjudication, as Porat and Cohen-Eliya explain, proportionality structures decision making between competing rights and interests by:

> basically requiring that any interference with rights be justified by not being disproportionate. It consists of four (or three, depending on your perspective) stages: whenever the government infringes upon a constitutionally protected right, the proportionality principle requires that the government show, first, that its objective is legitimate and important; second, that the means chosen were rationally connected to achieve that objective (suitability); third, that no less drastic means were available (necessity); and fourth, that the benefit from realizing the objective exceeds the harm to the right (proportionality in the strict sense).

Note that, as in the case of punishment, proportionality is here envisaged as legitimating and facilitating power in the very process of symbolizing its constraint.

We must, of course, be open to the possibility that the role of appeals to proportionality, as well as the specific institutional and doctrinal form which they take, has developed in different ways in different substantive areas. But across these undoubted differences, as I shall argue, we see some important common themes, notably in the way in which proportionality invokes ideas

---

17 Jefferson, op. cit., n. 9, quoted in Whitman, id.
18 Notably in Article 10(2) of the Prussian General Law of 1794. See Porat and Cohen-Eliya, op. cit., n. 10, ch. 2; M. Cohen-Eliya and I. Porat, 'American Balancing and German Proportionality: The Historical Origins' (2010) 8 *International J. of Constitutional Law* 263; S. Baer, 'Equality: the Jurisprudence of the German Constitutional Court' (1999) 5 *Columbia J. of European Law* 249; M. Loughlin, *Foundations of Public Law* (2010) ch. 14.

of rationally limited power, contributing to the law's claim to play a central role in the delivery of modern governance. Indeed we can usefully think about this in terms of the trajectory of modern political orders and ideologies: as the value attached to individual freedom and the claims of individuals of bearers of civil and political rights – as well as the complexity and ambition of state activity – increase, there is a growing need to develop discourses as well as institutional arrangements capable of legitimating the state's power and bolstering its credentials as both rational and reasonable.

These appeals to the metaphor of proportionality in the law derive a good part of their power from the way in which they connect the exercise of legal power with doctrines and ideas of reason, fairness, fittingness, and order circulating within broader political and indeed cultural discourse. As we have seen, the appeal to proportionality had long featured in just war theory in both classical and natural law traditions; from the seventeenth century, it began to be more specifically associated with the image of legitimate governance. Hence we might cite, for example, the role of rationality, order, and proportionality not merely in the treatises of Beccaria and Bentham or the reforms of Jefferson, but also, yet earlier, in Montesquieu[19] – all of them core founders of the political projects of the Enlightenment and its long aftermath. Moreover these images of order, proportion, and reason surface regularly in cultural texts such as novels, in which authors debate the excesses of arbitrary power under the *ancien régime*. Consider, for example, Oliver Goldsmith's indictment of the disorder of disproportionality in *The Vicar of Wakefield*, its language reminiscent of Beccaria (whose treatise on crime and punishment was published two years before Goldsmith's novel):

> When by indiscriminate penal laws a nation beholds the same punishment affixed to dissimilar degrees of guilt, from perceiving no distinction in the penalty, the people are led to lose all sense of distinction in the crime, and this distinction is the bulwark of all morality; thus the multitude of laws produces new vices, and new vices call for fresh restraints.[20]

Law, Goldsmith argues, should be made the protector, but not the tyrant of the people.

Of course, appeals to notions of order or 'proper place' may take radically different forms. Take, for example, this passage from Sarah Fielding, talented sister of the (inevitably more famous) playwright, novelist, essayist, and magistrate Henry, himself an eloquent critic of the cruelty and irrationality of the excesses of arbitrary power. Fielding extols something reminiscent of the ontology – and aesthetics – of balance, order, and reason to which the metaphor of proportionality invariably appeals:

> [I]t is in the power of every Community to attain it [real happiness], if every Member of it would perform the part allotted him by *Nature*, or his *Station in*

19 Montesquieu, Beccaria, Jefferson, and Bentham, op. cit., n. 9.
20 O. Goldsmith, *The Vicar of Wakefield* (1766/1974) 150; compare Beccaria, id.

*Life*, with a sincere Regard to the Interest and Pleasure of the whole ... [I]f he acts his Part well, he deserves as much *Applause* – and is as useful a Member of Society – as any other Man whatever: for in every Machine, the smallest Parts conduce as much to the keeping it together, and to regulate its Motions, as the greatest. That the Stage is a Picture of Life, has been observed by almost every body, *especially since* Shakespeare's *Time*: and nothing can make the Metaphor more strong, than the observing every Theatrical Performance spoiled, by the great Desire *each Performer shews of playing the Top-part* – In the Animal and Vegetable World there would be full as much Confusion as there is in human Life, – was not every thing kept in its proper Place.[21]

Note that the ontology which Fielding evokes leaves open the question of the source of its conception of 'proper Place' and harmony, with the reference to 'station in life' suggesting a notion of fixed status relations which was precisely what the emerging ideas of rational and limited governance were straining against. Yet while the metaphor of proportionality evokes a horizontal relationship of equivalence rather than one imposed from above, the very idea of equivalence seems to participate in some sort metaphysical or ontological claim.

## 2. *Appeals to proportionality across space: nations and regions*

The idea of proportionality is pervasive in modern, Western legal systems: it transcends the civilian/common law and other classificatory divisions.[22] Appeals to proportionality are not, however, invariant across space. (Much the same can be said of the metaphor of balancing, as convincingly demonstrated in Jacco Bomhoff's comparison of United States and German constitutional law.)[23] While proportionality, as we have seen, operates explicitly within foundational texts in the emergence of both English and American criminal justice systems, and in the early development of Prussian administrative law, and while strong family resemblances around images of natural order, reason, and rationally limited power inform each of these appeals, the trajectories of appeals to proportionality in different jurisdictions have varied widely, and are always coloured by the cultural, political and institutional context in which they arise. Hence, as Porat and Eliya-Cohen have noted, proportionality has had relatively restricted airtime in twentieth-century American constitutional law discourse, at just the time during which it has been travelling rapidly across European jurisdictions, including the common law system of England and Wales, in large part as a result of the jurisprudence of the European Court of Human Rights and the

---

21 S. Fielding, *The Adventures of David Simple Containing an Account of his Travels through the Cities of London and Westminster in Search of a Real Friend* (1741/ 2007) 234; compare H. Fielding, *Tom Jones* (1749/1998).
22 M. Damaska, *The Faces of Justice and State Authority: A Comparative Approach to the Legal Process* (1986).
23 Bomhoff, op. cit., n. 11.

parallel and rather different proportionality jurisprudence of the European Court of Justice.[24] Conversely, proportionality played a key role in American criminal justice reforms of the 1970s and 1980s, as in the reforms of a wide range of countries from Australia to Sweden. And this variation, of course, raises fascinating questions of comparative law – and indeed of comparative social science more generally – about the conditions or events which prompt appeals to proportionality at particular times and in particular places.

### 3. *Appeals to proportionality across different subject matter*

Finally, even within legal arenas, as we have already seen, proportionality features in a vast range of areas of law, and has accordingly spawned an enormous literature, particularly over the last twenty years.[25] For obvious reasons, it finds its origins in, broadly speaking, public law – operating in criminal justice, in administrative law, and, most recently, in human rights and in areas such as anti-discrimination law, to temper, moderate, and legitimate power, bringing it within the limits dictated by ideals of modern democratic governance, keenly attentive to the potential for abuse of public power. Yet it has also found a place in private law – perhaps reflecting the recognition that gross inequalities of private power, along with the increasing involvement of private bodies in exercising public functions and hence wielding quasi-public power, are rendering the development of analogous checks on the power deriving from money or commercial influence – or, at least, the symbolism of such checks – relatively more important. In a world in which power is closely allied with money and 'spheres of justice' become increasingly blurred, the traditional distinction between

---

24 Porat and Eliya-Cohen, op. cit., n. 10, p. 3: they attribute this variation to underlying differences in American and European attitudes to governmental power.

25 In addition to the references mentioned at n. 10 above, see N. Emiliou, *The Principle of Proportionality in European Law; A Comparative Study* (1996); D. Beatty, *The Ultimate Rule of Law* (2004); A. Baker, 'Proportionality and Employment Discrimination in the UK' (2008) 37 *Industrial Law J.* 305; V.C. Jackson, 'Being proportional about proportionality' (2004) 21 *Constitutional Commentary* 803; A. Stone Sweet and J. Mathews, 'Proportionality, balancing and global constitutionalism' (2008) 19 *Columbia J. of Transnational Law* 72, at 162; A. Stone Sweet and J. Mathews, 'All things in proportion? American rights doctrine and the problem of balancing' (2011) 60 *Emory Law J.* 101; M. Poto, 'The Principle of Proportionality in Comparative Perspective' (2007) 8 *German Law J.* 835; M. Andenaes and S. Zleptnig, 'Proportionality: WTO Law in Comparative Perspective' (2007) 42 *Texas International Law J.* 371; A.D. Mitchell, 'Proportionality and Remedies in WTO Disputes' (2007) 17 *European J. of International Law* 985; D. Grimm, 'Proportionality in Canadian and German Constitutional Jurisprudence' (2007) 57 *University of Toronto Law J.* 383; A. Ristroph, 'Proportionality as a Principle of Limited Government' (2005) 55 *Duke Law J.* 263. For a useful review of the range and trajectory of appeals to proportionality in different areas of law, see Engle, op. cit., n. 6, pp. 6–10.

37

public and private power calls for deconstruction, and necessitates the development of doctrines and practices limiting private as much as public power.[26] If private power can, in effect, enable or constrain public rights, then the same legitimation needs which I have argued to underpin the appeal to proportionality in public law resonate in private law. I will return to this issue below.

## DECONSTRUCTING PROPORTIONALITY: THE CASE OF CRIMINAL JUSTICE

How should we interpret the pervasive appeal to proportionality across so many areas of legal argumentation in so many contemporary systems? At one level, we might be tempted to deconstruct this as a widespread instance of ideological obfuscation. What have been the effects of the appeal to proportionality, with its promise of determinate limits on power? Might we not argue that what has been thought of as proportionality is, after all, not a naturally existing relationship, but a product of political and social construction, cultural meaning making, and institution building, and that the purported appeal to a naturally existing relationship is therefore a proper object of careful critique or even of suspicion? For example, the appeal to proportionality in the 'neoclassical' retributive revival in the United Kingdom and, most vividly, the United States, has been accompanied by a marked increase in the exercise of the state's penalizing power, inviting the sceptical thought that appeals to proportionality are little more than rhetorical window-dressing. On this view, such appeals are, in the original sense of the term, ideological in that they obscure our view of social reality. It is of particular significance in this context that proportionality operates to legitimate as well as purporting (indeed, by purporting) to constrain the exercise of power.

In a recent paper,[27] Hanna Pickard and I mounted precisely this sort of critique of the appeal to proportionality in penal law and policy debate. We argued that the capacity of appeals to proportionality to limit power was contingent upon its articulation with cultural and institutional features of the surrounding context. In an effort to understand the way in which contemporary appeals to proportionality as a limiting principle in criminal justice have had such different effects in different countries, we contrasted the cultural and institutional structure of not only different contemporary advanced democracies, but also early modern systems in which a more symbolic, less rationalist conception of proportionality seems to have been at

---

26 The recent 'cash for honours' scandal in British government is a spectacular example of this sort of blurring: on the case for distinctive spheres of justice, see M. Walzer, *Spheres of Justice: A Defense of Pluralism and Equality* (1983).
27 Lacey and Pickard, op. cit., n. 1.

work in legitimizing and stabilizing broadly talionic punishments.[28] In essence, we argued that the capacity of early modern systems to coordinate punishment in such a way that it was perceived as fitting to the crime derived from a hierarchical social order, an association of certain forms of penal and political authority with the sacred, and the currency of a distinctive symbolism of equivalence. Though inconsistent with modern ideas of proportionality, particularly in the discretionary power which implied uneven application of penalties, we suggested that these three features of the context in which penal practice went forward in very different societies shed light on how substantive criteria of fittingness or equivalence depend upon background social and cultural conditions. We then drew on this analysis to argue that the neoclassical revival of the late twentieth century was problematic from its inception, because the metaphors of 'desert' and proportionality, particularly in certain countries, were no longer so obviously grounded in the widely shared symbolic systems representing agreed social norms, or in the forms of political or religious authority, which previously animated and stabilized substantive judgments of equivalence or fittingness.

We might summarize these developments as moving from a conception of fittingness grounded in appeals to divine command or reason – a form of vertical authority if you like – to a conception of fittingness grounded in the more horizontal – still allegedly 'objective' , but purportedly more rational – concept of proportionality. In relation to punishment, Beccaria[29] and Bentham[30] are, with good reason, thought of as the key figures in this modernization of the rationale of the state's exercise of its power towards a neoclassical aspiration, though even here there is significant variation. Beccaria is of particular importance in that his work stands as an important modern source of both of the two main ideas which have coincided and competed with one another as justifications of state punishment. These are, first, the argument that punishment is in some sense a morally appropriate equivalent to an offence, and is thus constrained by the requirement of proportionality, reviving ancient ideas of a natural order (an argument to be found in pure retributive form in the work of, for example, Kant, who further saw the imposition of deserved punishment as obligatory rather than merely permissible); and, second, the utilitarian argument that punishment, as a prima facie evil, can only be justified by countervailing good consequences, achieved through specific or general deterrence, incapacitation, rehabilita-

---

28  With due respect to Engle, op. cit. n. 6, the *lex talionis* is in my view a clear case of distributive justice in Aristotle's sense, and accordingly a close analogue of proportionality. On the logic of early punishments, see, in particular, P.C. Spierenburg, *The Spectacle of Suffering: Executions and the evolution of repression: from a preindustrial metropolis to the European experience* (1984).
29  Beccaria, op. cit., n. 9.
30  Bentham, op. cit., n. 9.

tion, restitution or moral education (an argument worked out, with a rigour approaching obsession, by Bentham).[31]

But what is the potential of this modernist, rationalist appeal to proportionality to limit penal power in practice? Empirical studies indicate a noteworthy degree of consensus, even across different countries, on the relative seriousness of standard offences – so-called 'ordinal proportionality'.[32] But they reveal no such consensus about what this implies in terms of what penalty is suitable – 'cardinal proportionality'.[33] In 'core' areas of criminal law, appeals to ordinal proportionality may therefore provide some basis for institutional arrangements such as sentencing guidelines.[34] The consensus of powerful epistemic communities in the legal and political spheres allowed for a concrete institutionalization of agreed norms of proportionality through the enactment of the various programmes of sentencing reform launched in many jurisdictions in the wake of the just deserts movement. And these provide plentiful examples of successful institutionalization of stable relativities between penalties. To this extent, proportionality has indeed been successfully concretized in the criminal justice context. But the lack of any comparable consensus about cardinal proportionality implies that appeals to proportionality are unlikely to be a successful basis *in and of themselves* for institutionalizing substantive criteria of a punishment's 'fitness': the actual content and level of the scale as a whole cannot be constrained by an appeal to proportionality in the absence of consensus

31 Again, with due respect to Engle (op. cit. n. 6), I would regard the utilitarian tradition as containing a distinctive iteration of the appeal to proportionality – as indeed is explicit in Bentham, id.

32 P.H. Robinson, R. Kurzban, and O.D. Jones, 'The origins of shared intuitions of justice' (2007) 60 *Vanderbilt Law Rev.* 1633; P.H. Robinson and J.M. Darley, 'Intuitions of Justice: Implications for Criminal Law and Justice Policy' (2007) 81 *Southern California Law Rev.* 1; and P.H. Robinson and R.O. Kurzban, 'Concordance and Conflict in Intuitions of Justice' (2007) 91 *Minnesota Law Rev.* 1831.

33 It is further the case that, while there is also evidence that the perceived severity of an offence predicts the intensity of the response judged by experimental subjects to be appropriate, perceived severity does not predict whether subjects opt for a punitive or a reparative response: M. Bang Petersen, A. Sell, J. Tooby, and L. Cosmides, 'Evolutionary psychology and criminal justice: A recalibrational theory of punishment and reconciliation' in *Human Morality and Sociality: Evolutionary and Comparative Perspectives,* ed. H. Hogh-Oleson (2010) 72. See below for discussion, and N. Lacey and H. Pickard, 'To blame or to forgive? Reconciling punishment and forgiveness in criminal justice' (2015) *Oxford J. of Legal Studies,* published online April 2015 at doi:10.1093/ojls/gqv012.

34 Even ordinal proportionality may be much harder to motivate beyond 'standard' offences, and hence across the wide terrain of so-called 'regulatory' offences or areas such as corporate crime. And yet more widely, changing attitudes, at different paces in different countries, relating to offences as disparate as driving under the influence of alcohol, insider trading, and various forms of sexual conduct may complicate assessments of ordinal proportionality, even in areas traditionally regarded as wrong in themselves.

around conventions about where the scale should be pitched (consensus moreover which both common sense and empirical research show to be lacking in many social contexts).[35] Hence the constraining power of the appeal to proportionality is contingent upon other aspects of the context and system in which it operates.

Proportionality, in short, does not have an independent effect: where it 'works' to limit punishment, this is because of its articulation of, and resonance with, deeper conventions, normative systems, political institutions, and social structures. The challenge, accordingly, is to try to understand the conditions under which proportionality both gains its appeal and has some potential to limit power: whether through consensus within a powerful epistemic community such as a judiciary, and/or through its being situated within detailed rules, doctrines, and institutional arrangements.

## RECONSTRUCTING PROPORTIONALITY

In effect, then, Pickard's and my deconstruction of the appeal to proportionality in contemporary criminal justice claimed that this metaphorical trope amounts to no more than a first step in the crucial and complicated processes of meaning making, consensus building, and institutional development necessary to limit punishment and appropriate to current conceptions of political and social authority. In early modern systems, state authority was, if not explicitly theological, invested with at least some form of sacredness: social orders were formed around a cosmology or system of meaning in which there appears to have been a remarkable degree of consensus about appropriate penalties notwithstanding their disproportionate use against the poor, in a context of extraordinary levels of inequality and deprivation. Of course, by the latter part of the eighteenth century, the legitimacy of the relevant social, political, and penal systems was under question, and they were comprehensively reformed over the following century. But this process of rationalizing and modernizing reform undoubtedly extinguished certain governmental resources which cannot be revived in contemporary conditions.

What relevance does this argument about appeals to proportionality in the context of criminal justice have for other areas of law in which they increasingly feature? Needless to say, there are likely to be significant differences attendant on the different functions, doctrinal structure, and institutional embedding of different areas of law. Yet some of the same problems and opportunities can be observed – in particular, the challenge of grounding and making concrete the power-constraining potential of appeals to proportionality. The institutional solutions and background conditions

---

35 See nn. 32 and 33, above.

may be different, but the basic structure of the challenge is similar. What is more, as Poole notes,[36] it is far from clear that modern appeals to proportionality have really abandoned the metaphysical pretensions of their classical forbears. And giving a clear shape to a renewed vision of that underlying cosmology in more sceptical, rationalist times is no easy task. As Poole elaborates:

> The task of the decision-maker applying proportionality is to identify those elements and values and then to fashion them in a way that produces a harmony of the parts and therefore justice. Now, this task (or at least the first stage of it) might not be too difficult in practice. The values at stake might be obvious. But where they are not, there is a danger that either the judges would be rudderless or the direction they steered would not have been agreed already by the polity at large. Both problems loom larger for us (perhaps) than for those who articulated the classical model.[37]

In light of this difficulty, our task must be one of more thoroughgoing institutional and normative reconstruction which coheres with the resources which are now regarded as legitimate and meaningful.

Our deconstruction of appeals to proportionality, however, is not inconsistent with a recognition of the need to engage in that sort of reconstructive project. In this concluding section, I want to suggest that such a project must engage with two further questions. First, it must ask what has prompted the resurgence of appeals to proportionality in so many countries and across so many doctrinal areas – while holding in mind the likelihood that there will be different explanations across different areas. Second, it must work towards a better understanding of the conditions under which, in differently structured modern legal and social systems, appeals to the metaphor of proportionality are most likely to have the limiting effect which they claim – and, conversely, it must be alive to the power of this metaphor to obscure the realities of power by holding out a promise of limits which remains purely rhetorical.

Turning to the first question: why has proportionality experienced such a marked increase in its pervasiveness as one of law's legitimating metaphors? As we would expect, the reasons vary across doctrinal areas. In criminal justice, the resurgence of appeals to proportionality has been a function of the neoclassical revival in the wake of the collapse of the rehabilitative ideal in the United States, Britain, Australia, and many other European and Nordic countries. It has also been a tool wielded by legislators in an effort to constrain judicial discretion. In public law, the growth of appeals to proportionality has been a product of the rapid growth of the field of human rights and has delivered significant interpretive power to judges. This set of developments was of course prompted in large part by the traumatic abuses of governmental power which culminated in the Second World War. The

36 Poole, op. cit., n. 6, p. 389.
37 id., p. 390.

determination to avoid such excesses in future directly informed the development of the United Nations and of the European Convention of Human Rights. These political developments have been further underpinned by transnational legal institutions such as the European Court of Human Rights and, in a separate line of development, the European Court of Justice, which have allowed concepts nested within a particular system to travel to other systems, adapting themselves in the process to their new environments, and which have increased the power and significance of judicial review of governmental power at both national and transnational levels. In public international law, again fostered by its engagement with human rights norms and by the growth of humanitarian law and the explosion of specialist courts, the long-standing role of proportionality in just war theory has experienced a renewed momentum and a wider significance. Moreover, ideas of proportionality have found their way into entirely new areas such as the regulation of international trade, via the framework of the World Trade Organization. So one might simply regard the current pervasiveness of the metaphor of proportionality as the outcome of a number of contingent and, to some extent, unrelated institutional developments.

But to see the current emphasis on proportionality exclusively in these terms would be, I think, to beg the question of just why this metaphor – out of many others which might have had a resonance in relation to the need to limit punishment – has such appeal, and in doing so to miss something of importance to socio-legal studies. Certainly, there is much merit to Stone Sweet's and Mathews's suggestion[38] that proportionality tests appeal to judges because of their capacity to underpin a wide measure of judicial discretion: indeed, this is precisely an upshot of the indeterminacy of the concept of proportionality already noted in our discussion of criminal justice. But there is surely more to be said about why, specifically, this particular discretion-legitimating concept has gained such traction. Speculative though any such suggestion may be, I would like to argue that there is indeed some more general significance to the current salience of proportionality across systems and contexts. Just as there was a certain counter-intuitiveness to the resurgence of ideas of 'community' in the 1980s, as politics in the advanced democracies was moving in an ever more individualistic and even libertarian direction,[39] much the same might be said about the pervasive appeal to proportionality in a world ever more organized around the sway of unconstrained market forces and the naked power of money. Greater and greater numbers of the world's inhabitants experience themselves as living in a market culture – sometimes loosely characterized as 'neoliberal' – apparently intent, in Wendy Brown's resonant phrase, on *Undoing the Demos*.[40]

38 Stone Sweet and Mathews, op. cit., n. 25.
39 See Lacey, op. cit., n. 3.
40 W. Brown, *Undoing the Demos: Neoliberalism's Stealth Revolution* (2015).

And many advanced democracies have witnessed a significant attenuation of the welfare and other social and political institutions designed to provide a measure of distributive justice and to counter pure market power. In such a context, the idea that we have in place legal arrangements still capable of constraining – indeed proportioning – power along the lines of long-standing constitutional aspirations may have particular force, just as the warm if unspecific appeal to 'community' provided a comforting fantasy of connection and interdependence in an increasingly atomistic and competitive world of 'ontological insecurity'.[41] This speculative thesis would speak in particular to proportionality's expansion into the terrain of private law.[42]

If this speculation has any merit, it implies that we must attend carefully to the dangers as well as the positive potential of law's metaphors. For it is precisely through their method of carrying meaning over from one thing to another that they bear the potential to mislead: to conjure up a legitimating image which is distant from the realities of the power relations embedded in law as enforced. And here, to move to our second question, it becomes truly important to focus on context, and, in particular, on the features of different contexts which affect the capacity of appeals to metaphors such as proportionality to deliver the values or outcomes to which they aspire and through which they add their persuasive and legitimating force to legal discourse. In criminal justice as elsewhere,[43] it is where metaphors such as proportionality are articulated with widely-held attitudes or well-established institutional practices which help to coordinate expectations that they hold their greatest potential to limit power in something like the way that their rhetorical force promises. Our evaluation of law's metaphors, in short, must not be confined to their conceptual structure, their discursive form or even their doctrinal elaboration: it must also attend to the institutional arrangements which provide the framework for their interpretation and enforcement, and to the interests and power relations which shape their development and implementation.

---

41 A. Giddens, *Modernity and Self-Identity: Self and Society in the Late Modern Age* (1991).

42 For a recent example illustrating the potential for appeals to proportionality in private law, see *Cavendish Square Holding BV* v. *Talal El Makdessi* [2015] UKSC 67. In this case, Lord Mance (para. 32) cited disproportionality as the basis for constraining an exercise of private power in the form of the imposition of an excessive damages clause in a contract: proportionality was a condition for the court legitimately to give this aspect of the private agreement legal authority. See, also, S. Shiffrin, 'Remedial Clauses: The Over-Privatization of Private Law' (2016) *Hastings Law Journal* (forthcoming), at <papers.ssrn.com/s013/papers.cfm?abstract_id=265842>, arguing that the – analogous – presumption against the enforcement of liquidated damages clauses in American law reflects the fact that remedies in private law themselves depend on an exercise of state power which should be conditioned by public values, proportionality among them.

43 See Lacey and Pickard, op. cit., n. 1.

JOURNAL OF LAW AND SOCIETY
VOLUME 43, NUMBER 1, MARCH 2016
ISSN: 0263-323X, pp. 45–65

# Flesh of the Law: Material Legal Metaphors

ANDREAS PHILIPPOPOULOS-MIHALOPOULOS*

*Existing legal metaphors, even the predominantly spatial and cor-
poreal ones, paradoxically perpetuate a dematerialized impression of
the law. This is because they depict the law as universal, adversarial,
and court-based, thus ignoring alternative legalities. Instead, there is a
need to employ more radically* material *metaphors, in line with the
material turn in law and other disciplines, in order to allow law's
materiality to come forth. I explore the connection between language
and matter (the 'flesh' of the law) through legal, linguistic, and art
theory, and conclude by suggesting four characteristics of material
legal metaphors.*

Ex-voto, 'for a favor granted':
for a life saved, an image.
It's the contract of the ex-voto, exemplary painting.[1]

## LEGAL METAPHORS: WHY AGAIN, WHY NOW?

Legal metaphors are no longer an original topic, neither in legal research
specifically, nor linguistics in general. The research credentials hark back to
Thomas Hobbes, Jeremy Bentham, and Lon Fuller,[2] complemented more
recently by a surge of mainly North American literature either specifically

* The Westminster Law and Theory Lab, University of Westminster, London
W1W 7UW, England
andreaspm@westminster.ac.uk

I am grateful to the IUAV University, Venice, for funding this research, and to Roswitha
Gerlitz, Anna Grear, Steve Greenfield, Sakis Kyratzis, Mirko Nikolic, and Elias
Avramidis for their feedback.

1 P. Falguières, *Danh Vo: mothertongue* (2015), exhibition flyer, The Norwegian
Pavilion, Venice Biennale.
2 T. Hobbes, *Leviathan* (1660); J. Bentham, *Theory of Legislation* (1871); L. Fuller,
'Legal Fictions' (1930–31) 25 *Illinois Law Rev.* 363.

45

on the topic of legal metaphors,[3] or the broader cognitive science of law field, in which metaphors feature heavily.[4] Equally, legal metaphors have been endorsed with gusto by linguists as case studies for linguistic theories;[5] and by philosophers in order to explore the laws of metaphor,[6] to confine metaphors to their literal statements,[7] to think of the normative appeal of disease metaphors,[8] to explore the speculative laws of object oriented ontology,[9] and to analyse the normative connection between language and biology.[10] There have been critiques of metaphors,[11] endorsements of metaphors,[12] and even exhortations to carry on metaphorically speaking because in this way the law can develop in more imaginative ways.[13] Lakoff and Johnson's conceptual metaphor theory[14] – a most influential analysis with a sizeable following in law – changed our understanding of metaphors from pure *language* construction to *thought*. So, while there are always new things to be said, the debate is so well established that it risks becoming part of the legal norm, adding nothing new to the frontiers of legal theoretical thinking. Why is it then that another text or indeed series of texts on legal metaphors is needed? What will it add and where will it take the discourse?

New research on legal metaphors is needed because the legal theoretical context is changing, or more precisely, *turning*. The law (and I am using this generic term deliberately for reasons I show below) is turning in a spatial, corporeal, and generally material way.[15] In the same way, I suggest, legal metaphors must also change. Standard spatial and corporeal metaphors on

---

3 See J.C. Rideout, 'Penumbral Thinking Revisited: Metaphor in Legal Argumentation' (2010) 7 *J. of the Association of Legal Writing Directors* 155.

4 See (2002) 67 *Brooklyn Law Rev.*, dedicated to Steven Winter's *Clearing in the Forest: Law, Life, and Mind* (2001), and, in particular, M. Johnson, 'Law Incarnate', 949.

5 M. Johnson, 'Mind, Metaphor, Law' (2007) 58 *Mercer Law Rev.* 845.

6 See, for example, P. Ricoeur, *The Rule of Metaphor* (2003).

7 R. Rorty, *Contingency, Irony, And Solidarity* (1989).

8 S. Sontag, *Illness as Metaphor* (1978).

9 I. Bogost, *Alien Phenomenology, or What It's Like to Be a Thing* (2012).

10 D. Haraway, *How Like A Leaf: An Interview with Thyrza Nichols Goodeve* (2000).

11 Rosi Braidotti's call against metaphors in 'Animals, Anomalies, and Inorganic Others' (2009) 124 *Theories and Methodologies* 526.

12 For example, L. Morra, 'New Models for Language Understanding and the Cognitive Approach to Legal Metaphor' (2010) 23 *International J. of Semiotics of Law* 387.

13 Johnson, op. cit., n. 5.

14 G. Lakoff and M. Johnson, *Metaphors We Live By* (2003).

15 Admittedly later than most social sciences and humanities. See B. Warf and S. Arias (eds.), *The Spatial Turn: Interdisciplinary Perspectives* (2009), which typically does not have a chapter on law. On law and matter, see A. Pottage, 'The Materiality of What?' (2012) 39 *J. of Law And Society* 167; A. Grear, 'Human rights, property and the search for world's other' (2012) 3 *J. of Human Rights and the Environment* 173; A. Philippopoulos-Mihalopoulos, 'A Sociolegal Metatheory' in *Exploring the Legal in Sociolegal Studies,* eds. D. Cowan and D. Wincott (2015); A. Philippopoulos-Mihalopoulos, 'Critical Autopoiesis and the Materiality of Law' (2014) 27 *International J. of Semiotics of Law* 165.

which the law traditionally relies, are useful (section 2), but at the same time paradoxically perpetuate law's *de*materialization and abstraction (section 3). Instead, I suggest something novel and more ambitious, quite unlike the standard endorsements or critiques of legal metaphors: what I call *material legal metaphors*, namely, metaphors that are more than mere figures of speech, but are rather *embodied in the very body of their emergence, the law itself.*[16] Understanding metaphors as *the transfer of meaning from one regime of signs to another,*[17] I suggest (in the fourth and fifth sections) that material legal metaphors are the bridge between the semiotic and the material, opening thus the way for a new conceptualization of justice. This is not an abstract, textual or even future justice, but an immanent, embodied, spatially embedded justice. This is how I understand the term 'flesh' of the title: as the crux between semiosis and materiality.

The term 'flesh' appears explicitly only towards the end of the article but pulsates throughout the text and especially the interlaced passages in italics. These passages refer to Titian's last ever painting, the *Pietà*, with the materiality of which I performatively engage here in order to shed some light on legal metaphors. I undertake a close reading of both the representation and materiality of the painting, and I begin with the contract for the painting; this contract sets the scene for the first metaphor of my analysis, namely, the fact that meaning is transferred from the legal (contract) to the object (painting). The commissioning church in Venice was justly perhaps expecting the standard representation of *Pietà*, not least because people would know how they were expected to *feel* when looking at a *Pietà*. In other words, the metaphor determined the object itself, involving affective predetermination and excluding alternative conceptualizations. This, I argue, is what happens with the existing corporeal and spatial legal metaphors: via their pre-conscious effect, they determine what the law is supposed to be while marginalizing alternative forms. Titian's *Pietà*, however, did not adhere to the accepted metaphor. It carved a new path, in exactly the way I suggest material legal metaphors operate. The painting was not well received since the contractual recipients were operating within a closed system of metaphors that precluded alternative explorations of meaning. What they missed, however, was a key to the *Pietà* that Titian masterfully included in the canvas. Purely for reasons of suspense, I shall not yet reveal what this 'key' to the painting was. But my argument is that through this, the whole painting

---

16 For this reason, I do not engage with distinctions referring to metaphors of, in, or about the law (see F. Makela, 'Metaphors and Models in Legal Theory' (2011) 52 *Les Cahiers de Droit* 397, for a comprehensive but potentially sterile classification), since I find them permeable: however internal ('in' law) metaphors might be, they end up annulling the distinction between law's operations and law's perception by the rest of society.

17 Lakoff and Johnson, op. cit., n. 14, offer the transfer definition. The regimes of signs I draw from G. Deleuze and F. Guattari, *A Thousand Plateaus* (1992).

becomes a material metaphor for a contract with a party that could not easily be pinned down: death. In the conclusion, I refer to two material legal metaphors whose function is parallel to that of *Pietà*, namely, an attempt to capture the very thing that the law is.

## LAW, LANGUAGE, AND METAPHORS

Metaphorical thinking is creative thinking.[18] Its creativity lies in the transfer (Greek μεταφορά, *metaphor*, meaning 'transfer') of meaning from one regime of signs to other regimes. I draw the term 'regime of signs' from Deleuze and Guattari, according to whom regimes of signs are the various modes (machines) in which society represents itself.[19] These modes are not just linguistic but also material, and provide a context for meaning. Nathan Moore puts it clearly when he refers to regimes of signs as including 'elements, such as bodies and things (including tones, exclamations, gasps, stutterings, and so on), excluded from language (*la langue*).'[20] A metaphor, therefore, is the transfer of meaning from and to signs that are neither exclusively linguistic nor exclusively material. As I show below, the law is a good example of the above, in the sense that it is both linguistic and material.

Ever since the influential *Metaphors We Live By* by linguist George Lakoff and philosopher Mark Johnson, we know that 'our ordinary conceptual system, in terms of which we both think and act, is fundamentally metaphorical in nature.'[21] This means that metaphors are not mere figures of speech but determine how *thought* is structured and evolving.[22] Of course, law's textuality can hardly be disputed. In the traditional, exclusively linguistic understanding, 'law as (fundamentally a system of) meaning is only accessible through (linguistic) signs and thus dependent on the process of interpreting the signs.'[23] Even this approach, however, has been diluted, and sign interpretation has moved towards a more emplaced, material understanding. So, rather than seeing law (and language) as *langue*, namely, the Saussurian term for the abstract structure of language for which the cognitive mediation of participants is of marginal effect, we are moving towards a semiotic understanding of law (and language) as an outcome of

---

18  Winter, op. cit., n. 4, p. 5.
19  Deleuze and Guattari, op. cit., n. 17, p. 182.
20  N. Moore, 'Icons Of Control: Deleuze, Signs, Law' (2007) 20 *International J. for Semiotics of Law* 33, at 41. See, also, J. Murray, 'Deleuze & Guattari's Intensive & Pragmatic Semiotic of Emergent Law' (2007) 20 *International J. for Semiotics of Law* 7.
21  Lakoff and Johnson, op. cit., n. 14, p. 3.
22  See, also, G. Lakoff, 'The Contemporary Theory of Metaphor' in *Metaphor and Thought*, ed. A. Ortony (1993) 202.
23  J. Engberg and K. Wølch Rasmussen, 'Cognition, Meaning Making, and Legal Communication' (2010) 23 *International J. for Semiotics of Law* 367, at 367.

concrete situations, devoid of a priori or unchanged structures. In a most informative passage, Engberg and Wølch Rasmussen put the two approaches clearly:

> if language and meaning is mainly a superindividual concept, then the process of establishing the legal meaning of, for example, statutory texts in concrete interactions is one of looking into the superindividual in order to find a meaning. . . . If, on the other hand, language is seen mainly as an entity applied by individuals in their communicative and meaning creating (= semiotic) activities, then the process of establishing legal meaning is one of negotiating with other individuals the *meaning relevant in concrete situations*, a process which leaves much more relevance to the opinions and the ideological stance of the people involved.[24]

The first approach has been steadily losing ground to the second, especially after the latter's further cognitivist development, confluent with the affective turn in social sciences and humanities.[25] Affects are neither immaterial nor necessarily communicable notions, but the embodied and spatialized circulation of information that takes place in *concrete situations*. For this reason, spatial and corporeal metaphors are the most frequent ways of meaning transfer (in our case, from space and body to law), largely to do with the simple fact that we have bodies that move in space.[26]

Thus, we talk about finding the *sources* of law, which denote a physical movement 'back' to the originary fountain. We talk about legal *grounds* in argumentation, giving the impression of something stable and unmoving; there is a *system* of law to contain with, with its disciplinary *boundaries*, its *jurisdictional* application, and its court *hierarchies* such as *high* and *low* courts; a judge *balances* and *weighs* interests, putting one party's interests on the one side, and the other's on the other; and there are legal *lacunas* and *gaps* in the law through which one can slide. In the same manner, there is legal *standing*, namely, to find one's footing in the space of the law and defend oneself.[27] Standing implies an erect and even respectful posture of one's body before the court, despite the fact that one might be burdened by the *carrying* of a right or an obligation. Even the law itself is a body, the *body of law*, the legal *corpus*, with its *long arm*, its equity *conscience*, its *blind* justice, even its fully developed, organismic *constitution*. Obviously, law is a brittle thing, for why else could one *break* the law? Still, law is larger than us: one can easily be *within* the law. But rest assured, there is *nowhere to hide from the law*.

One could go on. But what reads as an entertaining 'a-ha!' moment for those of us who have not thought of legal metaphors before, reveals this: that we operate with metaphors on a preconscious level, namely, a level where

24 id., p. 368, added emphasis.
25 See M. Gregg and G. J. Seigworth (eds.), *The Affect Theory Reader* (2010).
26 Winter, op. cit., n. 4; Lakoff and Johnson, op. cit., n. 14.
27 See S. Winter, 'The Metaphor of Standing and the Problem of Self-Governance' (1987–88) 40 *Stanford Law Rev.* 1371.

language is accepted unquestioningly. We are so conditioned by the ruling metaphors of law that a) we do not question them and b) we allow them to carry on determining the way we stand in relation to the law, since we cannot even imagine a different way. This preconscious conditioning of reality via metaphors begs the question: how far have legal metaphors penetrated society's skin? Can we still maintain that legal metaphors are just language?

In an influential article on law and metaphors, Johnson expands on the fact that concepts are 'learned automatically through our bodily interactions with aspects of our environment.'[28] Johnson has found that concepts are conceived as physical objects through our bodies. The meaning transfer from idea to object is what Steven Winter calls 'an acquisition or "taking in" of that object'.[29] This is crucial for our purposes because it confirms that the law is understood through metaphors – as Johnson writes in the conclusion of his study on metaphors of property, land access, and law, 'you cannot practice property law without metaphor!'[30] It also shows that legal metaphors are not merely figures of speech (language) but embedded in thought, in its turn embodied in the movement of bodies in space who perceive of ideas as physical objects. In sum, we can no longer talk of law and legal metaphors as mere symbolic entities, but as a shared surface between the semiotic and the material.

Importantly, metaphors rely on 'highly determinate "spatial" or "bodily" logics that support and constrain inferences.'[31] An example is offered by Norman Spaulding: 'doctrinally, the dominant, indeed controlling, metaphor for the constitutional guarantee of procedural due process is a courtroom trial.'[32] Spaulding classifies this as a *dead* metaphor, namely, an ossified, fixed metaphor that perpetuates law's *closure*, in exactly the same way as the courtroom *enclosure* is thought of as sealed off and independent, even when televised or thoroughly reported upon:

> Enclosure not only symbolized the independence of law from political, commercial, and social space; it served to restrict access, limit vandalism, minimize the disruption of trial, and, perhaps above all, encourage deference to the administration of justice in a democratic society perpetually anxious about the authority of law and lawyers.[33]

In other words, understood through the metaphor of bodies enclosed in a physical space, the trial is the outcome of law's (self-perceived) need of self-

---

28  What he calls 'image schemas': Johnson, op. cit., n. 5., p. 856. See, also, G. Lakoff and M. Johnson, *Philosophy In The Flesh: The Embodied Mind And Its Challenge To Western Thought* (1999) 3–5.
29  Winter, op. cit., n. 4, p. 53.
30  Johnson, op. cit., n. 5., p. 867.
31  id., p. 856.
32  N.W. Spaulding, 'The Enclosure of Justice: Courthouse Architecture, Due Process, and the Dead Metaphor of Trial' (2012) 24 *Yale J. of Law & Humanities* 311, at 315.
33  id., p. 316.

defence against society's doubts. To put it more radically, enclosure is the metaphor that defends law's legitimation by excluding the rest of the world. Think of what Ebbesson points out: 'few professional groups that define the rest of the world through a negation, i.e. as "non-lawyers". Ever heard of "non-plumbers", "non-taxi-drivers", "non-nurses" or "non-teachers"?'[34]

### *Pietà I: From Contract to Object*

*Venice, late 1500s. A contract is signed between the most renowned painter of the Venetian Renaissance, Titian Vecellio, and the Franciscans Brothers of the Church of* Santa Maria Gloriosa dei Frari. *Burial ground for Titian will be reserved in the church, in return for a specially commissioned painting. The contract stipulates the dimensions of the canvas, the material, and its exact location, the* Altar of the Cross.[35] *It is agreed that this painting will be the altarpiece on Titian's tomb.*

*Above all, the contract stipulates the topic of the painting. Titian is to paint an 'imago pietatis pietà',*[36] *or what we have come to know as* Pietà. Pietà *('pity', 'piety', 'mercy') is the accepted term for the depiction of the Virgin Mary holding the dead body of Jesus in her arms after his deposition from the cross. The term originates in the Byzantine iconography of the* Man of Sorrows *(Imago Pietatis), namely, the dead Christ with his arms crossed over his chest.*[37] *The signified developed to the presently known form after the Florentine Renaissance and, in particular, Michelangelo popularized it with his* Pietà *statue (1498–99).*[38]

*The term* Pietà *is a metaphor. The original transfer of meaning from the Byzantine theme to that of the Virgin Mary and Jesus, was a fitting dominant metaphor for the counter-reformation signification system of artistic demands, and eminently useful for the church of the* Frari. *A* Pietà *encouraged emotional identification and response from the viewer, combined with chaste meditation.*[39]

> *The Pietà ... represents an eternal moment, a theological epitome in which fundamental truths are manifested in an affective but ideal image.*

---

34 J. Ebbesson, 'Law, Power And Language: Beware Of Metaphors' (2008) 53 *Scandinavian Studies in Law* 259, at 261.

35 C. Ridolfi, *Le Maraviglie dell'Arte* (1648, reprint 1914–24).

36 L. Puppi, *Su Tiziano* (2004) 63.

37 S. Ringbom, *Icon to Narrative: The Rise of the Dramatic Close-up in Fifteenth-Century Devotional Painting* (1965).

38 A. Nagel, *Michelangelo and the Reform of Art* (2000) 50.

39 J.M. Saslow, 'Pietà' in *Eye of the Beholder*, eds. A. Chong et al. (2003); Ringbom, op. cit., n. 37.

*The beauty of the visual concept resides precisely in its synthesis of human pathos and liturgical symbolism.*[40]

*In other words, the metaphor was successful because the contemporary viewer would know, not only what the term meant pictorially, but also what she was expected to feel upon seeing a* Pietà. *A complex affect consisting of empathy with the pious stories of the Virgin and Christ, and a deeper understanding of Christian mercy, is transferred as part of the politics and religious art of the time.*

*There is a second metaphor at play. Every contract transfers meaning from the contractual regime of signs to that of the contractual object, whether this is an actual object, an action, a movement, and so on.*[41] *In Titian's case, meaning is transferred from the contractual object (a* Pietà*) to the material object (the* Pietà*). According to this metaphor, the contractual object was expected to be a* Pietà *in the manner of Michelangelo. But this metaphor, which was what the Frari understood as* Pietà*, was already dead for Titian. His* Pietà *is a different metaphor that breaks the enclosure of the contractual* Pietà *and hurls meaning into a new regime of signification.*

## THE ENCLOSURES OF LEGAL METAPHORS

Successful legal metaphors have three main characteristics.[42] First, they have to be part of a consistent metaphorical system – precisely like the contractual *Pietà* – that determines meaning expectations. A metaphor will only work and catch on if consistent with the existing metaphorical edifice. We have seen that for law, the dominant metaphor that determines the metaphorical system is the trial enclosure with its control over who moves, who stands, who sits higher, who sits in a box. The effect of such a metaphor cannot be underestimated. Victoria Brooks has produced a thorough reading of the affective edifice of the law as materialized in the courtroom. She finds that 'the courtroom contains and twists bodies into its tiny caverns and grand panelled auditoria, with walls built to ensure the painful silencing of already terrorized bodies.'[43] These hierarchical spaces legitimize themselves with the help of references borrowed from history and divinity (and each judicial space has different ways of

---

40  D. Rosand, 'Titian in the Frari' (1971) 53 *Art Bull.* 196, at 211.
41  Indeed, every contract is a metaphor: J.M. Lipshaw, 'Metaphors, Models, and Meaning in Contract Law' (2012) 116 *Penn State Law Rev.* 987; also, R. Posner, *Law and Literature: A Misunderstood Relation* (1988) 101, for whom Dr Faustus's contract with the devil is a 'metaphor for commitment'.
42  I focus on those of particular relevance to law. For a complete list, see Lakoff and Johnson, op. cit., n. 14.
43  V. Brooks, 'Interrupting the Courtroom Organism: Screaming Bodies, Material Affects and the Theatre of Cruelty' (2014) *Law, Culture and the Humanities*, doi: 10.1177/1743872114543767.

asserting itself[44]), both in terms of architecture and insignia.[45] An example of the power of metaphor is the meaningless *dieu et mon droit* ('god *and* my right'): in the metaphorical system of hierarchies, enclosures, walls, and corridors of direction, a sentence written in unintelligent French (it is an incomplete sentence even in French) serves its purpose. There are of course plenty of other forms, practices or typologies of law that fall outside the metaphorical enclosure. But the dominant metaphor of the law remains an enclosure. The meaning transfer in this case is this: the world is excluded, the law is reinstated.

Second, a successful metaphor needs to be repeated. Once is not enough, since it still hits the conscious level, as Christopher Rideout shows in his influential text on the legal penumbra and the intense controversy this metaphor has caused to the legal world in the United States.[46] When adequately repeated, however, it becomes part of the norm. Ann Cammett has recently argued that the repetition of such metaphors as 'Welfare Queen' in the North American context has led to the unquestioned understanding that specific people, namely, black women of poor background, constitute an unwanted social burden:

> Racism plays a central role in Americans' collective historical and cultural heritage. Metaphors in this context also act as 'carriers of cultural elements', shaping how we make sense of the world and what we value and privilege.[47]

Third, a successful metaphor must trigger a preconscious, affective response that engages physical, symbolic, and emotional elements – as we have seen in the emotional identification that occurred with the more traditionally defined *Pietà*.[48] A metaphor evokes in its target audience a sense of responsibility. The audience must understand the metaphor, must feel that they belong to the consistent system of the metaphor, and must elaborate the metaphor in the same way as the body (the brain and/or the body itself) of the utterer. Johnson writes:

> there is no human conceptualization or reasoning without a functioning human brain, which operates a living human body that is continually engaging environments that are at once physical, social, cultural, economic, moral, legal, gendered, and racialized.[49]

---

44 L. Mulcahy, *Legal Architecture: Justice, Due Process and the Place of Law* (2010).
45 id.
46 C. Rideout, 'Penumbral Thinking Revisited: Metaphor in Legal Argumentation' (2010) 7 *J. of the Association of Legal Writing Directors* 155.
47 A. Cammett, 'Deadbeat Dads & Welfare Queens: How Metaphor Shapes Poverty Law' (2014) 34 *Boston College J. of Law & Social Justice* 233, quoting C. Lawrence, 'The Id, the Ego, and Equal Protection: Reckoning with Unconscious Racism' (1987) 39 *Stanford Law Rev.* 317, at 322.
48 On the emotional response of metaphors, see J. Charteris-Black, *Corpus Approaches To Critical Metaphor Analysis* (2004) 19; also, W. Patry, *Moral Panics and the Copyright Wars* (2009).
49 Johnson, op. cit., n. 5., p. 846.

It is only through a commonality (actual or aspirational) of such environments that the transfer of meaning is successful. Law's metaphors posit precisely this responsibility. Uttered by lawyers, judges, members of parliament, politicians, or even TV shows, social networking sites, and other media, legal metaphors are expected to be understood and embodied, since they come from *above*, where the good stuff is. This is not only a national jurisdictional issue. The metaphorical distinction between above and below is so embedded that lies in the core of colonial and postcolonial oppression of North versus South,[50] capturing happiness ('I'm feeling *up*. That *boosted* my spirits. My spirits *rose*. You're in *high* spirits.'); abundance and health ('The numbers keep going *up*.' 'He's at the *peak* of health. He's in *top* shape.'); and even the future ('All *up* coming events are listed in the paper. What's coming *up* this week?'), while sadness, illness, poverty, and past lie down below, in the South.[51]

According to the above criteria, existing spatial and corporeal legal metaphors are successful. They are consistent with each other and the grander legal metaphorical system; they are repeated in judgments, media coverage, everyday vernacular; and they are used unaware of their metaphorical nature, thus triggering an affective response in whoever wants to be *within* the law and yet avoid its *long arm*. Existing spatial and legal metaphors are part of what conceptual metaphor theory describes as *container metaphors*, themselves a form of enclosure. Lakoff and Johnson employ the example of a running race which poses as a distinct unit 'having in it participants (which are objects), events like the start and finish (which are metaphorical objects), and the activity of running (which is a metaphorical substance).'[52] The courtroom trial, the lawyers/non-lawyers distinction, indeed the law as a whole, obeys the logic of container metaphor, with its distinct beginning and end, its participants, its spatiality, and its specific activity: all neat metaphors that allow us to construct the law as a discrete activity, taking place in designated areas, affecting only the ones that are part of a trial or some adversarial legal procedure, and crowned by the final administration of justice. Container metaphors are at the core of a human need for separation, enclosure, and boundary setting. It is what Teresa Brennan calls 'the foundational fantasy', namely, the necessity of constructing a difference between self and environment.[53] Through its metaphors, law feeds this fantasy.

The larger container metaphor of the law as courtroom trial promotes an understanding of law as legitimate, adversarial, and enclosed, which, in its turn feeds the law's metaphorical system. This is the ultimate enclosure as

---

50 N. Wey Gomez, *The Tropics of Empire: Why Columbus sailed South to the Indies* (2008).
51 All examples from Lakoff and Johnson, op. cit., n. 14, pp. 15–17.
52 id., pp. 30–1.
53 T. Brennan, *The Transmission of Affect* (2004).

© 2016 The Author. Journal of Law and Society © 2016 Cardiff University Law School

described by Niklas Luhmann: the autopoietic, that is, self-preserving, legal system only accepts notions that are consistent with its existing structure.[54] A consistent metaphorical system, therefore, provides two things: a way of filtering which metaphor is relevant; and a given direction in which bodies (metaphorical and otherwise) are expected to move. This happens in a circular way, as Winter shows when he discusses how rules necessarily depend on the cultural practices they are meant to regulate.[55] Legal metaphors aim at establishing, maintaining, and imposing certain structures, and in this way they can end up marginalizing and excluding not just parts of society but also different modes of law. Metaphors reify 'the' law as something stable, solid, measurable, and scientific – thus pacifying social expectations of law's reliability. Carel Smith writes that existing legal metaphors:

> add to the view that the law is something that exists 'out there' ... The use of spatial metaphors to describe law, in short, might explain that lawyers are still attracted to the dubious idea that legal adjudication could be performed neutrally, as detached as a scientist who measures the distance between the Milky Way and the Andromeda Galaxy.[56]

Metaphors are characterized by a duality: 'in allowing us to focus on one aspect of a concept ... a metaphorical concept can keep us from focusing on other aspects of the concept that are inconsistent with that metaphor.'[57] Legal metaphors describe one kind of law and one kind of relation to the law, all in the service of maintaining the law's facade of weighed objectivity and blind impartiality, as well as the legal compulsion for adversarial resolution. They highlight precision, scientific balancing, and equity in terms of confrontation, and they obscure both the input of the hand of the judge and its weight, and other modes of dispute resolution such as contextual decision making, adjudication, consensus-based resolution, mutualism, and so on.[58] The fact that legal metaphors are used by advocates in potentially contradictory ways to illustrate their arguments and thus affect the court decision does not alter the fact that adversarialism remains the main legal container metaphor. Most often, legal metaphors highlight law's connection to order, balance, and justice, emphasizing thus a legal monopoly on it, while revolt, civil disobedience, or different kinds of balance lie on the other side of the law. Susan Sontag writes: 'political events started commonly to be defined as being unprecedented, radical; and eventually both civil disturbances and wars come to be understood as, really, revolutions.'[59] On

54 N. Luhmann, *Law as a Social System* (2004).
55 S. Winter, *A Clearing in the Forest: Law, Life and Mind* (2001).
56 C. Smith, 'The Vicissitudes of the Hermeneutic Paradigm in the Study of Law' (2011) 4 *Erasmus Law Rev.* 21, at 37.
57 Lakoff and Johnson, op. cit., n. 14, p. 10.
58 G. Barak, 'A Reciprocal Approach to Peacemaking Criminology: Between Adversarialism and Mutualism' (2005) 9 *Theoretical Criminology* 131.
59 Sontag, op. cit., n. 8, p. 80.

the other hand, current legal metaphors obscure the fact that law is self-legitimizing,[60] while highlighting the law's social expectations aspects, and thus feeding into the need for more policing, more security, more laws. Legal personification has comparably unequal effects, as Ebbesson finds:

> the metaphor of person contributes to legitimising why some categories (such as legal persons) are bestowed with human rights without being humans, while other categories are excluded, even though the legislation may be intended to protect them (for example environmental law and animal welfare law).[61]

There is another, to my mind deeper issue with the standard spatial and corporeal legal metaphors. Rather than actually bringing forth the materiality of the law, these metaphors offer a sliver of controlled spatiality and corporeality which advance the purposes of legal abstraction. This is often the irony of the metaphor, or what Sontag has called its contradictory application:[62] spatial and corporeal legal metaphors turn the law *away* from capturing its legal spatial and embodied meaning. Henri Lefebvre has written on how legal metaphors deny the body to which they refer by discursively breaking it down into pieces.[63] Heeding these metaphors, one would think that the law is still something that resides exclusively in the courtroom, that is hierarchical and adversarial by nature, that has an actual origin able to provide the law with its much needed legitimacy, that it is different from politics, economics, culture, religion, and so on. But we now know that the law is everywhere,[64] that its courtroom-based form is losing ground to other forms of adjudication,[65] that its disciplinary boundaries are arbitrary constructions that serve disciplinarian means according to various interests,[66] that jurisdiction is not actual geographical space but what the law makes of geographical space,[67] and that, finally, the law is not abstract but embodied in all the bodies of its emergence whether human or nonhuman.

From innocuous figures of speech to reality-determining distinctions,[68] illuminating while obscuring, and appeasing the need for particular application of the law while upholding law's abstraction, current spatial

---

60  Luhmann, op. cit., n. 54.

61  Ebbesson, op. cit., n. 34, pp. 263–4.

62  Sontag, op. cit., n. 8.

63  H. Lefebvre, *The Production of Space* (1991).

64  A. Sarat, ' "…The Law is All Over": Power, Resistance and the Legal Consciousness of the Welfare Poor' (1990) 2 *Yale J. of Law and the Humanities* 343.

65  O. Fiss, 'Against Settlement' (1984) 93 *Yale Law J.* 1073; L. Webley, 'When is Mediation Mediatory and When is it Really Adjudicatory?' in *Mediation and Religious Arbitration,* eds. S. Bano and J. Pierce (2016).

66  M. Foucault, *Society must be Defended* (2003).

67  A. Philippopoulos-Mihalopoulos, *Spatial Justice* (2015).

68  'The textual apparatus is transformed into a libidinal apparatus, a machinery for ideological investment.' F. Jameson, *The Political Unconscious* (1981) 15.

and corporeal legal metaphors are in the service of what Deleuze has called *control society*. Legal metaphors have become *control signs*. Moore puts it thus:

> the control sign functions to make reality and representation indistinguishable. On this basis, it becomes possible for control to not only manipulate reality as if it were a sign (the two obvious examples being marketing and religion), but also to insist upon any regime of signs as an inevitable and inescapable 'reality' or fact (for example the 'war on terror').[69]

**Titian, *Pietà*, 1576, Gallerie dell'Accademia, Venice**

69 Moore, op. cit., n. 20, p. 52.

57

*Venice is being ravaged by the plague. Titian, of already advanced age, paints his* Pietà *as a plea for mercy ('pietà'), a standard practice of the time. But mercy is not granted. Titian dies from the plague, the* Pietà *left in a seemingly unfinished state.*

The painting was never hung in the Frari Church. We can only hypothesise, but this seems to be the main reason: what Titian produced was not a Pietà. *Thematically, it contained no divine redemption or promise of eternal life. It had little to do with the salvation of the* Altar of the Cross.[70] *There is no Michelangelo elegance here – the container* Pietà *metaphor. Titian's* Pietà *is dark, haunting, sparse. The vanishing point is neither Christ nor Virgin, but another metaphor: Titian employs his teacher's Giovanni Bellini's serene, golden apses, but turns them into a dark, tomb-like, haunted, empty awning. Bellini's sacred conversation becomes Titian's howl. The apse transfers the meaning of eternity, from Bellini's limpid, luminous faith in a crystal-clear future, to a space filled with the dread of death. Stylistically, the painting could be rejected as unfinished.[71] Yet this is also part of Titian's metaphor: in his later paintings, Titian developed a technique that did not accord with the accepted standards of Venetian – or any other, for that matter – painting. He used his fingers rather than the brush;[72] he applied thick impasto to accentuate a drama too coarse for conservative Venice; he courted violence and darkness that could only be justified by describing the paintings as unfinished.*

In rejecting the painting, the Frari were operating within the consistent system of metaphors that had determined what a Pietà was, what an appropriate altarpiece should look like, what constitutes a finished piece of art, and what constitutes an adequate metaphorical object of contract. Titian's Pietà *would not fit any of them.*[73]

---

70  Ridolfi, op. cit., n. 35.
71  Rosand, op. cit., n. 40, p. 210. However, E. Tietze-Conrat, 'Titian's Workshop in His Late Years' (1946) 28 *The Art Bulletin* 76, at 80, finds that the composition 'is established in every detail.' See, also, R.S. Winter, 'Of Realizations, Completions, Restorations and Reconstructions' (1991) 116 *J. of the Royal Musical Association* 96, at 97. See F. Pedrocco, *Titian* (2000) on Palma il Giovanne's contribution.
72  T. Nichols, *Titian and the end of Venetian Renaissance* (2013).
73  id. The Frari were always slow to appreciate Titian, as evinced in their reluctance to hang Titian's first altarpiece, the *Assunta.*

In an interview on the body of her work, Donna Haraway says:

> I find words and language more closely related to flesh than to ideas ... Since I experience language as an intensely physical process, I cannot *not* think through metaphor ... I experience myself inside these constantly swerving, intensely physical processes of semiosis.[74]

Haraway's embodied metaphor goes somewhat further than the conceptual metaphor approach. This is no longer about how metaphors are produced, in the conceptual metaphor sense of the brain and body's participation. For Haraway, feminist philosopher with a biology background, the linguistic body is as physical as any material body.

> Understanding the world is about living inside stories. There's no place to be in the world outside of stories. And these stories are literalized in these objects. Or better, objects are frozen stories. *Our own bodies are a metaphor in the most literal sense.* This is the oxymoronic quality of physicality that is the result of the permanent coexistence of stories embedded in physical semiotic fleshy bloody existence. None of this is an abstraction.[75]

Haraway's metaphors are always material, co-extensive with the body of their emergence. Not only do we conceive ('taking in') of concepts as physical objects, as Winter, and Lakoff and Johnson have argued above; rather, concepts have their own physicality. We do not merely construct them as objects. They *are* objects.

As we have seen, standard legal spatial and corporeal metaphors discount law's materiality. But what is law's matter? And how do we reconcile it with the fact that law is *also* and at least at first instance, textual? I have written on law's materiality elsewhere,[76] so here I will limit myself to the following observations. First, it is important to consider law's materiality broadly, and not as something limited to legal files, court spaces, and so on.[77] Law is not confined to what is semiotically understood as legal, but permeates life in terms of bodies, objects, and spaces. From the simple example of the evolution of the legal profession that accepts that an increasing amount of previously reserved activities can now be performed by non-lawyers,[78] to the more complex issue of legal agency attributed to corporations, rivers, and

---

74 Haraway, op. cit., n. 10, pp. 85–6.
75 id., p. 107.
76 Philippopoulos-Mihalopoulos, op. cit, n. 15 and n. 67.
77 B. Latour, *The Making of Law: An Ethnography of the Conseil d'Etat* (2004); Pottage, op. cit., n. 15.
78 A. Perlman, 'Towards the Law of Legal Services' (2015) 37 *Cardozo Law Rev.* 2284; L. Webley, 'Legal Professional De(re)regulation, Equality, and Inclusion' (2015) 83 *Fordham Law Rev.* 2349.

networks,[79] the law is unfolding its material nature in increasingly more evident ways. Critical socio-legal research is overwhelmingly showing that embodiment (in the broadest sense of bodies as human and non-human) is the only way in which the law exists.[80]

The second point I would like to make is that the law has an interest in concealing its materiality. Law's greatest trick is to make us believe in its supposed abstract, universal, immaterial, merely semiotic nature. How else could this other favourite legal metaphor, that of blind justice, operate? Indeed, how else could law operate materially *and* control without making its presence asphyxiating? Take a walk and observe the law enabling, channelling, impeding, accelerating your movement; see the illegality of hoods in shopping malls, veiled women in Paris, unveiled women in Afghanistan, walking in the nude in London. And then try to touch these bodies – the law will stop you; sniff out how the law allows baking bread smell to circulate through a supermarket's air shafts, while prohibiting smells from a restaurant percolating the upstairs flat. And so on, without even talking about planning regulations, zoning, and privatization of public spaces. Life is thick with law, so thick that the law becomes invisibilized. So invisibilized that it is as if it *is not* matter, that indeed it *does not* matter. Law presents itself (without ever itself falling for this trick) as abstract, distant, and closed. Existing legal metaphors perpetuate the separation of matter and law by pacifying the quest for legal matter, and thus reinstating the exclusively semiotic nature of law. The challenge we are facing now is to understand law as both semiotic and material. In order to do this, we need to embrace what I call material metaphors, namely, metaphors that bring together the material and semiotic regime of signs.

Before focusing on these metaphors, let me briefly suggest a way in which meaning is transferred between the material and the semiotic through Spinozan ethics, and particularly his concept of *parallelism*.[81] Moira Gatens and Genevieve Lloyd explain that:

> nothing that happens in the order of thought depends causally on anything that happens in the order of material things, or vice versa. But the 'order of thought' and the 'order of things'... are mapped onto one another in a relation of correspondence.[82]

This is Spinoza's parallelism, which cultivates togetherness but also distance. In that sense, law is both matter and language, but these two withdraw from each other, offering only easy metaphors in their stead. At the

---

79 A. Grear, *Redirecting Human Rights: Facing the Challenge of Corporate Legal Humanity* (2010); B. Jessup and A. Jones, 'In one ear and out the other' in *Research Handbook on Human Rights and the Environment*, eds. A. Grear and L. Kotzé (2015); G. Teubner, *Networks as Connected Contracts* (2011).
80 Cowan and Wincott, op. cit., n. 15.
81 B. Spinoza, *Ethics* (2000) Book III, E2p7.
82 M. Gatens and G. Lloyd, *Collective Imaginings: Spinoza, past and present* (1999) 3.

same time, legal matter and legal language evolve together, although not causally dependent on each other. Parallelism is Spinoza's way of populating the vast oneness (god or nature) that for him determined everything, while allowing for difference between matter and mind. I would like to think of Spinoza's parallelism as the *law's flesh*: neither just a thing nor just a concept, *flesh* is the parallel co-existence of both legal matter and legal language, brimming with legal texts, statutes, decisions, opinions, symbols, but also bodies and spaces that would seemingly be outside the usual symbolic expanse of the law, yet in reality they are in the core of what it means to be legal.

This is what Haraway means when she refers to 'the materialized semiosis of flesh'.[83] Legal matter and legal language are inextricable. Our responsibility as scholars given to the burden and delight of interdisciplinary research, is to try and take in matter and mind together, without succumbing to easy separations.

### *Pietà III: The Last Metaphor*

*On the bottom right-hand corner 'a painting inside the painting recalls the rules and the contract.'[84] Titian has included an* ex-voto, *a votive image depicting two men, one aged and one younger, praying to a floating* Pietà. *The two men have been identified as Titian and his son Orazio, whom Titian expected to take over the workshop after his death.[85]*

*The ex-voto is the material metaphor of the painting, reaching out from within.[86] By including it in the canvas, Titian tells us many things: first, this might not be a traditional* Pietà *but through the votive image as the interpretative key, the painting* becomes *a* Pietà. *Second, this new metaphor changes the whole reference system. The ex-voto renders the whole altarpiece a votive offering.[87] Titian makes sure that this, 'the most poignant conceit in the composition' as David Rosand*

---

83 Haraway, op. cit., n. 10, p. 86; see M. Merleau-Ponty's 'The Flesh' in his *The Visible and the Invisible*, tr. A Lingis (1968); also, G. Deleuze, *Francis Bacon: The Logic of Sensation* (2003).

84 Falguières, op. cit., n. 1.

85 E. Panofsky, *Meaning in the Visual Arts* (1982).

86 'Metaphors can be constructed in modes other than language, for example in visual images. Accompanying verbal text, however, plays a crucial part in focusing and shaping the visual metaphor.' H. Stöckl, 'Metaphor Revisited: Cognitive-conceptual versus Traditional Linguistic Perspectives' (2010) 35 *AAA – Arbeiten aus Anglistik und Amerikanistik* 189, at 202. The ex-voto operated as the accompanying text, since the viewers would know exactly that it meant to denote.

87 '[T]he votive pictorial conventions ... effectively transform the large painting into a votive image.' M. Holmes, 'Ex votos: Materiality, Memory and Cult' in *The Idol in the Age of Art*, eds. M. Cole and R. Zorach (2009) 180.

*put it,*[88] *does not escape the attention of the viewer. He allows only one source of light in the painting, and that is the bottom right corner of the painting, where the* ex-voto *lies. The painting is structured along this luminous diagonal: bodies, glances and hands are aligned to this one perspective. Even a part of the apse is highlighted by the metaphor, thus insinuating a sliver of hope. It is Titian's way of asking the plague to pity him and his son.*

*Orazio, however, also dies in the plague, more or less at the same time as Titian. Titian's final contract was honoured by neither party, whether the Frari or death.*

## LAW'S MATERIAL METAPHORS

How can we perceive of the flesh of the law? My answer is, through *material legal metaphors*. I define material legal metaphors as fleshy, pulsating metaphors that emerge from within the body of law, determined by and in their turn determining how the law, in its fleshy, that is, material and textual dimension, is to be understood. These are novel rather than fixed ('dead') metaphors and generally operate as conceptual metaphors do, with some fundamental differences in relation to the traits discussed above in section 3:

*first*, material metaphors make explicit their material provenance, not only in their name (so not only in terms of figures of speech) but fundamentally in the way they attempt to grapple with both matter and law.

*second*, material metaphors do not operate as a container in a consistent system whose boundaries are closed and determined; rather, even when in the form of enclosures, they remain contingent and undetermined.

*third*, although they rely on repetition and affective response, they are, at least at first, *counter-intuitive*. They are often neologisms or even forced combinations of terms that cause questioning rather than preconscious acceptance.

*fourth*, they do not control the perception of legal reality as singular, nor do they guide perceptions in a certain direction, but allow a fleshy malleability of perception that can take different paths – exactly as the law is.

Law as a whole is a material metaphor.[89] No doubt to talk about law generically and without specification, risks essentialization, shedding light on one side of it (whatever the author wants to emphasize) and obscuring other sides of law. This is a real risk but also, I think, a risk worth taking, if only to avoid another risk: to perpetuate the impression that the law can be compartmentalized into public law, private law, property law, EU law, and

---

88 Rosand, op. cit., n. 40.
89 Strictly speaking, this is a synecdoche, but the metaphorical operation of meaning transfer occurs here too.

so on. The classic understanding of *areas* of law (another metaphor) imparts the false idea of legal difference according to subject matter. But we know that these are epistemological conventions. In reality the law spills over, knows no internal boundaries, needs the rest of the law in order to stand. The same applies to the law in relation to other disciplines. Law is not politics, economics, geography, chemistry, medicine, psychology, and so on. But is that really the case? All these disciplinary distinctions collapse at a single trial or a single statutory instrument. In practice, the law has always been a cross-disciplinary excursus, where lawyers and judges and even legal academics need to have a passable level of knowledge of some other discipline. For these reasons, I do not object to the use of the generic term 'law'. If anything, the metaphor is palpable, and through it one can perceive law's embodiment and spatialization not as an exception, but as everyday occurrence. We need to carry on using the metaphor of *the law* because the law needs to be further banalized. What initially would not seem like the law (a pavement or a caress or a flood) becomes the law.[90] Talking about the 'law' is a fundamental material metaphor, emerging from the core of the law yet allowing it to form contractual synapses with other disciplines as well as with bodies and spaces. The material metaphor of the law breaks the habitual metaphor system that determines what the law is, and resemiologizes objects as the law.[91]

In the concluding part of this text, I would like to focus on what I consider the most fundamental material metaphor for the law, 'the most poignant conceit in the composition':[92] justice. At first instance, the metaphor of justice as Justitia, the blind, scale-balancing, sword-cradling woman, seems perfectly fleshy, that is, both material and discursive. This woman, however, is a puppet. As feminist critique has convincingly shown,[93] Justitia's fetishized blindness and its token sword threat reek of masculine construction. It is a

---

90 This is what I have called (Philippopoulos-Mihalopoulos, op. cit., n. 67) *the lawscape*, a material metaphor that moves beyond the standard corporeal and spatial legal metaphors and contains the semiotic and the material in one epistemological and ontological tautology.

91 Examples of other material metaphors in law can be found in Grear, op. cit., n. 79, a particularly good example of fleshy resemiologization of current corporate metaphors. In A. Philippopoulos-Mihalopoulos, *Absent Environments* (2007), I suggested the material metaphor of waste as both a physical and a legal concept. Another material metaphor has been the Derridean 'deconstruction is justice', in J. Derrida, 'Force of Law' (1990) 11 *Cardozo Law Rev.* 920 – see A. Moser, 'Justice Of Metaphor – Metaphor Of Justice' in *Philosophische Perspektiven*, eds. O. Neumaier et al. (2005) 199.

92 Rosand, op. cit., n. 40.

93 J. Resnik, 'Reconstructing Equality: Of Justice, Justicia, and the Gender of Juris-diction' (2002) 14 *Yale J. of Law and Feminism* 393; J. Resnik and D. Curtis, *Representing Justice: Invention, Controversy, and Rights in City-States and Democratic Courtrooms* (2011); R. Lee, 'Justice for All?' (2012) 217 *Vanderbilt Law Rev.* 217; on gender blindness and supposed impartiality, see M. Minow, 'Justice Engendered' (1987–1988) 10 *Harvard Law Rev.* 10.

product of the father law, an Athena jumping out of Zeus's head, or an Eve carved out of Adam's rib. Justitia is devoid of flesh, artificially propped up on top of courthouses, her strings pulled by a paternalistic law that hides behind a female appeal and offers itself to the male gaze.[94] She is so excessively surrounded by the symbols of her borrowed power that she collapses under the weight of her own gravitas.[95] As a metaphor, Justitia highlights a certain understanding of female power, while at the same time obscuring its status as derivative, paternalistic, and patronizing. Its materiality is subsumed in its desperate symbolism. Blind justice is a 'conceit', but not a material metaphor.[96]

What is left then? What is the material metaphor of the law that guides the law from within while at the same time expanding its horizon? What is the immanent metaphor of law's *ex-voto* that will capture the end of law, in the same way that Titian's *ex-voto* tried to capture death? In this quest, it is important to maintain justice as the absolute immanence of the law, its horizon and ultimate goal. It must remain the interpretative 'key' to the whole legal system, guiding the law from within legal operations. But it must also remain a contingency, as Luhmann puts it, namely, what *might* happen when the law applies – but there is no guarantee.[97] At the same time, justice must be embodied and spatialized, fully materialized, away from paternalistic depictions; its contingency must not be blind, but must look into the particulars of each body and the differences across the spatial continuum; finally, it must not be anthropomorphized, obeying token rules of attribution and enabling facile identification.

I have called this material metaphor *spatial justice*: a post-human take on existing discourses of spatial justice,[98] which challenges identification by keeping on repeating the question 'why am I positioned in this way?' This is not a metaphysical but a physical quest, beginning with the violence inherent in the fact that every body necessarily occupies a certain space to the exclusion of other bodies. Spatial justice as a question emerges when a body (individual or collective) moves into the space of another body (individual or collective). This movement is a constant occurrence. Spatial justice ques-

---

94  Resnik and Curtis, id. I. Bennett Capers, 'On Justitia, Race, Gender, and Blindness' (2006) 12 *Michigan J. of Race & Law* 203.

95  See L. Mulcahy, 'Imagining Alternative Visions of Justice' (2011) 9 *Law, Culture and the Humanities* 311, at 322; see, also, Resnik and Curtis, id., commenting on the Venetian Justitia, surrounded by male figures and their symbols.

96  P. Goodrich, 'The Foolosophy of Justice and the Enigma of Law' (2013) *Yale J. of Law and the Humanities* 141, at 143, makes a valid point of Justitia's metaphorical value and, more generally, of the 'visible structures and plastic forms that constitute the immediate and recognized presence of law', ultimately, however, subsumed into 'the imaginary of justice that lawyers sometimes remember to address.'

97  Luhmann, op. cit., n. 54.

98  I define spatial justice, op. cit., n. 67, in contrast to the current understanding of the notion which, I argue, is fundamentally aspatial and with no connection to the law.

tions the rightfulness of such a movement, and the way the various geopolitical, ecological, but also quotidian conflicts are supposedly resolved, namely, on arbitrary historical, ethnic, economic, and other grounds.

Spatial justice operates as law's material metaphor because, first, it brings together materiality and law; second, it is not a container metaphor that determines a process arbitrarily separated by a paper-thin skin from its horizon, but a constellation of potentialities that open up in the violence of space without given direction. In that sense, it does not follow a fetishized description of the liberal body as separate, self-contained, and given to teleology (habitually fed by current container legal metaphors) but sees the body for what it is, namely, in a neuronic material continuum with space and other bodies; third, it causes questioning (why only spatial? why not temporal? what has space to do with justice? and so on) initiating rather than closing off the debate; and, fourth, it does not attempt to prescribe a singular solution but allows a negotiation of fleshy bodies to determine its outcome.

Material metaphors are not easy things. They are counter-intuitive and do not easily catch on; they frequently test new ground for which no vocabulary exists; they escape the given system of metaphors yet they are also inscribed in it; finally, they refuse to separate matter from language. But perhaps more importantly, they aim for something that remains difficult to capture and even harder to negotiate with. Space, body, law: their materiality is vast, all-informing, omnipresent. Any term would by definition leave out a great deal of their complexity. The problem with all these issues with which material metaphors are grappling is not that they are transcendental. Rather, very much like death in Titian's *Pietà*, they are constantly around us, with us, in us.

JOURNAL OF LAW AND SOCIETY
VOLUME 43, NUMBER 1, MARCH 2016
ISSN: 0263-323X, pp. 66–84

# The Trials of Lizzie Eustace: Trollope, Sensationalism, and the Condition of English Law

IAN WARD*

*The Eustace Diamonds was published in 1872. It was the third of Anthony Trollope's famed Palliser series. It represented, however, something of a diversion, telling the story of the 'cunning' Lizzie Eustace who declines to return a priceless diamond necklace to the estate of her recently deceased husband. Critics have supposed that* The Eustace Diamonds *can be read as a contribution to the contemporary genre of 'sensation' novels. Sensation novels were full of sex, crime, and scheming young women like Lizzie Eustace. The law should of course have brought to Lizzie to justice. But it does not; indeed it barely tries. For the law in* The Eustace Diamonds, *as in so many 'sensation' novels, is conspicuous only in a failure that is as metaphorical in purpose as it is prosaic.*

## INTRODUCTION

The idea that writers might deploy the law as a metaphor for something else is not new, and neither is the more particular idea that Victorian authors might have done so in order to nurture broader reflection on the 'condition' of England. Charles Dickens's *Bleak House* is commonly read in these terms. Dickens did not have much time for lawyers, especially those he created, and not much patience with legal process. But it was not just Dickens. Travesties of procedural justice lie at the heart of novels such as Thackeray's *The Newcomes*, George Eliot's *Adam Bede*, and Mary Gaskell's *Mary Barton*, whilst egregious lawyers can be found constantly wandering throughout the pages of the Victorian canon. Nowhere, however, was the failure of law so commonly deployed than in the so-called 'sensation' novel of the 1860s and early 1870s. The sensational 'moment' was relatively brief. But it was long enough, too long according to many. English literature was

* Newcastle Law School, Windsor Terrace, Newcastle upon Tyne NE2 7RU, England
ian.ward@newcastle.ac.uk

never the same again.[1] It was not simply that the sensation novel was written differently. So too was it read differently. The purpose of this article is to take a closer look at the sensational moment and, more particularly, at one novel which was intended to be read perhaps at the margins of the sensation genre, Anthony Trollope's *The Eustace Diamonds*. Trollope was a rather evasive sensationalist, as we shall see, but when his devoted readers encountered the first serialized parts of his novel in late 1871, they found much with which they had elsewhere become all too familiar. There was sex, crime, and a wicked woman; and there was a legal system which was patently unable to do much about the sex, the crime or the wicked woman.

## THE SENSATIONAL MOMENT

In the Preface to the second edition of his *The English Constitution*, published in 1872, Walter Bagehot invited his readers to contemplate England 'in the time of Lord Palmerston'. It was not, in terms of strict chronology, much of a reach. Palmerston had died in October 1865. In terms of constitutional 'reform', however, the intervening seven years represented an 'age'; or at least it did to Bagehot. Palmerston had known that placing 'power in the hands of the masses' only 'throws the scum of the community to the surface'.[2] But barely two years after the 79-year-old Palmerston's heart had given out, whilst groping a maid on the billiard table at Brocket Hall, the Tory administration of Derby and Disraeli had recklessly enacted a second 'mischievous and monstrous' Reform Act, as a consequence of which England was now a very different place, and a much more worrying one. There had, Bagehot soberly advised, been 'great changes in our politics', changes of a 'pervading spirit'. The 'bovine' masses had been given the vote, for which reason he could predict only 'calamity' and socialism.[3] Even Derby famously conceded that the Act represented a 'leap in the dark'. But he was persuaded of the evil necessity. As Disraeli averred, the 'times' were 'tempestuous' and without another Act there would likely be revolution in the streets of London.[4]

---

1 See here P. Brantlinger, 'What is "Sensational" about the "Sensation Novel"?' (1982) 37 *Nineteenth Century Fiction* 1, at 1–2. In Brantlinger's influential genealogy, the 'sensation' novel can be placed between late Gothic and the emergent genre of detective fiction. If there had been no sensation 'moment', there would not, the surmise runs, have been a Sherlock Holmes or a Hercule Poirot. Winifred Hughes places the sensation novel at the same 'transitional' point: see her *The Maniac in the Cellar: Sensation Novels of the 1860s* (1980) 70.
2 M. Bentley, *Politics Without Democracy* (1996) 161.
3 W. Bagehot, *The English Constitution* (2001) 194–5, 197–8, 201–2; A. Buchan, *The Spare Chancellor: The Life of Walter Bagehot* (1959) 138, 144–5, and 208, commenting on the tone of 'settled melancholy' which characterizes the 1872 Preface.
4 A. Briggs, *The Age of Improvement* (1959) 497.

67

R.H. Hutton would later, famously, acclaim Bagehot as the 'greatest Victorian'.[5] The compliment was as much representational. Asa Briggs suggested the same a few years later in an essay on mid-Victorian constitutionalism. Bagehot, Briggs ventured, was representative of a certain mid-Victorian state of mind; intellectually liberal, viscerally conservative, necessarily troubled. It was moreover a common predicament. Lots of Victorian gentlemen, for whom the 'age of improvement' had morphed into a 'world of nightmare', felt much the same.[6] And their metaphors had darkened accordingly. Derby did not invoke a leap in the light. Neither did Thomas Carlyle. His essay on the 1867 Act was entitled *Shooting Niagara: And After?* It was, of course, the same Carlyle who, forty years earlier, had first supposed that England was 'sick and out of joint' and suffering from a debilitating 'condition'.[7] Little had happened in the intervening decades to make him any less grumpy. Nothing was to be gained by looking back to 1832 he opined. 1790 was the pressing historical referent. Dickens, fresh from publishing his *Tale of Two Cities*, agreed. The 'general mind' of England as the 1860s advanced was much like that of revolutionary France.[8] There would in the end be no revolution. But the fear that the next riot was only, quite literally, a stone's throw away remained. There were in sum plenty of reasons to worry in mid-Victorian England; too many voters, too many closet Jacobins, too many cities and too many people moving to them, too few going to church, too few finding employment, too much sex, and too much crime.

And too many people reading stuff too. Literacy levels were rising inexorably. The 1851 census revealed that 31 per cent of men and 45 per cent of women were still functionally illiterate. By 1871 the figures were down to 19 per cent and 26 per cent. By 1860 there were over five hundred Mechanics' Institutes up and down the country running literacy classes. 1859 saw the publication of the first academic study of the novel. Eighty-six million newspaper stamps were issued in 1850. By 1864, the circulation figures for provincial weeklies was in excess of two and half million. There were five different dailies and five weeklies in Newcastle upon Tyne alone. Driffield had three weeklies. For the professional writer, a larger readership was a matter of celebration; more readers meant more money. For reformers such as John Stuart Mill it was furthermore an unarguable sign of progress. Others were less sure. Reading in general, Victoria's first Prime Minister Lord Melbourne observed, was the 'vice of the present day'.[9]

---

5 G. Young, 'The Greatest Victorian' in *The Collected Works of Walter Bagehot, Vol. 15*, ed. N. St John Stevas (1986) 209, 212.

6 Briggs, op. cit., n. 4, pp. 95, 102.

7 G. Himmelfarb, *The Spirit of the Age: Victorian Essays* (2007) 48.

8 G. Jones, 'Introduction' in *Charles Dickens, A Tale of Two Cities and the French Revolution*, ed. G. Jones (2009) 10.

9 L. Mitchell, *Lord Melbourne* (1997) 22, 25.

More especially there were all the novels, especially those which were commonly termed 'sensational' and which had burst onto the literary scene at the very dawn of the 1860s. The 'sensation' novel was of course a particular expression of a broader 'sensational' moment. Whilst Westminster bickered about the merits and demerits of further franchise reform, the attention of the rest of England had turned to an epidemic of moral and sexual degradation which was spreading through its alleyways, gin-houses, and drawing rooms. Godless, leaderless middle England, as the readers of the morning papers daily discovered, had lost its moral compass; a supposition the credence of which was seemingly enhanced by the joyously salacious accounts of proceedings which were being brought before the newly established Divorce Court. And then there were all the murders. Countless column inches were taken up with the lives, and deaths, of the 'Doncaster poisoner' William Palmer, of the murderous teenager Constance Kent who preoccupied the celebrated Mr Whicher for so long, the notorious Madeleine Smith who was accused of poisoning her lover in Glasgow, but who sensationally escaped the noose with a 'not proven' verdict, and so many others. It was all so thrilling. Sex and crime, it seemed, was everywhere. England was teeming with psychopathic daughters and murderous lovers, whilst behind every twitching net-curtain might be found a bored and bigamous housewife.

Many of whom were also, and of course, reading sensation novels, the most successful of which invariably contained three essential ingredients: sex, crime and, most importantly, a beautiful young woman who was either traduced by wicked men or who, conversely, had devoted her life to traducing them. The gender connotation was defining, the expectation pressing, as the hugely successful Mary Elizabeth Braddon acknowledged. There was 'nothing', Braddon recognized, that 'English men and women enjoy more than' a 'really good murder', except perhaps for a spot of salacious extra-marital sex.[10] So that is what she and her fellow sensationalists gave them, along with myriad instances of spousal violence, rape, fraud, bigamy, even the occasional 'criminal' conversation. The 'palette' of the sensation reader, she remarked on a different occasion, 'requires strong meat, and is not very particular as to the qualities thereof'.[11] The presence of crime moreover necessitated the presence of law, for which reason there would invariably be a scattering of generally clueless detectives and mendacious lawyers; not, of course, to provide any reassurance, but rather to serve as a chorus of the contemptible.

---

10 The sentiment found famous expression in George Orwell's analysis of Victorian sensationalism, entitled 'The Decline of the English Murder' in *The Penguin Essays of George Orwell* (1968) 351–4.

11 J. Carnell and G. Law, 'Our Author: Braddon in the Provincial Weeklies' in *Beyond Sensation: Mary Elizabeth Braddon in Context*, ed. M. Tromp (2000) 150; R. Wolff, *Sensational Victorian: The Life and Fiction of Mary Elizabeth Braddon* (1979) 155–6, 163.

Two of the novels commonly regarded as announcing literary sensationalism, Braddon's *Lady Audley's Secret* and Ellen Wood's *East Lynne*, both move around the myriad lies of adulterous women who think nothing of transgressing moral and legal norms in order to realize their marital and amorous ambitions. The latter is perhaps unusual in presenting readers with a relatively positive depiction of a worthy, if crushingly dull, lawyer: the cuckolded Archibald Carlyle, whose wife runs off to France with her lover. There are no similarly worthy lawyers, dull or otherwise, in any of Braddon's novels. There are, however, lots of bored and beautiful young women, and lots of cuckolded men. In *Lady Audley's Secret* there is perhaps the most beautiful and most pathological of all. The eponymous Lucy Audley rampages across Braddon's blockbuster, marrying and murdering a series of besotted men until her crimes are finally uncovered by an acquaintance of one her unfortunate victims. Of course the idea of prosecuting Lucy before the law is barely countenanced. Instead she is sent to a far worse fate, to live the rest of her life in Belgium.

The consonance between England's 'condition' in the 1860s and the rampant popularity of the sensational genre was commonly appreciated by variously disapproving critics, alongside the especially troubling gender implication. Amongst the more perceptive was a young Henry James who, in a review of Braddon in 1865, observed of sensational novels that their:

> novelty lay in the heroine being, not a picturesque Italian of the fourteenth century, but an English gentlewoman of the current year, familiar with the use of the railway and the telegraph. The intense probability of the story is constantly reiterated. Modern England the England of today's newspaper crops up at every stage.[12]

Sensation novels, James appreciated, were set in the here and the now, and whilst they might have sought recourse to all manner of familiar Gothic tropes, in fact purported to present something that was intensely real and ordinary. The perceptive James was one of the few to take a more reflective view of sensationalism. Fraser Rae, though hardly approving of the literary 'abomination', likewise noted that Braddon's particular success lay in her ability to present crime as 'the business of life'. So did an anonymous reviewer in the *Christian Remembrancer* who invoked a Carlylean resonance in concluding that the sensation novel was clearly a 'sign of the times'. Others eschewed perception for a simpler, more visceral, disgust. The Reverend Paget expressed himself to be 'utterly demoralised' by the sensation novels that he was invited to review; 'so licentious and so horrible'. The Very Reverend Henry Longueville Mansel, Dean of St Pauls, indomitable literary reviewer and self-appointed guardian of the nation's morals, agreed. There was 'something unspeakably disgusting in this ravenous appetite' for sensationalist 'carrion'.[13]

---

12 In I. Ward, *Sex, Crime and Literature in Victorian England* (2014) 65.
13 id., pp. 61–2, 64–5.

Prospective audience was a common concern, pathological metaphors a common recourse. The *Westminster Review* suggested that the 'sensational mania' was a species of 'virus' for which there was no known treatment. According to Mansel, sensation novels were written to satisfy 'the cravings of a diseased appetite'. The blame lay more closely with those women writers who failed to appreciate their responsibility to the coming 'genera-tion'.[14] In due course Braddon would admit that a novel such as *The Doctor's Wife*, a blatant plagiarism of Flaubert's *Madame Bovary* which she churned out in 1864, was 'not a story' which should be 'placed in the hands' of a 'young person'.[15] But that was much later. In 1864 she just banked the cheques and kept on writing her stories of wicked women, gullible husbands, and ripped bodices. And in this she was certainly not alone, as was only too patently, and painfully, apparent.

As the 1860s unfolded, middle England was assailed by countless similar tales, and not just from the more familiar culprits, Wood and Braddon, Wilkie Collins and Charles Reade. A new generation sensed an opportunity. A young Thomas Hardy managed to kick-start his career in 1871 with the strategically entitled *Desperate Remedies*. It said everything the circulating library reader needed to know; and Hardy never looked back. And then there were the more established and hitherto more respectable who, to the evident horror of their erstwhile critical admirers, appeared to succumb to the demands of the market and the lure of very large advances. Amongst their number might be counted the Charles Dickens who published *Great Expectations* in 1861 and who, a decade on, died midway through *The Mystery of Edwin Drood*. Another, perhaps, was the novelist who, in his essay on the mindset of anxious mid-Victorian England, Briggs placed alongside Walter Bagehot as representative of what Lord Brougham famously termed the 'intelligence of the country': Anthony Trollope.

## THE TRIALS OF LIZZIE EUSTACE

As a self-styled 'advanced conservative liberal', Trollope like Bagehot was caught between a residual fear of revolution and a broader appreciation of 'improvement'. He too was an avowed admirer of Palmerston, and the kind of pragmatic, if increasingly arcane, species of Whiggery which had apparently died that same morning in October 1865. It has been suggested that the entire series of Palliser novels, which Trollope had begun in late 1864, can be read as a kind of extended encomium to the virtues of 'old' Whiggery. There is certainly much that is 'old' Whig in the lead character of Plantagenet Palliser, not least the determination not to allow the practice of government to be derailed by fanciful ideologies. Bagehot termed it 'dull-

14  id., p. 64.
15  Wolff, op. cit., n. 11, p. 61.

ness', and meant it as a compliment. Trollope later suggested that in casting the irredeemably dour and dedicated 'Planty' Plantagenet he had come closest to creating the 'perfect gentleman'.[16]

Back in 1867, as the second Reform Act was struggling through Parliament and Bagehot was wrestling with the various essays which made up his *English Constitution*, Trollope was still basking in the critical acclaim which accompanied the publication of the last two Barset 'chronicles' and the first Palliser novel *Can You Forgive Her?* By 1872, conversely, his star had waned slightly, despite the relative success of the second Palliser novel *Phineas Finn* in 1869. Whilst some kind comments had been made regarding *Ralph the Heir*, which appeared in 1871, other recent novels such as *Linda Tressel* and *Sir Harry Hotspur* had failed to generate much critical applause or much money, whilst the current serialization of *The Golden Lion of Granpere* was hardly making waves. There was however another novel which had begun serialization in the latter part of 1871. It was entitled *The Eustace Diamonds*, and was written as the third of the Palliser novels. The final instalment appeared at the very end of 1872, the full-length novel a few months later. A little later, Hugh Walpole would acclaim the novel as 'one of the first comedies in the ranks of the English novel'.[17]

There is a brief account of *The Eustace Diamonds* in Trollope's *Autobiography*, sandwiched between a muse on the hassles of moving house and the rather different stresses which came with organizing a visit to Australia.[18] The novel, Trollope summated, is nothing other than the 'record of a cunning little woman of pseudo-fashion, to whom, in her cunning, there came a series of adventures unpleasant enough in themselves, but pleasant to the reader.'[19] Allusions were made to Thackeray and Wilkie Collins. As he wrote, the 'idea constantly presented itself to me that Lizzie Eustace was but a second Becky Sharp', whilst in regard to the plot, Trollope further surmised, his 'friend' Collins would probably have 'arranged' it better.[20] But, in regard to the *Autobiography* at least, that was it. Trollope was not inclined to dwell too long on *The Eustace Diamonds*. He was clearly not too impressed with his own handiwork. He had 'written much better'.[21]

It is certainly true that everything moves around the 'cunning' Lizzie, wife of the recently deceased Sir Florian and in contested possession of a necklace of diamonds estimated to be worth £10,000. Lizzie claims that Sir

---

16 See A. Trollope, *Autobiography* (1996) 229, and also P. Brantlinger, *The Spirit of Reform: British Literature and Politics 1832–1867* (1977) 209–10.
17 H. Walpole, *Anthony Trollope* (1928) 99. More modern critics have tended to be kinder too. Victoria Glendinning suggests that it is 'one of his best novels', see her *Trollope* (1992) 403.
18 Trollope, op. cit., n. 16, pp. 217–19.
19 id., p. 218.
20 id. Not that Trollope was much of an admirer of Collins's style. With Collins, he observed, 'it is all plot'.
21 id.

Florian intended her to keep the jewels. They are, she maintains, 'altogether my own', given her 'forever and ever'. No one believes her. Nothing more than 'downright picking and stealing' Lady Lithlithgow opines (p. 91).[22] Such 'a necklace', as Lord Fawn recognizes, 'is not given by a husband even to a bride in the manner described by Lizzie'. In fact they were merely lent 'for the purpose of a special dinner party'. At first the Eustace family is inclined to let things rest for 'the sake of tranquility'. The family lawyer Mr Camperdown, however, is determined that the 'swindler' Lizzie cannot be allowed to get away with her 'robbery'. He will 'jump upon' her (pp. 75, 264). Lizzie however refuses to relinquish possession. Nor is it clear that she should. She knows that the diamonds were 'not really' her own, but is genuinely 'not sure' in law whether she must relinquish them. Her 'ideas about law and judicial proceedings were very vague' (p. 93).[23] In this she is not alone. As Lizzie digs in, an increasingly frustrated Camperdown casts around for alternative legal strategies. But the more he casts around the more frustrated he becomes. He seeks recourse to the esteemed Mr 'Turtle' Dove, barrister and 'learned counsel' of unquestioned authority, for an opinion on the law of heirlooms (pp. 261–2). If the diamonds can be considered heirlooms, then it would not have been within Sir Florian's power to give them to Lizzie, for which reason she would not be entitled to keep them.

Conscious of the criticism which had attached to a previous attempt to navigate his way through the 'meshes' of the law in the earlier *Orley Farm*, published in 1860–1, Trollope asked his friend and fellow Garrick Club member, Charles George Meriwether QC, to draft Dove's opinion.[24] It was certainly comprehensive, replete with five legal authorities and eleven further judicial opinions. Unfortunately what it did not provide was much legal clarity. The diamonds, Mr Dove resolves, cannot be proven to be 'heirlooms' since Lord Eustace as 'devisor' did not item them as such in his will. Moreover, the idea that 'any chattel may be made an heirloom by an owner of it' is anyway mistaken. And so is the belief that the law of heirlooms is concerned with 'trinkets only to be used for vanity and orna-ment'. In sum there is 'much error about heirlooms'. And the situation would not necessarily have been resolved if the diamonds were considered to be heirlooms, for they might then be deemed 'paraphernalia'; articles of per-

---

22  All references given internally are to A. Trollope, *The Eustace Diamonds* (2004).

23  See here S. Daly, 'Indiscreet Jewels: *The Eustace Diamonds*' (2005) 19 *Nineteenth Century Studies* 69, at 72; also W. Kendrick, '*The Eustace Diamonds*: The Truth of Trollope's Fiction' (1979) 46 *ELH* 136, at 145.

24  The reference to the 'meshes' of the law is found in *Phineas Finn* and is generally agreed to be an allusion to the difficulties he encountered in *Orley Farm*. See A. Pionke, 'Navigating "Those Terrible Meshes of the Law": Legal Realism in Anthony Trollope's *Orley Farm* and *The Eustace Diamonds*' (2010) 77 *ELH* 129; also M. Wan, '*Stare Decisis*, binding precedent, and Anthony Trollope's *Eustace Diamonds*' in *Reading the Legal Case: Cross-Currents Between the Law and the Humanities*, ed. M. Wan (2013) 205–6.

sonal property which can be retained after marriage. The law, Mr Dove confirms, 'allows claims for paraphernalia for widows'; at least in 'limited' form, most of the time. In Lizzie's case a claim that the diamonds were 'paraphernalia belonging to her station' might be 'doubtful', but arguable still (pp. 262–3, 297).[25] There was rather too obviously a lot that was 'doubtful'; about Lizzie, about the diamonds, and about the law which was supposed to govern their proprietary relation.

Camperdown, hitherto the epitome of cold reason, is driven to distraction: 'A pot or pan may be an heirloom, but not a necklace! Mr Camperdown could hardly bring himself to believe that this was the law.' He muses obsessively on the inability of the law to deal with 'an evil-minded harpy' such as Lizzie. It is:

> a thing quite terrible that, in a country which boasts of its laws and of the execution of its laws, such an imposter as was this widow should be able to lay her dirty, grasping fingers on so great an amount of property, and that there should be no means of punishing her (pp. 289–92).[26]

Thoroughly distressed, Camperdown visits Mr Dove in his Chambers for further explanation. Pressed to explain why the diamonds would not be considered to be an heirloom, Dove opines that whilst a single diamond might be so determined, a necklace would not for the simple reason that its setting might be changed at will from one generation to another. It could hardly thus be deemed to be 'precious'. Camperdown is incredulous. It is in part a problem of 'error', but it also a problem of uncertain precedent and the finest of interpretive semantics. Camperdown has devoted his entire professional life to the law. But when he needs it most, it disappoints. All, he concludes bitterly, after hours of pouring over precedents, settings, and settlement deeds, is 'confusion' (pp. 184–5, 295).

And it is not just Camperdown who despairs. 'As far as I can see', Lord Fawn tells another of the family lawyers, Hittaway, 'lawyers are always wrong'. The young barrister Frank Greystock muses on his chosen profession, one which trains its practitioners in the art of obfuscation, of 'mastering the mysteries of some much-complicated legal case which had been confided in him, in order that he might present it to a jury enveloped in increased mystery' (p. 155). Readers of Trollope would have been entirely familiar with the perception. Trollope held his lawyers in much the same regard as

---

25 For commentaries on Dove and his opinion, see Pionke, id., pp. 145–6; N. Lacey, 'The Way We Lived Then: The Legal Profession and the 19th-Century Novel' (2011) 33 *Sydney Law Rev.* 599, at 606; L. Goodlad, 'Anthony Trollope's *The Eustace Diamonds* and "The Great Parliamentary Bore"' in *The Politics of Gender in Anthony Trollope's Novels*, eds. M. Marwick, D. Morse, and R. Gagnier (2009) 105; Wan, id., pp. 210–14.

26 See, also, J. McMaster, *Trollope's Palliser Novels: Theme and Pattern* (1978) 96, 101.

74

Dickens held his.[27] 'I have an idea that lawyers are all liars', Lucius Mason had concluded a decade earlier in *Orley Farm*, an observation which lent some justification to his own lawyer's rueful observation that 'we lawyers' are indeed 'much abused now-a-days'. Not least, it might be supposed, by writers such as Trollope who created women such as Lizzie Eustace to torment them.

And it is not just the lawyers who fail to inspire. Trollope's detectives are every bit as useless when it comes to solving, or resolving, things. Later called in to investigate the apparent theft of the diamonds, it quickly becomes apparent that they have no clue as to where they might be or what might have happened.[28] And much the same can be said of the successive magistrates Lizzie fools. The magistrate in Carlisle to whom she swears a false statement in regard to the supposed theft is far too easily gulled, the magistrate before whom she is summoned in London only to eager to believe the barely credible excuses she provides in order to deflect intimations of her own perjury.[29] Lizzie may be genuinely terrified of the prospective consequence of this perjury being uncovered; to be kept 'upon the treadmill and bread and water for months and months', Mrs Carbuncle supposes (p. 690). But the terror only serves to sharpen her performance. Floods of tears and a little judicious handwringing are enough to win over the sitting magistrate who, by the end, 'was altogether on her side'. 'Poor ignorant, ill-used creature – and then so lovely', the narrator observes of proceedings, 'That was the general feeling' (p. 716). The law is no match for Lizzie's theatrics.[30] It is rarely much of a match for anyone's theatrics. Trollopian trials invariably dissolve into little more than arcane rhetorical games.[31] The trials of Lizzie Eustace are no exception. When she is asked to return to London to give evidence at the subsequent trial of the real thieves, Lizzie

---

27 See J. Kincaid, *The Novels of Anthony Trollope* (1977) 14–15, suggesting that Trollope's depiction of lawyers in *The Eustace Diamonds* makes for particularly grim reading.
28 The narrator reports that when the matter of the diamonds becomes a matter of public interest, the 'newspapers had been loud in their condemnation of the police' (p. 553).
29 Lizzie determines to carry the diamonds in a strong box with her on a journey to her Scottish estates. On her return journey, the box is stolen at Carlisle. Lizzie had removed the diamonds from the box, but claims that they have been taken too. She hopes that by so lying Camperdown will halt his threatened Chancery action for the recovery of the diamonds. The box is found shortly after, and suspicion falls on one of her footmen. Suspicions however quickly grow in regard to the veracity of Lizzie's story. All a bit 'fishy', Lady Linlithgow reflects (p. 460). Shortly after, the diamonds are indeed stolen.
30 Kincaid, op. cit., n. 27, pp. 204–5 suggests that Lizzie is one of the most accomplished of Trollope's actors.
31 For a commentary on the presentation of Trollopian trials as little more than verbal jousts, see G. Fisichelli, 'The Language of Law and Love: Anthony Trollope's *Orley Farm*' (1994) 61 *ELH* 635, at 635–44, and C. Lansbury, *The Reasonable Man: Trollope's Legal Fiction* (1981) 91.

75

declines feigning illness. The clerk of the court is despatched to check. But Lizzie refuses to see him. Despite their 'anger' at Lizzie's 'fraudulent obstinacy', it is resolved that nothing can be done, or at least the officers of the court cannot bring themselves to try to do anything (pp. 749–50). Lizzie escapes, again.

And this matters because, as the reader is informed from the very start, Lizzie is not just a 'selfish, hard-fisted little woman' but also a habitual liar. 'It may', accordingly, 'seem unjust to accuse her of being stupidly unacquainted with circumstances and a liar at the same time; but she was both.'[32] She may not have been sure whether her retention of the diamonds was lawful. But she thinks nothing of spinning a complicated weave of fibs in order to enhance her chances of keeping them. Within a few pages she is already lying about the diamonds, telling creditors that she does not have them, signing promissory notes on false pretences, raising imaginary finances, and secretly pawning the jewels. And so it goes on. The more Lizzie lies, the more she is obliged to lie again in order to cover her original sin: the claim that the diamonds belong to her.[33] Her success is due entirely to the skills she displayed in court. Lizzie is a consummate 'actress', as the narrator repeatedly confirms, coaching herself 'before the glass', so that she can 'tell her story in a becoming manner' (p. 54). 'When there came to her any fair scope for acting', the narrator observes, 'she was perfect', whereas in 'the ordinary scenes of ordinary life' she 'could not acquit herself well'. There 'was no reality about' Lizzie. Her cousin Frank is torn between disapproval and admiration. John Eustace wonders if, had the law permitted it, Lizzie would not 'make an excellent lawyer' (p. 699). The narrator is less ambivalent, observing that her performance was 'too' perfect. There was 'too much of a gesture, too much gliding motion, too violent an appeal with the eyes.' Perhaps, but it is sufficient to take in an awful lot of men, and indeed women, who should have known better.

There is of course an immediate context to the vexed question of who owns the diamonds in law; the often heated debates which moved around the passage of the 1870 Married Women's Property Act. The Act established the right for married women to retain a legal right to money earned and property inherited. In effect it established a right to 'separate' property akin to that which had been developed in equity during the previous century. The peculiarities which surround 'paraphernalia' would be writ all the larger. The 1870 Act did not go as far as many campaigners wished, and it was only with the passage of the 1884 Married Women's Property Act that the most obviously deleterious consequences of the ancient doctrine of coverture were finally redressed. In the perception of its critics, however, the 1870 Act had

---

32 It has been suggested that Lizzie is the first of three reprehensible upstarts whom Trollope presents successively, to be followed by Melmotte in *The Way We Live Now* and Lopez in *The Prime Minister*. See Kendrick, op. cit., n. 23, pp. 136–7.

33 id., p. 143.

already gone much further than it should. Notably, many suspected that the real motivation for the 1870 Act was not so much a principled concern for the situation of married women than a wish to address instances of collusive marital fraud. The instance of marital fraud in *The Eustace Diamonds* may not have been collusive, but it was resonant. Whilst Lizzie had little intention of working for a living, she certainly intended to marry for one, for which reason her rights as a married woman, and then a widow, were immediately pertinent. In securing marriage to Sir Florian she 'had played her game well, and had won her stakes' (p. 46).

The same critics worried more generally that by enhancing the proprietary rights of women the 1870 Act would hasten the fragmentation of the family. The Victorian conservative invested much social and cultural capital in the sanctity of the family, the 'true key to English happiness'.[34] It was for this very reason that sensation novels generated such critical consternation. They intimated rebellion, intended to be read as 'narratives' of 'active resistance'.[35] There is little doubting that Lizzie was inclined to rebel. As she confides to the thoroughly obedient Lucy Moore it is not 'my plan to be tame' (p. 176). It has been suggested that in her rebellion Lizzie 'challenges the Establishment by resisting the legal system that attempts to define her as only a wife, mother and widow but not as a legally independent human being', and she does so by creating an alternative 'fictional text of her life'.[36] The creation of a rebellious Lizzie does not of course mean that Trollope was a feminist writer; far from it. In the *Northern American* he quipped notoriously that the 'best right a woman has is the right to a husband'.[37] And Lizzie is certainly not the only negatively drawn female in *The Eustace Diamonds*. Lots of thoroughly dislikeable women walk through its pages, or more commonly sit gossiping in its sitting-rooms. Lady Hittaway is a compulsive muck-spreader, Lady Linlithgow an inveterate card cheat, whilst Lady Fawn will say anything to anybody who might be persuaded into marrying one of her odious children.

The Trollopean canon is full of disagreeable women. But there are a lot of agreeable ones too, like indeed the angelic Lucy Moore, who is written as a very obvious counterpoint to the 'cunning' Lizzie. And, it might be noted, a lot of disagreeable men, such as Sir Griffin Trewitt. The newly married Trewitts have a minor place in *The Eustace Diamonds*. But Sir Griffin's view of marriage is clear. He does not 'mean to have any ill-humour' from his

---

34 In the words of Sir Alexander Patterson. Quoted in E. Koonce, 'Lizzie's Sensational Public Invasion and her Rewriting of British Legal History in Anthony Trollope's *The Eustace Diamonds*' in *The World as a Global Agora: Critical Perspectives on Public Space*, eds. L. Touaf and S. Butkhil (2008) 174.

35 The expression is Lisa Surridge's. See her *Bleak Houses: Marital Violence in Victorian Fiction* (2005) 9–10.

36 Koonce, op. cit. n. 34, pp. 171–2. The same thesis is suggested in Kendrick, op. cit., n. 23, pp. 138–43.

37 In Goodlad, op. cit., n. 25, p. 107.

wife; she will have 'the worst of it if there is'. As the Trewitts depart the novel, the reader is left with an image of his wife Lucinda sitting by the fire exhausted by the violence of the previous night, waiting for Sir Griffin to return with a 'look of fixed but almost idiotic resolution' on her face, and a poker in her hand (pp. 675–7). There are too many couples like the Trewitts in Trollopian England: too many lost loves and distant husbands, too many intimations of violence, too many tears, and too many lies. If the 'condition' of England was looking a little less rosy in 1872, the condition of its women had been desperate for a very long time. In Lady Glencora Palliser, Trollope created one of his favourite characters. Lady Glencora was intended to be very different from Lizzie Eustace, except perhaps in one way. Trapped within a desperate and loveless marriage herself, Lady Glencora cannot help but admire Lizzie Eustace, not least her boldness in 'wearing' her diamonds in public (p. 195). The actions of Lizzie Eustace could never be condoned. But they might be understood.

## GREAT DIVISION IS MADE

The case for including *The Eustace Diamonds* in the pantheon of literary sensationalism remains contestable. The *Spectator* clearly had its suspicions. It was the 'element of sordidness' which ultimately made the novel such a 'depressing' read. The author had 'given too much rein to his pleasure in coarse-painting, and has not quite produced upon his readers the sense of complete verisimilitude' that might have been preferred. Ultimately, however, it was the 'breathing pretence and dissimulation' of its protagonist Lizzie Eustace which the reviewer found so troubling.[38] Across the Atlantic, the *Nation* took a slightly different view, albeit working with the same referent. Whilst *The Eustace Diamonds* might be 'dull at times', it was 'more entertaining than half a hundred of the parodies of sentiment which forever attract hungry readers.'[39] The *Times* eschewed the contention and simply concluded that it was an 'excellent novel', whilst the *Saturday Review* was pleased to announce that 'Mr Trollope is himself again'.[40] The latter review was perhaps the most perceptive of all. Noting that the character of Lizzie was 'certainly well drawn', it commended most especially her credibility:

> She likes talking and making confidences, and saying pretty things; she is capable of keen enjoyment in the exercise of her powers, whether she is abusing her absent acquaintances in select epithets, which is her notion of friendship, or following the hounds at the risk of her neck in the hunting-field. She longs to confide in her associates, only it is not in her nature to trust a woman. Her designs are not colossal. A secret is a real burden. She is too

38 In D. Smalley, *Trollope: The Critical Heritage* (1969) 372–3.
39 id., p. 375.
40 id., pp. 374, 376.

clever, and the use she makes of her ignorance is a feminine feature. A great many women would have utilized their ignorance of law as she does, and stuck to the diamonds with a like pertinacity.[41]

At the end of the day it was this ordinariness which troubled. Sensation novels traded on the paradox: the consequences of extraordinary crimes committed by ordinary people.[42] In endeavouring to retain her diamonds, Lizzie does what many if not most girls of her age and in her circumstance might have been expected to do. She knows the score. In matters of love, as she informs Frank, 'Honesty in a woman the world never forgives' – and in most other matters too (p. 481). Lizzie Eustace is a classic example of the kind of 'equivocal heroine' who populated so many sensation novels.[43] Not only does she do what any girl might have done, she feels the same frustrations and, as a consequence, makes the same, in many ways predictable, mistakes. It is the 'companionableness', as the *Saturday Review* concluded, 'a life and spirit, about which keeps her within the bounds of humanity.' What again troubled so many critics of the kinds of novel in which the kind of women like Lizzie lived was the possibility of reader empathy. Lizzie should have been condemned, and reformed, then maybe pitied a bit. She was not supposed to be admired, still less her actions understood or condoned.[44]

There was certainly a lot about Lizzie that might have appealed to the devotee of the sensation novel, as Trollope well knew. Whilst *The Eustace Diamonds* might have been nominally placed within the Palliser series, it is not about politics or indeed the Pallisers. Plantagenet Palliser has a walk-on part, his wife Lady Glencora flits in and out serving as a kind of ancillary narrator. But the novel is squarely about the scandalous life, and lies, of the 'exquisitely lovely' Lizzie Eustace, dark-haired, possessed of a sultry voice and the kind of eyes that would 'ravish you' (pp. 54–5, 147). The loveliness is vital, for not only did the sensation novel reveal the extraordinary beneath the ordinary, but so too did it reveal the presence of evil behind the mask of beauty.[45] Lizzie has the same temperament, pathological, calculating, 'incapable of real anger', as Braddon's eponymous and similarly beautiful Lucy Audley (p. 55). And she reads the same kind of books as so many similarly misguided heroines, the wrong books, romantic, French.[46] She

---

41 id., p. 376.
42 For a discussion of this defining 'paradox', see Hughes, op. cit., n. 1, pp. 16–18, 60.
43 id., p. 46.
44 The cultivation of empathy was of especial importance to Trollope, as Stephen Wall has emphasized, for which reason the creation of credible characters, rounded as much by their flaws as much as their virtues, was critical. See S. Wall, *Trollope and Character* (1988) 10–13.
45 An expression of the 'generic principle of doubling', as Winifred Hughes puts it: Hughes, op. cit., n. 1, p. 20.
46 She keeps a copy of the Bible next to her as she reads her favourite French novels, so that in the event of a surprise visit she might quickly make a swap (p. 121).

certainly adores the wrong poet, wiling away her hours dreaming of Byronic 'corsairs' who might come to her rescue. To all appearances Lizzie is a quintessential sensational 'heroine', as Lady Linlithgow appraises, 'what with her necklace, and her two robberies, and her hunting, and her various lovers' (p. 570).

Of course, by 1872 the sensational 'moment' had nearly passed. If Trollope had intended to catch the sensationalist wave he had rather missed the flow. There again there was still money to be made, and few Victorian novelists were more sensitive to commercial trends than Trollope.[47] The place of *The Eustace Diamonds* in the *Autobiography* is again suggestive, just after a muse on the estimated £800 he had lost in selling his house at Waltham. The inference to Collins's *The Moonstone* a few lines later is just as telling.[48] Trollope knew what he was doing when he wrote *The Eustace Diamonds*, in precisely the same way that Braddon knew what she was doing when she wrote *Lady Audley's Secret*. He knew what his readers wanted, and he knew what they would buy. At the same time, he also knew what defences he might deploy when the critics, as was to be expected, began to sharpen their pencils.

A first defence is didactic. It was this defence which saved Wood's *East Lynne* from a still more savage critical reception, at least in some quarters. According to the *Conservative*, in casting *East Lynne* before her devoted readers, Wood had 'served the interests of morality in holding up to society a mirror in which it may see itself exactly reflected'; a conclusion that was both reassuring, and at the same time, thoroughly unsettling.[49] The *Saturday Review* adopted much the same tone in regard to *The Eustace Diamonds*. There was 'much not only to amuse but to learn from, if people will accept the conduct of most of its actors as a warning', adding that its author, after all, 'only paints society as it is shown to him'.[50] Interestingly, on publication of Trollope's *The Way We Live Now*, just three years later, the *Times* adopted the same tone. It:

---

47 In his *Autobiography*, he famously took the trouble to present an account of his earnings to date, in 1876. They amounted to just under £69,000. It was in sum 'comfortable, but not splendid': Trollope, op. cit., n. 16, pp. 231–2. For a comment on Trollope's commercial sensitivity, see Wall, op. cit., n. 44, pp. 4–5.

48 Trollope, id., p. 218. It has even been suggested that Trollope was endeavouring to recast a 'realist' version of Collins's novel. Trollope was an ambivalent critic of Collins, with whom, he observed in the *Autobiography*, 'it is all plot'. The idea that Trollope might have been consciously writing a realist version of Collins's novel is reinforced by evident parallels in their respective accounts of the diamonds' origins. In both cases, the diamonds come into the hands of English families as a consequence of the military campaign launched by the British against Tipu Sultan in Mysore at the very end of the eighteenth century.

49 Ward, op. cit., n. 12, p. 52.

50 Smalley, op. cit., n. 38, p. 376.

should make us look into our own lives and habits of thought, and see how ugly and mean and sordid they appear, when Truth, the policeman, turns his dark lantern suddenly upon them, and finds such a pen as Mr Trollope's to write a report of what it sees.[51]

It is certainly a defence which Trollope was keen to deploy.[52] 'Gentle readers', Trollope had observed at the close of *Ralph the Heir*, published just a few months earlier, 'the physic is always beneath the sugar, hidden or unhidden.'[53] Half way through *The Eustace Diamonds*, the narrator pauses to emphasize that the story of Lizzie Eustace is intended to provide a 'true picture of life', to 'show men what they are, and how they might rise' (p. 357). And the same intent is repeatedly asserted in the *Autobiography*. A writer must 'please', but so too 'must' he 'teach whether he wish to teach or no'.[54] Whilst 'nothing can be more dull or more useless' than simply relating a 'string of horrible events', of 'horrors heaped upon horrors', if the larger purpose is to promote reader reflection on the 'truth' of 'human nature', then the 'higher aim' justifies the means:

> Let an author so tell his tale as to touch his reader's heart and draw his tears, and he has, so far, done his work well. Truth let there be – truth of description, truth of character, human truth as to men and women. If there be such truth I do not know that a novel can be too sensational (p. 147).

This latter sentiment gestures towards the second defence. In the third of her sensationalist blockbusters, *The Doctor's Wife*, published a decade earlier, Braddon had endeavoured to write an ironic pastiche of the sensation genre. This did not, as her many critics observed, mean that the novel was not sensational, still less did it absolve her of the responsibility of writing it. But Braddon was adamant that it was, as a consequence, a more 'serious' work. The irony reinforced the pretended didacticism, the titillation justified as a means to the better education of her readers. The same can be inferred in *The Eustace Diamonds*. Whilst Lizzie's 'story' was 'absolutely false in every detail', the narrator confides, the public appetite for 'sensationalized stories is great', and the 'little mystery' of the diamonds 'is quite delightful'; so much so that Lady Glencora hopes that it will never be solved (pp. 470–1). There is, for sure, a distinctly Swiftian tone in the division of the drawing rooms of England into rival camps of 'Lizzieites and anti-Lizzieites'.[55] The former hold that their heroine has been 'very ill-treated'. The latter suppose that she is 'bold' and 'rapacious'. The schism even reaches into Westminster, threatening incredibly enough to bring down the government. When her dithering fiancé, the Liberal Lord Fawn, finally abandons Lizzie, his

51 In F. Kermode, 'Introduction' to A.Trollope, *The Way We Live Now* (1994) 23.
52 Kincaid, op. cit., n. 27, pp. 201–2, suggests that *The Eustace Diamonds* is perhaps Trollope's most didactic novel.
53 A. Trollope, *Ralph the Heir* (1978) 425.
54 Trollope, op. cit., n. 16, p. 143.
55 Brantlinger, op. cit., n. 16, pp. 211–12.

© 2016 The Author. Journal of Law and Society © 2016 Cardiff University Law School

Conservative opponents rally to her cause. But when Lady Glencora, wife of the prospective Liberal Prime Minister Plantagenet Palliser declares that Lizzie must have been a 'victim', all the pieces shift. The anti-Lizzieite Liberals are 'obliged' to swear a new allegiance, for which reason all the Tories turn against her (pp. 455–6, 531). The governance of England moves around what people think of Lizzie Eustace. As Walter Kendrick shrewdly observed of Trollope's writing in general and *The Eustace Diamonds* in particular, 'the paradox' of Trollopian 'realism is that it lives on the energy of what it condemns: only the lie of fiction allows the truth to be told.'[56]

This paradox found variant expression in a famous passage in the *Autobiography* in which Trollope challenged the idea that there was anyway a clear binary distinction between the 'sensational' and the 'anti-sensational' novel:

> Among English novels of the present day, and among English novelists, a great division is made. There are sensational novels, and anti-sensational; sensational novelists, and anti-sensational; sensational readers, and anti-sensational. The novelists who are considered to be anti-sensational are generally called realistic. I am realistic … All this I think is a mistake – which mistake arises from the inability of the imperfect artist to be at the same time realistic and sensational. A good novel should be both – and both in the highest degree. If a novel fail in either, there is a failure in art.[57]

The testamentary assertion is telling. Trollope, like Wood, wanted the best of both worlds; to be esteemed as a respectable author, and to be rich. And in regard to the critical 'mistake', he may have been right. The nature of the 'sensationalist' still troubles modern critics, in large part for the reasons which Trollope insinuated.[58] Nicholas Daly has suggested that it represented a mutant species of realist 'condition of England' literature, assuming a radically different approach to articulating and 'encoding' the same underlying fears. Certainly the critical existence of a 'sensationalist' genre of literature cannot be denied, regardless of how contestable, and how stable, its generic boundaries might be.[59] And *The Eustace Diamonds* looked, and read, like a sensation novel. All the necessary ingredients were present: the beautiful heroine, perhaps not as wicked as some, but wicked enough, the intimations of sexuality, and the crime. Stealing diamonds from gullible husbands might not seem quite as sensational as murdering them. But it is troubling enough.

56 See Kendrick, op. cit., n. 23, p. 156.
57 Trollope, op. cit., n. 16, p. 146.
58 For an overview of these critical travails, see A. Maunder, 'Mapping the Victorian Sensation Novel' (2005) 2 *Literature Compass* 1, at 5–8, 26, concluding that the genre, in sum, 'remains contradictory', a mass of ambiguities and inconsistencies, and also, rather earlier, Hughes, op. cit., n. 1, pp. 47–57.
59 See N. Daly, *Sensation and Modernity in the 1860s* (2009) 6–7, 17, 27, likewise suggesting that it may be treated as an 'aberrant strain' of the complementary genre of domestic novel. Much the same suggestion can be found in Brantlinger, op. cit., n. 1, p. 27.

And then there is the hopeless inability of the law to somehow stop beautiful, scheming women from doing what they want. The failure of law is not, as we noted before, a peculiarity of the 'sensational' novel. But its failure served an especial purpose in a genre of literature which traded so obviously on a popular fascination with sexual and criminal transgression. Moreover, Lizzie cuts a curious and still more troubling figure within the genre, for the simple reason that she so obviously gets away with it. Most sensationalist heroines are brought to some kind of justice. It might take the form of a criminal trial, despatch to a continental asylum or, as in the case of Ellen Wood's Isabel Vane, a harrowing deathbed torment. But not Lizzie Eustace. At the end of the novel Camperdown confesses to being 'ashamed' at the amount of money 'he had wasted' on his futile attempt to bring Lizzie to justice. Indeed, it is not just that Lizzie has somehow escaped justice. The law never really tried. Ultimately, despite all the money and all the legal machinations, at no point has any serious 'attempt' been made to 'punish her'. In the case of Lizzie versus the law, Lizzie had 'triumphed' (pp. 753, 755).

The law is present in *The Eustace Diamonds* because the plot moves around a criminal act. But it is conspicuously absent as a mechanism for effecting justice. The presence of this absence gestures towards another of the defining paradoxes of the genre, and the age; the thoroughly distressing thought, as Winifred Hughes puts it, that life was 'ruled by coincidence rather than logic', by chance and 'circumstance', good luck and ill.[60] Some murderous wives might be brought to justice, as might some thieving widows, but some would not; just as some unjustly incarcerated girls might be rescued from asylums whilst others would remain trapped for years and years.[61] The depiction of sclerotic procedures, stuffy courtrooms, and dim-witted detectives insinuated a deeper regulatory malaise. And another critical ambiguity, for having expressed the absence, and its deleterious consequences, the sensation novel assumed the role of regulatory surrogate.[62] The didactic defence was premised on precisely this assumption, and whilst few narrators were quite so readily moved to judgement as those commonly found in Ellen Wood's novels, most evinced a similar prejudice. This did not mean that justice was ever assured. But it did mean that the reader might be guided towards a proper appreciation of what was right and what was wrong.

There is an immediate and very obvious parallel to be drawn here, with the demise of another institution in which Englishmen and women had, for

---

60 Hughes, op. cit., n. 1, pp. 22, 58.
61 See Daly, op. cit., n. 59, pp. 33–4, discussing this paradox in the immediate context of Collins's *The Woman in White*.
62 The broader thesis was ventured, influentially, in D. Miller, *The Novel and the Police* (1988), and M. Knight, 'Figuring out the Fascination: Recent Trends in Criticism on Victorian Sensation and Crime Fiction' (2009) 37 *Victorian Literature and Culture* 323, at 327–8, picking up on the obviously Foucaultian resonance.

83

centuries, placed so much regulatory faith. Trollope certainly noted it, fashioning his celebrated Barchester 'chronicles' around the trials and tribulations of the established Church. Matthew Arnold's *Dover Beach* provided a despairing poetic complement. Half a generation later, Thomas Hardy would confirm the moment of God's 'funeral'.[63] The absence of praying complemented the absence of law and the absence of moral abstinence. Henceforth, according to Thomas Carlyle, the morals of mid-Victorian middle England would be shaped by a very different kind of clerisy; a 'Priesthood of the Writers of Books'.[64] The prospect hardly reassured those who regarded themselves in more familiar clerical guise. London may have been teeming with Jacobins, its drawing-rooms populated by any number of lascivious lovers, murderous mistresses, and thieving wives, but in the opinion of John Henry Newman, far and away the greatest threat to the sobriety, and the sanctity, of mid-Victorian England was to be found in men and women who read too much and as a consequence had 'views' on 'matters of the day'.[65] From a very different perspective, Wilkie Collins articulated much the same concern in an essay published in *Household Words* in 1858, wondering about the consequences of writing for a 'public to be counted by millions; the mysterious, the unfathomable, the universal public.' One consequence, of course, would be his fortune. Another would be that of his good friend Anthony Trollope.[66]

---

63 For a commentary, see A. Wilson, *God's Funeral* (1999) 3–15.
64 T. Carlyle, *Selected Writings* (1986) 247.
65 In Himmelfarb, op. cit., n. 7, p. 25.
66 Not that either ever seemed to feel other than financially pressed. No matter how much Trollope earned, he always seemed to spend more. Financial pressures are a recurrent theme of his *Autobiography*.

JOURNAL OF LAW AND SOCIETY
VOLUME 43, NUMBER 1, MARCH 2016
ISSN: 0263-323X, pp. 85–104

# M. NourbeSe Philip's *Zong!*:
# Metaphors, Laws, and Fugues of Justice

Anne Quéma*

*Focusing on* Gregson v. Gilbert, *the article considers colonialism as a historical chain of events with the Middle Passage as a major locus of association among humans, things, the sea, trade, transportation, maritime law, and finance speculation. Out of this assemblage emerged slavery as a racist socius through which the metaphor of the human-thing circulated. In citing* Gregson v. Gilbert, *M.N. Philip's poem* Zong! *seeks to bear responsibility to the reified bodies of the murdered Africans by generating a poetics of relationality that disassembles and reassembles the legal words as sign-objects on the page. Her gendered address to the law exposes the rape that Africa endured. Bearing witness to this trauma, her poem speaks to and with the dead, recognizing the singularity of the Africans' languages, of which as human-things they were deprived. Gathering readers and listeners, the poem creates an event through which an ethics of justice might materialize.*

> How do you/we relate to the law when it once said that we were things,
> and upheld all of these decisions that supported that view?[1]

The legal document *Gregson v. Gilbert*[2] records a trial that took place on 6 March 1783 that was to have major repercussions on the movement for the abolition of slavery. The trial concerns the *Zong*, a captured Dutch ship that departed Africa for Jamaica in August 1781 with 442 slaves aboard. According to James Oldham:

* *English and Theatre, Acadia University, Wolfville, Nova Scotia B4P 2R6, Canada*
*aquema@acadiau.ca*

1 In P. Saunders, 'Defending the Dead, Confronting the Archive: A Conversation with M. NourbeSe Philip' (2008) 26 *Small Axe: A Caribbean J. of Criticism* 63, at 66.
2 *Gregson v. Gilbert* (1783) 3 Doug 232, 99 E.R. 629.

The ship reached Jamaica, but Captain Collingwood mistook the landfall for Hispaniola (Haiti/Dominican Republic) and sailed into open sea. When the mistake was discovered, the water supply on board was waning, and weather and currents made beating back to Jamaica difficult (Cuba was nearer, but was in Spanish hands and inhospitable). The first mate, James Kelsall, swore that there was only enough water for four days, but ten to thirteen days would be required to regain Jamaica. Dozens of slaves had already died on board when a decision was made to sacrifice additional slaves in order to save the rest ... approximately 130 slaves were thrown overboard, and the lawsuit in the court of King's Bench was brought by the owners against the underwriters to collect insurance for the slaves claimed to have been lost by absolute necessity (valued at £30 per head). The jury verdict was for the plaintiffs. A motion for a new trial followed, argued in Easter term 1783.[3]

As Jane Webster indicates, Olaudah Equiano informed Granville Sharp of the *Zong* event and trial, and Sharpe organized the recording of the litigation. At the time, Sharp along with Thomas Clarkson spearheaded the anti-slavery abolitionist movement in England.[4]

Emerging from Oldham's and Webster's analyses alone is a series of events that created linkages among entities as disparate as sailing, water, a lawsuit, the coast of Africa, underwriters and mariners, the Caribbean Islands, winds and currents, and abolitionists, among others. Circulating among this web of connections is the metaphor of the human as thing on which slavery depended for its definition and practices. It is the same metaphor that has circulated from one account of the *Zong* event to the next. Whether we consider the representation of the massacre at a commemorative event, in a scholarly analysis, a poem, a film, a painting, or a legal text, we see displacements occur from one site to the next, performatively yielding social meaning. In this context, and reactivating the etymological meaning of 'metaphor' as the carrying and transfer of meaning,[5] my concern is not so much with metaphor in law. Instead, I begin with: how does a metaphor function as it transits from one locus to the next, and what are its performative effects?

Drawing on Latour's conception of the social as described in his Actor-Network-Theory, I propose to consider colonialism as a historical chain of transformative events with the Middle Passage as a major locus of association among humans, things, the sea, trade, transportation, law, and finance speculation. Out of this assemblage emerged slavery as a particular social and racist configuration. For Latour, the social is not a given to be

---

3 In J. Oldham, 'Insurance Litigation Involving the Zong and Other British Slave Ships, 1780–1807' (2007) 28 *J. of Legal History* 299, at 299–300.

4 See J. Webster, 'The Zong in the Context of the Eighteenth-Century Slave Trade' (2007) 28 *J. of Legal History* 285. The Society for Effecting the Abolition of the Slave Trade was established in 1787. The slave trade was abolished in 1807; slavery was abolished in England in 1833.

5 See etymology in the OED. at <http://www.oed.com/view/Entry/117328?redirected From=metaphor#eid>.

identified with social structures. Instead, it presents itself at the performative outcome of a series of links among entities that in their assemblage produce an event and manifest the social. Thus:

> the word 'social' ... is the name of a movement, a displacement, a transformation, a translation, an enrollment. It is an association between entities which are in no way recognizable as being social in the ordinary manner, *except* during the brief moment when they are reshuffled together .... social ... is the name of a type of momentary association which is characterized by the way it gathers together into new shapes.[6]

Checking 'how much energy, movement, and specificity our own reports are able to capture',[7] anthropologists network processes of association among humans and non-humans that beget the social. Latour's rejection of a traditional sociology revolving around the analysis of structures in favour of the study of the social as performative outcomes may seem extreme. In contrast, one could invoke Bourdieu's analysis of structural reproduction through hexis, habitus, and schemes, all of which would shed light on law and slavery. However, Bourdieu's focus on (performative) social structures and Latour's focus on circulation and exchange through acts of association are not antinomic. While Bourdieu speaks to the weight and persistence of power through structures, Latour offers a pragmatic method to trace the mobility and circulation of power through encounters and collisions, as when the poem *Zong!* meets law, finance capitalism, and insurance policies.[8]

In the first section of this argument, I will focus on linkages among some of the entities constituting the social or 'socius' of the Middle Passage to suggest that the metaphor of the human as thing acted as a crucial mediator of social configuration: circulating metonymically through the colonial socius, it accumulated meaning from one locus to the next. Drawing on analyses of maritime law, insurance policies, and finance capitalism, I will offer a preliminary networking of a series of associations that semantically relied on this key metaphor and that are part of a historical chain of traumatic violence to this day.

In the second section, I will suggest that M. NourbeSe Philip's poem *Zong!* (2008) presents itself as a relay in this colonial chain of traumas and their reiterative violence. Both critique and commemoration, the poem seeks to bear responsibility to the reified and abjected bodies of the Africans aboard the *Zong*. In this experimental long poem in six sections, Philip draws on *Gregson* v. *Gilbert* as a linguistic matrix to generate her text thereby constituting a performative address to the law that takes the path of citation. Citing, fragmenting, and recombining law's formulas, *Zong!* strives to liberate the memory of the African Ancestors from the prison-house of

---

6 B. Latour, *Reassembling the Social: An Introduction to Actor-Network-Theory* (2005) 65.

7 id., p. 131.

8 M. NourbeSe Philip, *Zong! As Told to the Author by Setaey Adamu Boateng* (2008).

language and mediates an alternative poetics of relationality that throws time out of joint, proceeding along the principle of dis/re-assembling among sign-objects on the page. To this extent, Philip shares with Derrida 'a *politics* of memory, of inheritance, and of generations'[9] that is predicated on responsibility and that makes the advent of justice possible. As Derrida writes:

> no justice – let us say no law and once again we are speaking here of laws – seems possible or thinkable without the principle of some responsibility, beyond all living present, within that which disjoins the living present, before the ghosts of those who are not yet born or who are already dead, be they victims of wars, political or other kinds of violence, nationalist, racist, colonialist, sexist, or other kinds of exterminations, victims of the oppressions of capitalist imperialism or any of the forms of totalitarianism.[10]

The poem's fractal and combinatory poetics transforms the *ratio decidendi* of the *Zong* trial from a speculative investment in the human-thing into an ethical question of justice.

In the third section, I will argue that, in response to the massacre of Africans on *Zong*, Philip's poem addresses the law by mediating a concatenation of agencies among humans, things, sea, ship, languages, trade, finance capital, and maritime law which generates a performative critique. Through their metonymic and fractal processes, the various sections of the poem tear away at the assemblage through which the metaphor human-thing circulated and that the courts sanctioned at the *Zong* trial. Central to Philip's critique is rape, which is all at once a singular act of violence and a collective trauma. This gendered address to the law therefore turns upon the obscene injury to African women's bodies on which law, church, and finance capital turned a blind eye.

In the final section, I will pause on the reconfiguration of the act of bearing witness in Philip's poem. In its desire to bear witness to the past, the poem transforms the Western concept of the witness by speaking *to* and *with* the dead, not *about* the dead. This address to the Ancestors seeks to do justice to the African slaves and to recognize the singularity of their languages, of which as human-things they were deprived. I will conclude by suggesting that, both on the page and on stage during poetry readings, *Zong!* becomes the performative occasion for the social when readers, listeners, viewers, and reciters reassemble the various languages and media of the poem. Out of this socius may emerge justice as an event through which an ethics of hospitality and relationality might materialize.

9  J. Derrida, *Specters of Marx*, tr. P. Kamuf (1994) xviii–xix.
10  id., p. xix.

Developing exponentially for several centuries, the colonial circuit of the Middle Passage sought to maintain itself through renewed links among maritime law, trade, church, sovereignty, bureaucracy, and finance capitalism that produced slavery as a particular social configuration. The practices surrounding slavery revolved around a key metaphor that is both appallingly simple and politically complex: slavery rests on the notion that a human being is a thing, and that as such it can be owned and shipped as cargo across the Atlantic, then be exchanged as a commodity for trade.[11] The metaphor is this politically laden trope that ferried over meaning from the word 'human' to the word 'thing' and that produced a dislocation in the conception of the human. Shedding a Latourian light on metaphor, one can suggest that if the social is the outcome of reassembling, then the slave metaphor is the trope that, in assembling human with thing, created this catachrestic hyphen that obtained as slavery in the Middle Passage. Thus the human-thing joined the chain connecting sugar, rum, tobacco, guns, beads, pigs, port, cowries, bills of exchange, and promissory notes, all of which enacted the triangular trade. This historical reification of human beings, which slave mutinies and the struggle for independence in Haiti proved fallacious, derived from the belief in the principle of property ownership which English law authorized and legitimized. Blackstone thus asserted that the possession of property 'is that sole and despotic dominion which one man claims and exercises over the external things of the world, in total exclusion of the right of any other individual in the universe.'[12] These words resonate with the violence of three centuries of despotic dominions over land and humans turned into things. They also demonstrate law's capacity to invoke with decisive authority principles to fill in the hiatus between incommensurable entities such as human and commodity.[13]

From a discursive standpoint, the metaphor of the human-thing functions as a floater travelling among the various elements of the sea, maritime law, the barracoon, sovereignty, ship, cargo, trade, and credit-based exchange that in their assemblage produced colonialism. Therefore, at work is not only the trope of the human-thing, but also its exposure to a metonymic process whereby the trope functions as a relay among heterogeneous entities and fosters a circulation of meaning and practices. The metaphor acts as a crucial mediator of social configuration, metonymically circulating through the circuit of the colonial socius, and accumulating meaning from one locus to the

---

11 See Eric Williams's landmark study, *Capitalism and Slavery* (1944).

12 In M.S. Ball, *Lying down Together: Law, Metaphor, and Theology* (1985) 119.

13 Thus Latour argues, 'The linkages of law have ... this distinctive feature: through the intermediary of a particular hiatus they allow means to follow a highly original trajectory in a series of leaps from facts to principles': B. Latour, *An Inquiry into Modes of Existence: An Anthropology of the Moderns* (2013) 365.

next. In this sense, the metaphor of the human-thing functions according to Roman Jakobson's notion that metaphor and metonymy work in combination.[14] For him, the analysis of the metaphor as a trope outside the syntagmatic context of the sentence makes no sense. Instead, the metaphor, which rests on the process of selecting paradigms of meaning, makes sense insofar as it is correlated with the metonymic process of combining the selected paradigms of meaning. In other words, metonymy and metaphor work hand in hand to produce meaning through selection and combination. Thus, the human-thing metaphor not only selects but also hyphenates two paradigms of meaning that historically engendered a web of performative practices with material effects in law, trade, state sovereignty, and capitalist economies of exchange.

To demonstrate the circulation of this metaphor and its relaying function, one can focus on the rhetoric associated with the sea in maritime law and its subsequent combination with insurance law and slavery. In his study of maritime law, Ball refers to metaphors that operated in clusters sharing 'family resemblances',[15] thereby creating ideological links among disparate elements such as law, trade, and ontology. These clusters originated in two conceptions of the sea. In 1609, Hugo Grotius published *Mare Liberum* in which he argued that:

> legally free seas prove and serve fulfillment of human life in community …
> Divine justice has established that each nation requires the supplies of others.
> The necessary mutuality of this order of distribution is to be realized through
> unrestricted navigation and the open access of each nation to all. By nature and
> purpose, the sea is a bond of human fellowship.[16]

In 1635, John Selden counter-published *Mare Clausum* (drafted in 1618) in which he maintained that:

> the law of the sea effects a division that allows the English to keep their seas
> … The practice of dividing the sea and excluding others protects exhaustible
> resources. Its purpose is to increase the efficiency of exploitation and to slow
> the loss of profit.[17]

One metaphor associated the sea with fluid exchange and fellowship, the other linked the sea to a bulwark against economic loss and exhaustibility. Both focus on trade as the exchange of commodities of which the slave would become one. Both metaphors also shed ironic and tragic light on slavery whereby the metaphor of the sea as a bond of human fellowship was downtrodden, and whereby the notion of the sea for market profit and sovereignty enabled the practices of slavery.

While the sea was either a mediator of free trade from one continent to another, or one of regulated transactions for the benefit of the nascent British

---

14  R. Jakobson, 'Linguistics and Poetics' in *Language in Literature*, eds. K. Pomorska and S. Rudy (1987) 62.
15  Ball, op. cit., n. 12, p. 101.
16  id., p. 39.
17  id., p. 41.

Empire, it remained a site of perils and risks to be insured against. And it is in the terminology of insurance policies that we can see the metaphoric cluster of the-human-thing-commodity-cargo reappear and circulate, this time linking law, trade, and sovereignty onto capitalist practices and concepts. Discursively, this assemblage assumes new meaning in the standard Lloyd's marine insurance policy that 'took shape during the 1600s, achieving printed form in a policy dated 20 January 1680/81 covering the Golden Fleece and its cargo from Lisbon to Venice',[18] and that was used throughout the eighteenth century. Here is an excerpt:

> Touching the Adventures and Perils which we the Assurers are contented to bear and do take upon us in this Voyage, they are, of the Seas, Men-of-War, Fire, Enemies, Pirates, Rovers, Thieves, Jettisons, Letters of Mart and Countermart, Surprisals, Takings at Sea, Arrests, Restraints and Detainments of all Kings, Princes, and People, of what Nation, Condition or Quality soever, Barratry of the Master and Mariners, and of all other Perils, Losses and Misfortunes that have or shall come to the Hurt, Detriment, or Damage of the said Goods and Merchandises and Ship, &c., or any Part thereof.[19]

At work in this catalogue is a Latourian series of association among entities that, if it were not for the ominous reference to goods and merchandises, would sound poetically fantastic.

The terms of the standard insurance policy prepared the ground for and legitimized the metaphor of the human-thing to be shipped across the Atlantic, with the ship itself operating as yet another actant ensuring the circulation of goods for the sake of economic transactions. As Oldham explains:

> distinctions relating to human cargoes clearly imply that what was being insured was not the 'life' of a slave as such, but his or her status as cargo: that is to say, the status of the enslaved as goods in transit. Human cargoes (slaves) in transit on the sea occupied a problematic, liminal position in maritime law – a position somewhere between personhood and property.[20]

This liminal position is also what links insurance policies to maritime law and eventually to *Gregson* v. *Gilbert* through which judges legitimized the metaphoric cluster of the human-thing-commodity-cargo in transit. As scholars and Philip herself emphasize, at stake at the trial was not whether Captain Collingwood was to be tried on murder charges, but whether the jettisoning of slaves who had not rebelled constituted a necessary act that was subject to compensation.

Furthermore, Ian Baucom's analysis of slavery helps us network the links among the sea as *mare liberum* and *mare clausum*, maritime law, and speculative capitalism. He describes a major shift from a hierarchy organized around landed property, aristocracy, and state war making to a culture of

18 In Oldham, op. cit., n. 3, pp. 301–2.
19 id., p. 301.
20 id., p. 296 (footnote omitted).

public credit, debt-financing mechanisms of war making, and power relations between creditors and debtors. Attending this transformation is a standard subjectivity redefined through the financial system and its attendant practices of speculation, exchange, trustworthiness, credibility, and calculations. Above all, this culture functioned in the allegorical mode whereby im-material, imaginary, and financial values were generated by means of credit-based transaction and bills of exchange. In sum, the vast allegory of capitalism had the effect of occulting materiality, that is to say, things. What is the place of slavery in this allegorical drama? According to Baucom, slavery as a type on interest-bearing money lies at its heart:

> on reaching the slave markets of the Caribbean or the Americas, a vessel would assign its cargo to a local factor or sales agent .... That factor would then sell the slaves (by auction, parcel, scramble, or other means) and then, after deducting his commission, 'remit' the proceeds of the sale in the form of an interest-bearing bill of exchange. This bill amounted to a promise, or 'guarantee', to pay the full amount, with the agreed-upon interest, at the end of a specified period, typically from one to three years ... The Caribbean or American factor had thus not so much sold the slaves on behalf of their Liverpool 'owners' as borrowed an amount equivalent to the sales proceeds from the Liverpool merchants and agreed to repay that amount with interest. The Liverpool businessmen invested in the trade had, by the same procedure, transformed what looked like a simple trade in commodities to a trade in loans.[21]

These practices, Baucom argues, explain why Collingwood proceeded to jettison the slaves off the ship: ill and valueless, they could no longer serve in this credit-based transaction, yet their loss as insured property could be invoked to obtain compensation. What this dematerializing and speculative logic implies is that, in legitimizing the principles of maritime law and finance capitalism, *Gregson* v. *Gilbert* equally disembodied the Africans of the Middle Passage, legitimizing what Achille Mbembé referred to as the creation of '*death-worlds*, new and unique forms of social existence in which vast populations are subjected to conditions of life conferring upon them the status of *living dead.*'[22] In this context, Baucom's analysis is highly per-suasive and complements Mbembé's attribution of the origins of necro-politics to the governance of colonial plantations that displayed the 'the first syntheses between massacre and bureaucracy, that incarnation of Western rationality.'[23] *Gregson* v. *Gilbert* stamped this rationality with legitimacy.

However, one should bear in mind that the allegorical mechanism of Baucom's description depends on the metaphoric cluster of the human-thing-commodity-cargo. Without the hyphenation, the slave cannot be the object of credit and speculation, even though his or her body is dematerialized. To

21  I. Baucom, *Specters of the Atlantic: Finance Capital, Slavery, and the Philosophy of History* (2005) 61.
22  A. Mbembé, 'Necropolitics' (2003) 15 *Public Culture* 11, at 39–40.
23  id., p. 23.

grasp this fact, one needs to remember that what occasioned the litigation at King's Bench is an event that presented itself precisely as this linking among colonial power over bodies, capitalist speculations, sovereignty, and military competition at sea. A series of interconnected decisions can be listed as follows: (i) In loading the cargo aboard the Zong, Collingwood activates the metaphor of the human-thing; (ii) the cargo has to be insured; (iii) the cargo has lost its value; (iv) asking for compensation will minimize the loss; (v) he jettisons the cargo to be in a position to receive compensation. While decisions (ii), (iii), and (iv) unfold according to the principles of speculative finance, decisions (i) and (ii) attend the materialization of the human-thing metaphor. Triggering inhuman and catastrophic consequences, Collingwood acted upon the metaphor, unwittingly returning the cargo to humanity: this is what Granville Sharpe understood: 'negroes exist / for the throwing' (*Zong!* p. 34).[24] For there can be murder only if the embodied nature of the slaves is affirmed: 'suppose the law not / — a crime / suppose the law a loss' (*Zong!* p. 20). Sharpe's documented attempt to obtain a trial on murder charges sought to mediate and thereby affirm the dignity of the Africans' lives, whose bodies had become the target of domination. As Agamben argues, 'the politicization of bare life as such ... constitutes the decisive event of modernity and signals a radical transformation of the political-philosophical categories of classical thought.'[25] The passage from human to thing to human does make manifest the bodies of the Africans and their exposure to bare life. Thus, the metaphor both masks and manifests the visibility of the colonial socius of racism towards Blacks. In this sense, it is not so much the allegorical exchange-value of the slave that makes legal trouble but the metaphor of the human-thing, insofar as murder and genocide can only happen to embodied human beings.

The human catastrophe of the *Zong* trial, in which the metaphor of the human-thing played a central role, stands as a link in a historical chain through which the metaphor is still running its course, accumulating, diffusing, and refracting the original trauma and violence. This violence can be connected to Derrida's identification of the violence at the foundation of law:

> the operation that consists of founding, inaugurating, justifying law (*droit*), making law, would consist of a *coup de force*, of a performative and therefore interpretative violence that in itself is neither just nor unjust and that no justice and previous law with its founding anterior moment could guarantee or contradict or invalidate.[26]

24 See A. Rupprecht on Sharpe in '"A Very Uncommon Case": Representations of the Zong and the British Campaign to Abolish the Slave Trade' (2007) 28 *J. of Legal History* 329, at 336.

25 G. Agamben, *Homo Sacer: Sovereign Power and Bare Life* (1998) 4.

26 J. Derrida, 'Force of Law: The "Mystical Foundation of Authority"' (1989–90) 11 *Cardozo Law Rev.* 920, at 941, 943.

The violence of law's authority reverberates through the historical evolution of American courts' decisions revolving around discrimination against Blacks and the establishing of affirmative action programmes.

Thus, focusing on the metaphors of brand, badge, and stigma that circulated in the antebellum period and that kept appearing in cases such as *Dred Scott* v. *Sandford* and *Plessy* v. *Ferguson*, Brook Thomas begins with yet another originary and reiterative moment of law's violence. In *Dred Scott* v. *Sandford*, Justice Roger Brooke Taney declared that:

> Various discriminatory legislation enacted by states against free blacks had … 'stigmatized' them by impressing upon them 'deep and enduring marks of inferiority and degradation'. Since there was only one class of citizens in a republic and since, at the moment of founding, states had 'deemed it just and necessary thus to stigmatize' those of African descent, they were excluded from the community that originally constituted the sovereign people of the nation.[27]

This reiteration of law's foundational violence leads Shoshana Felman to ascribe to law the power to inflict trauma on a cumulative and historical basis:

> Legal memory is constituted, in effect, not just by the 'chain of law' and by the conscious repetition of precedents, but by a forgotten chain of cultural wounds and by compulsive or unconscious legal repetitions of traumatic, wounding legal cases.[28]

Further, the cumulative and refracting violence of the metaphor of the human-thing has traveled from the courts to the administrative policies and practices ruling supermax prisons.

In an anthropological and legal investigation of United States high security units, where the dream of the panopticon has come true through the electronic eye monitoring prisoners' each and every move, Joan Dayan argues that the legal code of slavery has migrated towards the penal system:

> Legitimacy, reasonableness, and necessity. These words recur throughout the Code Noir of the French islands, the West Indian slave laws of the eighteenth century, the black codes of the American South, and contemporary legal decisions maintaining prison security. The language of the law, amid the current spectacle of chain gangs, control units, and executions, preserves the memory of slavery.[29]

---

27 In B. Thomas, 'Stigmas, Badges, and Brands: Discriminating Marks in Legal History' in *History, Memory, and the Law*, eds. A. Sarat and T. Kearns (2002) 250.

28 S. Felman, 'Forms of Judicial Blindness: Traumatic Narratives and Legal Repetitions' in Sarat and Kearns, id., p. 30.

29 J. Dayan, 'Held in the Body of the State: Prisons and the Law' in Sarat and Kearns, id., pp. 183–4. Philip also states (in Saunders, op. cit., n. 1, p. 68): 'In a way we have always been outside of *that Law*, in a philosophical sense. We are still outside of the law today (and yet trapped by it) in the way the law is used to police and confine black bodies in the new prison industrial complex.' Beyond the courts and supermax prisons, the legacy of slavery is manifest in American welfare policies and their

It is as a mediator and relay in this historical chain of traumatic and reiterative violence that I propose to read Philip's *Zong!* Both critique and commemoration, the poem unfolds as a reiterative and performative event whose potential outcome consists of a social transformation in the name of justice.

## FROM HUMAN-THING TO RELATIONAL SIGN-OBJECTS

The critique of the colonial socius requires a counter-discourse that escapes the calculus of profit and loss that turned the sea into a battlefield of domination where, in complicity with finance capitalism and insurance, law suspended the humanity of beings. Exposed to bare life on a ship of fools, the Africans were subject to a state of exception that prowled above and below deck. In her 'Notenda' to the poem, Philip explains that she sought to create anti-meaning to counter the effects of colonial and legal domination. Through this anti-meaning the poem seeks to remember the Africans by returning them to the embodied and spiritual character of human beings. Hence the titles of four of the five sections: 'Os', 'Sal', 'Ventus', and 'Ferrum'. Just as African groups, languages, animals, body parts, crew, food and drink, nature, and women who wait are made manifest at the end of the book (*Zong!* pp. 185–86), human beings who were murdered are made manifest through sounds, languages, ululation, and moans throughout the poem.

The resuscitation of this community creates a paradox which Sarah Dowling posits as follows: while '*Zong!* emphasizes the enfleshed voice', the 'attempt to constitute community must fail: Philip demonstrates the impossibility of communing with bodies that have been absented or silenced, with bodies that have disappeared beneath the ocean.'[30] Taking Dowling's analysis one step further, I suggest that the pause on bodies also enacts a fundamental address to the law in the name of *ius* or justice,[31] and bears witness to the dehumanized and abjected bodies of the Africans aboard the *Zong*. A dilemma lies at the origin of this address: what language should one use when addressing the law? Using law's language runs the risk of getting enmeshed in its doctrines and procedures; not using law's language will lead

---

metaphorical rhetoric: see A. Cammett, 'Deadbeat Dads & Welfare Queens: How Metaphor Shapes Poverty Laws' (2014) 34 *Boston College J. of Law & Social Justice* 233.

30 S. Dowling, 'Persons and Voices: Sounding Impossible Bodies in M. NourbeSe Philip's *Zong!*' (2011) 210–11 *Canadian Literature* 43, at 57, 58.

31 Here I draw on the notion of truth as an event, which Adam Gearey borrows from Johan Van der Walt, who analysed the South African Truth and Reconciliation Commission's work in performative terms: A. Gearey, ' "Tell All the Truth, but Tell it Slant": A Poetics of Truth and Reconciliation' in *Law and Literature*, eds. P. Hanafin, A. Gearey, and J. Brooker (2004) 46.

the law to lend a deaf ear to the address. And using or not using the language of law is pre-empted by the fact that the 'negro' remains outlawed, neither in or out, but both. This dilemma accounts for the experimental and paradoxical aspect of the poem. Indeed, the address unfolds, wrestling in the textual grip of the text of *Gregson* v. *Gilbert*.

As explained by Philip and as underlined by critics,[32] the poem presents itself as an experiment over-determined from the start by a linguistic constraint: the text of *Gregson* v. *Gilbert* constitutes the matrix of the first twenty-six subsections constituting 'Os' – the alpha and omega of the western alphabet – while its subsection 'Dicta' defies the calculus of gain and loss by offering six unnumbered poems that nevertheless spin into serial and combinatory verse. The next five sections draw and expand on this initial legal cache memory, unfolding in the lyrical, dramatic, oratory, and fugal modes. The constraint, which the archival calligraphy of the five sections' titles inscribes, is both linguistic and ethical: the syntax of the lawsuit report aims to make legal sense and to deliver a judgment, but running through this procedural and semantic coherence is the silenced incoherence and madness of the metaphor human-thing upon which the *ratio decidendi* of *Gregson* v. *Gilbert* turned. Philip's writing proceeds to confound the law by fragmenting its formulas, seeking to liberate the memory of the African ancestors from the prison-house of legal language. Here are two examples of the process of dis-assembling and recombination taking place in the poem:

> where the ratio of just / us less than / is necessary / to murder / the subject in property / the save in underwriter / where etc tunes justice / and the *ratio* of murder / is / the just in ration / the suffer in loss (*Zong!* pp. 25–26)

> my once queen / now slave / there be / no free / on / board / under / writers /tire /of writs / writ fine / with sin (*Zong!* p. 86)

Furthermore, the legal text functions as a synecdoche, as it stands for language as a whole from which Philip must generate meaning. Arguing that 'Philip metaphorizes the possibilities of resuscitation by reviving the legal transcripts documenting the massacre',[33] Baucom sees in her task a metaphor enacting the passage from tomb to resuscitation.

It is worth mentioning that the words 'resuscitate' and 'citation' share the same etymological origin, which is to move, stir, excite, or mobilize. Thus, if Philip's politics of memory revolves around an address to the law, it is by means of citation, as the following use of the deictic 'the' indicates: 'the that fact / the it was / the were / negroes / the after rains' (*Zong!* p. 5). Mobilizing the words of maritime law as an originary and historical matrix, she engages

---

32 For a subtle analysis of the role of the epic catalogue in *Zong!*, see E.M. Fehskens, 'Accounts Unpaid, Accounts Untold: M. NourbeSe Philip's *Zong!* and the Catalogue' (2012) 35 *Callaloo* 407.
33 Baucom, op. cit., n. 20, p. 332.

in a metonymic series of citational displacements: 'there is bone / a secret race under / writers / lives of writ s / & rent s / cede / the truth' (*Zong!* p. 80). In citing the legal text, Philip deflects the terms of reasoning from speculative interest to an ethical question of justice: 'should they have / found being / sufficient / a necessity / (portion that question) / should they have / found the justify / for exist' (*Zong!* p. 27). Stirring law's use of language, she transforms the poetic page into a heterotopic site for an event where a process of metonymic dis-assembling takes place that aims at breaking the syntagmatic principle of an unjust language.[34]

This fractal and combinatory poetics submits the linearity and one-sidedness of legal language to a critique while creating a *mise en scène* through *a mise en page* in which signs function like objects on the material page. Acknowledging Baucom's analysis, the poem bears the traces of Philip's reflection on the chimeras of finance speculation – 'invest in / tin / in / rum / in slaves / in / negroes serve / the preserver / the jam / and jamaica' (*Zong!* p. 73) – and on the possibility of a pre-capitalistic sea untouched and unstained by the metaphors of free trade and bulwark. Seizing the actuarial logic by the throat, she shuffles the key words of the litigation and recombines them serially in an impossible pre-lapsarian, pre-capitalistic state of being (*Zong!* p. 49). Philip describes her poetics of interaction among words, letters, and blank spaces as follows:

> The organizing principle, once I had found the form of the cluster, was a relational one. Each word or word cluster is in relation to each other, particularly on sequential lines, and, further, no word or word cluster can come directly below another cluster of words. Another way of looking at it is that each cluster of words is seeking the space or the silence above. And this creates a number of alternatives for meaning and reading.[35]

Activated by the acts of reading, these clusters of sign-objects act the way that Latourian objects interact, mediating and performing an event whose social outcome depends on the reader's deciphering and interpretation.

While this poetics of relationality proceeds along metonymic dis/re-assembling among sign-objects, it also draws on key metaphors. In 'Notenda', Philip offers the metaphor of the grand boggle game to explain what poetic process she went through as she sought to create the patterns on the page. In the poem itself, one comes across the metaphor of sailing creating a cat's cradle on the sea (*Zong!* p. 85), which strikes one as a self-referential statement, materializing for the reader what her eyes have been doing throughout the pages: weaving imaginary lines of connection from one

---

34  Sharpe suggests that the poems of *Zong!* 'work through their own logic of association, word play and sliding signification of words and syllables, whose meanings change with the insertion of a different letter or transference into another language or through alliteration': J. Sharpe, 'The Archive and Affective Memory in M. NourbeSe Philip's *Zong!*' (2014) 16 *Interventions: International J. of Postcolonial Studies* 465, at 473.
35  In Saunders, op. cit., n. 1, p. 72.

**Figure 1.** *Zong!* p. 106

l eau lave l eau                                                         lave l eau je
                          me lave je
            me lave de sin                                        sure
                              as the sun any
sane man can                                                      see no sin
            in the net of                              our life our
                  lies bodie s                          in situ in
                  sand in                                            water geld
                        the negro now
and wash the                                      water of all sin
                  èsù                                              oh l eau
            l eau wash
      the water                              wash
            the water èsù oh                              èsù
                        save
                              the                            us
            in you the ius
                                    in us
      no sin no                  sane man can no                  sane men au
            sein de in
                                    the midst of gore
      de goré e sing
a song                                    for rose un
      son la son le                              son for
                  rosa a san                  man                  for rose they
                  hoe                  the field the toad
                        hops his ship                  on
      the lip                                    of ruin her
            every where                              his hip his
      sore toe            too                  much                  port rest
            rest rosa                              a hero rosa
            says                  is ever                  alone
                        the deed must
            be done rest says                        rosa me
      want fu                  fu omi
                        water the dread                  deed dare
d                  & done drat                  the cat dear
      ruth dear dear                  ruth i                  won her was
                  wont to                  bed her bet

106

M. NourbeSe Philip, p. 106 of *Zong!* © 2008 M. NourbeSe Philip
Reprinted with permission of Wesleyan University Press

cluster of words to another, vertically, horizontally, diagonally. Through this ceaseless game of metonymic combination of units of meaning, the words extracted from *Gregson* v. *Gilbert* are let loose and morph into polysemy and polyculture (*Zong!* p. 106, see Figure 1). In fact, the very act of citing the poem cannot do it justice, as it destroys the relational quality of the clusters. Relentlessly anti-linear, the writing process defies not only the language of law, but also the language of the critic, a word that shares with law the etymologies of reading and judging.

Furthermore, the relations among the clusters create fantastic shapes of objects on the page and have prompted readers into metaphorical readings of the text. Critics have indeed detected the shapes of the account ledger, the window from which sailors could see these bodies fall, or the dendrita of sea shores.[36] Philip herself sees in her text the 'aesthetic translation' of slavery as legal containment and the escape from suffocation and enclosure, 'as if the words are seeking space to breathe'.[37] Whether it be through the grand boggle game, the cat's cradle, or the concrete object of poetry, the poem has upset the reifying metaphorical chain of the human-thing-commodity-cargo and redefined objecthood through a poietic event whereby sign-objects act on the page in a relational mode, addressing the text of the law but also the reader, listener, and viewer. Indented, fractal, and floating on the pages, the clusters under the movement of the reading eyes create a time out of joint, to quote Derrida, for whom the time of justice is one of disjunction.[38]


## PHILIP'S GENDERED ADDRESS TO THE LAW

It is through this metonymic process that the various sections of the poem tear away at the assemblage through which the metaphor human-thing circulated and that the courts sanctioned at the *Zong* trial. Philip disturbs the apparent composure of the law by disrupting its aspiration to totality and autotelic containment. The various links among church, sovereignty, trade, capitalism, property ownership, law, and the practices of mariners on *Zong* are scattered for all to see on the pages of the poem, and it is the readers' complicit eyes that make the ethical and political connections. The violation of African bodies through branding and lashing is linked through a history of imperial domination, combining political events with epic texts (Homeric and Virgilian) that to this day are regarded as the foundational master-pieces of western literature: 'a span / of pain / such / that / the / poet / of / the / trope / that is / troy can / not own / but there is / property i / say / in / pope / in /

---

36 See Fehskens, op. cit., n. 31, pp. 410, 420; F. Wah, 'Reading M. NourbeSe Philip's Zong!' (2013) *Jacket2*, at <http://jacket2.org/article/reading-m-nourbese-philips-zong>.
37 In Saunders, op. cit., n. 1, p. 73.
38 Derrida, op. cit., n. 8, p. xix.

99

troy in / rome / in / negro / in / guns / bam bam / our eyes / skim the sea for / bodie s for the law in *ius* in / us in /os in bone' (*Zong!* p. 87). The poem bears the traces of oration (as in o-ratio-n), Shakespearean drama, aria, odes, and Cartesian philosophy and its reflection on what constitutes subjectivity – the I/*yo/je/esse/sum/ego/ik* that do not include the Africans – as the cultural tools of the master which the various voices of the poem cite and mobilize. The moans of pain of the slaves are juxtaposed contrapuntally to the Christian symbolism of suffering and crucifixion, of dove and Eden, guilt and salvation, all of which the mariner-persona is mouthing, gnawed as he is by the sins he has committed aboard the ship. It is through this series of associations that the text reveals the ignominy that the Africans endured aboard the Zong and that the court occulted:

> negroes for sale the wig / w ogs   the nig /nogs   get / the tongs   the /irons
> hot / hot sing / sing       a       son/ g    of / sin such / a / din / such / a
> ding / ding       dong / sing / he sang / *ba ba iya* (*Zong!* p. 86)

Through the anagrammatic combinations of slave, lave, save, *ave*, and salve (*Zong!* p. 63), Philip conveys the tragic irony of a hallucinatory, raving Christian discourse that could not correlate the slaves to the very expression of human suffering that Christ is supposed to embody. The irreducible aspect of the text has led Veronica Austen to reflect on the relationship between power and the ethics of writing and interpreting the *Zong* massacre: 'How can Philip, or anyone, ethically represent the experience of the massacre's victims when to construct a representation means to hold power over those victims and their legacy?'[39] Seeking peace and release, this poetic address to the law cannot be but violent, not only because it represents acts of extreme and inhuman violence, but also because in engaging with the legacy of violence and injustice, the text inevitably generates its own violence against the tools of the master of which we are the complicit inheritors.

Central to Philip's address to the law is rape – 'rape this voyage' (*Zong!* p. 109) – which is all at once a singular act of violence and a collective trauma, and to which the various sections owe their reiterative temporality. The reference to rape recurs through the women/woman's words, 'de men dem cam fo mi' (*Zong!* pp. 68, 93, 94) and the mariner's lust and obsession – 'the wonder her / sex wet' (*Zong!* p. 112) leaving her scent on his skin. It is expressly stated towards the end of 'Ventus', the third section driven by the winds of the ocean and the venting of those to whom injustice has been done:

> we / sailed / up / the / cunt of / africa to / found/ an / out / caste / race can t /
> you add / a market /
> waits it fans the / deed s alms / for / the poet of / troy … mark them dem *j ai* /
> *faim j/ai soif*
> dindin dong / dung / don din / din don don ding / ding / dong done (*Zong!* pp.
> 97–8).

39 In '"Should We?" Questioning the Ethical Representation of Trauma' (2011) 37(3–4) *English Studies in Canada* 61, at 63–4.

The gendered address to the law turns upon the obscene injury – 'cut / her open her / shape tie her / ripe toes / round / and firm / the cord' (*Zong!* p. 71) – to African women's bodies on slavers and later on plantations where they functioned as breeders for the reproduction of a labour system.[40] Philip's attention to women and the pain they endured certainly demarcates her work from the postcolonial critiques that Baucom and Derrida offer. As the wars of the twentieth and twenty-first centuries indicate, women always bear the ravages of violence, 'the sack of troy the rage of men lives the poet writes' (*Zong!* pp. 94–5). In an allusion to the *Odyssey*, the mariner states: 'circe / waits / lips / hang / make s / fun / of / eros / of us / & / *ius* makes / pigs of / us' (*Zong!* p. 93). The word '*ius*' appears on the pages according to the combinatory and associative dynamic of the text that anagrammatically juggles the homonyms 'os', 'es', 'us' (*Zong!* pp. 68–9), but also connects the 'I' to 'us', the singular to the collective. It is perhaps in this single word and its poietic declensions that we see the strife for the just word in the name of justice.

Philip repeatedly refers to *Zong* as 'the story that cannot be told and must be told' (*Zong!* p. 196). This statement situates the poem between silence and language. The page enacts silence through the spatial relations between cat-cradled clusters and the blanks pocking the page.[41] It might be tempting to account for this silence by invoking the concepts of melancholy and the *unheimlich*, which are typically used to account for symptoms of trauma. The Freudian theory is well known: the self who endures a loss cannot grieve because it internalizes the object of loss and drifts through a reiterative process of mourning. For instance, Tim Armstrong argues that the story of the *Zong* demands a '"working through" which might deal with what is repressed and lost to understanding – though here we must understand "working-through" in a way that Freud only occasionally countenanced, as dealing with historical experience.'[42] However, what is striking is that this theory of melancholy and haunting perversely rehearses the theory of ownership: the self encrypts, that is to say, claims possession of the dead that it will not relinquish, while the dead claims possession of the living, who is in a perpetual position of debtor. The living becomes perpetually indebted through a mortgage of the dead. Are we, Westerners, so deeply ingrained

---

40 See A.Y. Davies, 'Outcast Mothers and Surrogates: Racism and Reproductive Politics in the Nineties' in *Feminist Theory*, eds. W.K. Kolmar and F. Bartkowski (2010) 447–53.

41 As Eichhorn states, 'In the final section of *Zong!*, the text appears in gray scale and many of the words are superimposed. Here, paradoxically, it is an excess of words rather than their absence, a discursive explosion rather than a constraint, that reproduces the silence that marks the historical and judicial conditions of the *Zong*'s fatal passage': K. Eichhorn, 'Multiple Registers of Silence in M. NourbeSe Philip's *Zong!*' (2010) 23 *Xcp: Cross-Cultural Poetics* 33, at 37.

42 T. Armstrong, 'Catastrophe and Trauma: A Response to Anita Rupprecht' (2007) 28 *J. of Legal History* 347, at 347.

with the concept of ownership that even the theoretical – speculative – account of our phantasms has to bear the capitalistic and legal signs of our culture? Is it not the case that, by dispossessing African people of their home, Western capitalism and law imposed the logic of the *unheimlich*, which is but the other side of Western individualism based on property, autonomy, and the suspicion of whatever is foreign or beyond bounds? In other words, the *unheimlich* is a white way of telling what cannot be told.[43]

## BEARING WITNESS FOR JUSTICE AS EVENT

Vital then is a practice of bearing witness to the past beyond the strictures of Western language and the idiom of melancholy. It is not so much that the law cannot deal with the past and, as Sarat and Kearns argue, through the principle of *stare decisis* (the doctrine of precedent)'in every legal act there is an insistent call to remember'.[44] However, if *Gregson v. Gilbert* reminds us of anything, it is that the Africans were not only reduced to things, but that the sailors on the ship asking them to jump and that the judges at King's Bench delegitimizing them as things addressed them in a language they could not understand. As Derrida reminds us, justice cannot be done if the language that law speaks remains impenetrable and inhospitable to people.[45] So the question again is how to bear witness to the past, especially when the singularity of one's language is not recognized? How to:

> exorcise not in order to chase away the ghosts, but this time to grant them the right, if it means making them come back alive, as *revenants* who would no longer be *revenants*, but as other *arrivants* to whom a hospitable memory or promise must offer welcome – without certainty, ever, that they present themselves as such. Not in order to grant them the right in this sense but out of a concern for *justice* ... which is desirable: *through* but also *beyond* right and law?[46]

I suggest that Philip's poem speaks *to* and *with* the dead, not *about* the dead, as a means of doing justice to the African people who were massacred on the *Zong*.

To make the dead or Ancestors manifest, Philip not only invokes them by name at the bottom of the poem's pages, she also meddles with the legal concept of the name of the author. Indeed, on the cover of her book, you can

---

43 Thus, Coppola argues that 'The poet reconceptualizes slavery not as an event consigned to the past, but as a powerful reassessment of contemporary politics of memory that imposes a reconsideration of our notion of modernity': M. Coppola, 'This is not was: M. NourbeSe Philip's Language of Modernity' (2013) 2 *Textus* 67, at 74.
44 A. Sarat and T. Kearns, 'Writing History and Registering Memory in Legal Decisions and Legal Practices: An Introduction' in Sarat and Kearns, op. cit., n. 27, p. 13.
45 Derrida, op. cit., n. 25, p. 948.
46 Derrida, op. cit., n. 8, p. 175.

read: *Zong! – as told to the author by Setaey Adamu Boateng*. Setaey – the Adam on the boat perhaps – is the ancestor bearing witness to and telling the untellable through the citational pilfering of the legal text. In the epigram to the 'Ratio' section, Philip quotes Paul Celan: 'there is no witness for the witness'. While the quotation partly refers to the death of those whose witnessing becomes a dead letter, Setaey Adamu Boateng's telling allows for a conception of witnessing other than that of taking the stand and telling the truth on the basis of a biblical oath. Not a mere third-party observer, Setaey is the survivor and decryptor of the untellable event that needs to be told to the future through the present. Philip turns the legal definition of *dicta* (a judge's statement that may be pertinent to the case but that has no direct bearing on the outcome of the lawsuit) into a dictation from the Ancestors, an impertinent witnessing addressed to the law for the sake of justice. As Clarke insightfully remarks,[47] the poem reads like a séance through which author, surrogate author, mariners, slaves, and readers communicate through a sensorial, affective, and sensuous stirring of the Ancestors. The medium is indeed the message. While Western law seeks to create a unilateral address without rebuttal other than through appeal, Setaey addresses not only the law but also the dead. While the court did not ask for a response, and in fact never provided any sense of what eventually took place, the poem engages in a posthumous dialogue. The aporetic approach, oscillating between haunt-ology and ontology – 'is being is / or / should / is is / is / be / being / or / been' (*Zong!* p. 37) – speaks to the profoundly ethical aspect of the poem whose author bears witness to the dead, which is none other than bearing witness to the living.

As such, the poem acts as a mediator of embodied responsibility and shifts the use of language from the mausoleum of the propertied and autonomous self to collective caring in the name of justice; from crypt to aqua; from melancholy to speaking *with* the dead; from dirge to song and fugues; and from 'the mother document' (*Zong!* p. 200) of *Gregson* v. *Gilbert* to the sea as matrix of languages. The fugal and multivocal dendrites of language perform socius, materializing not only the agonistic co-existence of masters and slaves on the *Zong* but also a potential exchange for an ethics of hos-pitality, regeneration, and justice.[48] In contrast to the lack of communication between the Africans and the masters, Philip opts for collective practices of trans-communication whereby Yoruba, Fon, Shona, Twi, West African Patois, Dutch, French, Latin, Portuguese, Spanish, Italian, Greek, and Hebrew – as well as sounds, onomatopoeia, assonances, and alliterations – commingle, disfigure and reconfigure English, drawing in the reader and listener. If the poem fails to recreate the community of the past, it

---

47 G.E. Clarke, 'Review of *Zong!* By M. NourbeSe Philip' (2008) 4 *Maple Tree Literary Supplement*, at <http://www.mtls.ca/issue4/writings-review-clarke.php>.
48 Dowling, op. cit., n. 29, p. 9, points out that 'The only word in this poem that is never broken apart into its constituent sounds is the word "our".'

nevertheless has the power to conjure a *socius* through the performative event of language in the plural: 'there are / suits there are / writs liens / & notes le mot / just e the just / word just / a word *ave* / *ave* to / the negroes and / *se*' (*Zong!* pp. 111–12).[49] In 'Ferrum', where the metal of tongs and irons transmutes into the medium of word smithery, the shock of tongues and their sound patterns are not cause for discord; instead, they irrigate the possibilities of exchange through the translation from one idiom to the next that is generative of being through meaning – the clusters of words relaying and transforming languages and their sounds.

The poem makes the voices of the Ancestors manifest, but this manifestation cannot occur without the work that is expected from readers, who have to engage (as actants) in a reiterative poiesis of sense making to which they co-respond through their own participation in the fashioning of meaning. In other words, bearing witness and responsibility takes the path of association among sign-objects, readers, listeners, and the poet-performer. Justice as an event of reassembling materializes at poetry readings of *Zong!*, which Margaret Christakos describes:

> The current engagement involves musicians, a circular arrangement of audience around the performance, and a spacious text-referential reading mode made available to all who attend with the invitation that every voice may become co-present in reading the text aloud, in synchronizing oration with the group, in diverging into personal timing, in vocally occupying the text at any of its many nodes in relation to a loosely conducted choral inhabitation of it. As multiple voices converge and diverge building a rough choral volume, Philip reads the text section by section, embarking into improvised attentions upon particular phrases, moving her body rhythmically, walking, bending, pulsing, pivoting incantatorily around segments whose crystallizing refrains later emerge as group memory for the entire assembly.[50]

On these public occasions, the poem does justice to the slaves through collective *and* networking acts of memory and the imagination. The page as relational bearer of signs becomes alive as the Africans of the *Zong* are made manifest to our eyes and ears. In these practical events, ghosts become hosts, and 'thought *becomes act*, and body and manual experience … labor but always divisible labor – and shareable.'[51]

---

49 In the 'Glossary', Philip refers to *àse* as signifying 'may it manifest' in Yoruba (*Zong!* p. 184).

50 M. Christakos, 'Crossing Over: Temporalities of Erasure and Recuperation in the Contemporary Long Poem, For Example, in Erín Moure's *The Unmemntioable* and M. NourbeSe Philip's *Zong!*' (2015) *Lemon Hound*, at <http://lemonhound.com/2015/02/20/13067/>. Christakos argues that 'Philip is enacting a "material metaphoricity" that gestures indigeneity through this linguistic and semantic decomposition.' Philip's reading performances are available at: <https://www.youtube.com/watch?v=my4eE4denus>; <https://vimeo.com/27014186>; <https://www.youtube.com/watch?v=HVl5sYePm0o>; <https://vimeo.com/78360574>; <https://vimeo.com/78360575>.

51 Derrida, op. cit., n. 8, p. 170.

JOURNAL OF LAW AND SOCIETY
VOLUME 43, NUMBER 1, MARCH 2016
ISSN: 0263-323X, pp. 105–22

# 'We Want to Live': Metaphor and Ethical Life in F.W. Maitland's Jurisprudence of the Trust

ADAM GEAREY*

*This article argues that reading F.W. Maitland's jurisprudence of the trust alongside Hegel's philosophy of social recognition offers insights into the way in which metaphors 'structure' the modes of ethical life that inform legal and social institutions. Conventional ways of reading Maitland (and John Neville Figgis) have obscured the affinities their work shares with Hegel, and limited the impact of a way of thinking about law and society.*

'[A] theme from the borderland where ethical speculation marches with jurisprudence.' F.W. Maitland[1]

'On the crossroads between magic and positivism.' Theodore Adorno[2]

## INTRODUCTION

The main thesis of this article may seem somewhat quixotic. I will argue that reading Maitland's jurisprudence through the Hegelian concept of social recognition can tell us something significant about law and metaphor. But, why read this most English of historians through German metaphysics? My

\* School of Law, Birkbeck College, University of London, London WC1E 7HX, England
a.gearey@bbk.ac.uk

Thanks to Piyel Haldar for perceptive comments on an earlier version of this article; and to David Gurnham and the anonymous reviewers whose advice also helped to improve its structure and focus.

1 F.W. Maitland, 'Ethical Personality and Legal Personality' in *The Collected Papers of Frederick William Maitland*, ed. H.A.L Fisher (1911) 304. The account of *sittlichkeit* is taken from G.W.F. Hegel, *The Phenomenology of Spirit* (1967) 466–82.
2 Theodore Adorno in a letter to Walter Benjamin, 10 November 1938, cited by G. Rose, *The Melancholy Science* (1978) 41.

argument will be that the received ideas about the differences between Maitland and Hegel conceal a much greater affinity. Reading Maitland and Hegel together can direct our attention to an understanding of metaphor that must inform any proper engagement with law, society, and ethics.

Hegel's thinking of the dialectic of recognition shows how an inherently metaphorical process articulates the ethos of legal institutions. Thus, although it is something of a free translation, we will use the Hegelian notion of *sittlichkeit* (or the social world in which 'we' recognise each other as citizens) as a way of thinking about the ethical life that is articulated by Maitland's idea of the trust. As we will see, thinking about ethical life is inseparable from the study of metaphor. In fact one might say that ethical life is defined by those metaphors by which we live. Maitland understood this truth. To read a metaphor is to be able to work between the literal and figurative, between the hidden and the revealed. But, as Maitland was also careful to point out, it is not 'always easy to say where metaphor begins'[3] and ends. The correct reading of history requires sensibility and discrimination. Indeed, we will pick up on Maitland's resistance to German metaphysics as central to an issue of style that is fundamental to his writing. Maitland's work is significant precisely because his writing has a certain 'grain of voice'. He is concerned with the presentation of a particular vision of equity to his fellow Englishmen. We will draw on Maitland's exercise in language to make some final points about the reception of his work in the early decades of the twentieth century. In particular we will examine how those developing a sociological jurisprudence misunderstood his relationship with Hegel and thus failed to appreciate the centrality of metaphors to the way in which we live the law.

The first section of the article focuses on notions of social recognition and ethical life. We will make reference to thinking on metaphor to show how the theory of *sittlichkeit* provides a distinctively 'modern' form of the social bond. Elaborating our understanding of social recognition, we will show how metaphors are central to the struggle over the definition of a social ethos. These arguments extend into Maitland's opposition between the artificial idea of corporation and the law of trust. Whilst Roman law thinking on the fiction of corporation feeds into theories of the social contract, the trust articulates a form of ethical life that rivals that great Latin fiction of the state. The trust provides a legal 'shell' which nurtures the genius of civil life. A final section will engage with the reception of Maitland through sociological jurisprudence and suggests that any development of his insights must take seriously the concern with a social ethos in which legal institutions are rooted.

3 Maitland, op. cit., n. 1, p. 403.

Our starting point is Hegel's theory of social recognition. *Sittlichkeit* can be thought of as the way in which a society 'comes into being' by recognizing itself as such. This might seems somewhat obscure but if we compare the concept of *sittlichkeit* with the more familiar notion of the social contract, we can get a good sense of its distinctive contribution to the analysis of 'modern' society. Liberal political theory sees the social contract as a way of thinking about the origins of mutual rights and obligations. The social contract defines the legal foundations of an order of association that considers itself rational, legitimate, and self-founding. However, the contract is only one way in which the concept of a social bond can be articulated. The theory of *sittlichkeit* seeks to discover 'something' that underlies the very idea of a social bond in the first place. Whatever form the legal or cultural vehicle takes (trust, contract or other device) it must be able to articulate a much broader ethos. Oliver Wendell Holmes (to whom we will return) provides us with a working notion of ethos as describing those 'felt necessities of the time, the prevalent moral and political theories, intuitions of public policy, avowed or unconscious ... the prejudices which judges share with their fellow-men [.]'[4] For Hegel, this complex of beliefs, values, representations, norms, and practices provide the terms in which 'we' recognize ourselves. As 'moderns' – or self-conscious, reasoning actors – we need to see ourselves reflected in our actions and in the institutions that form our world. Law will not bind rational people together unless it is embedded in an ethos that enables mutual recognition. So, in Hegel's social philosophy the interiority of reason must be able to find itself in the external world of others. In other words, 'I' must see myself in 'you' and 'you' must recognize yourself in 'me' and (to return to our first point) our institutions must give form to our mutual recognition.

We can think of this process of social recognition as mobilizing a complex of metaphors. The institutions of the social world provide us with metaphors of ourselves. 'We are' the institutions that we have created: we are our metaphors. The creative, negating power of reason thus enables us to recognize or 'come to' ourselves in what we are not: the external forms that give shape to our inner selves. This argument can be elaborated still further. Metaphor is a device or figure that presents one thing as another. The comparison is then suppressed (metaphor is not simile). Metaphor thus takes on a special meaning in our reading of Hegel's philosophy. In ethical life our institutions are effectively a metaphorical prosthesis or 'stand-in' for ourselves. We will return to the second feature of metaphor (the suppression of comparison) in a moment as I want to summarize our argument so far. Metaphor has to be understood in a special sense to think about the dialectic

4 O.W. Holmes, *The Common Law* (1881) 5.

of recognition. We need to stress the inherently social nature of recognition and the fact that it is an activity or set of practices and norms in and through which we work to create both ourselves and our world. The term spirit can also be used to describe this complex of recognition. I do not want to overuse this expression, but will make reference to spirit as a way of thinking about the social complex of recognition. Spirit can thus be understood in its more or less common sense application (as in the spirit of a culture) or – in this more precise Hegelian use (a slightly more sophisticated form of common sense) – as an understanding of the dialectic of social recognition. Thus when we speak of the spirit of a culture, or the spirit of the law, we are referring to the complex of metaphorical substitutions where a set of institutions and doctrines 'stand in for' or represent our understanding of ourselves as rational subjects rooted in our 'own' traditions and mores.

We can now turn to the suppression of comparison in metaphor. We have described rational ethical life as a 'stand-in'. As such, it must replace previous, historical modes of recognition and, by the same token, must also resist rival modes of recognition (Hegel is primarily concerned with the emotive bond of the family) in order to mandate the universal terms of recognition and belonging as subjects of a rational state. We can thus appreciate that an account of hegemony is implicit in Hegel's understanding of *sittlichkeit*. Most importantly, the dominant mode of ethical life must present itself as the best possible way in which social life can be articulated. This underlies the hegemonic notion that modern societies are best organized around rational markets structured by law and the state. Precisely because this claim rests on the forgetting of its metaphorical nature, any rival metaphor could challenge its hegemonic hold. This is exactly what is at stake in Maitland's work. The trust provides a 'plural' way of organizing social life and an alternative to the overwhelming might of the sovereign state. It also provides a different way of thinking about markets and the role that social actors play in commerce. Any engagement with metaphor is thus an examination of the terms of communal life.

Hegel is often misread on this point and it appears that Maitland and other 'English pluralists' failed to understand the true import of Hegel's philosophy. Hegel is not an apologist for the absolute state. The absolute state is only one form that *sittlichkeit* might take. Hegel shows that the hegemonic form of state, law, and market is, in part, a historical effect. Very crudely, this is why *The Phenomenology of Spirit* is such a big book. *The Phenomenology* shows that any account of the mode of recognition must present itself as the authentic working out of a historical pattern. However, history does not run towards some immanent telos. To return to our earlier point, any claim about the nature of the ethical bond is itself an interpretation of history by a hegemonic power. A brief reference to Hegel's understanding of metaphor can help us to appreciate why the construction of the social bond is such a careful construction – and entirely precarious.

In his discussion of metaphor in *The Aesthetics*, Hegel makes a distinction between invisible inner spirit and sensuous, material form. The inner and the outer have no necessary link, but are brought together by the 'wit' of the poet in metaphor (and allegory, parables, similes, and stories). Thus, a metaphor that compares a hero to an eagle or a lion does not embody the spirit of a hero so described. The lion or the eagle 'stands in' for something that it is not.[5] The link, then, is entirely contingent: a matter of invention. Scholars and poets who make use of metaphors might allow us to grasp something, but, they could also mislead us. For instance, in the nine flights of an Egyptian stair, the 'cognoscenti' may be able to 'sniff out' something recondite, but this may be a matter of pure invention: a problem in the work of the neo-Platonists, as well as that of literary critics. Metaphors are inherently slippery. Power is, in brief, the ability to mandate meanings and to limit the inherent play of metaphor. By analogy, any account of the social bond will be a dispute over the extent to which certain metaphors can reflect spirit. Poets, philosophers, historians, and law makers are involved in the same hermeneutic endeavours.

This takes us to Maitland. Maitland links the trust to the spirit or genius of English law. Despite what pluralist scholarship tells us, this is an application of Hegel's thinking rather than its avoidance. It is also an attempt to define the metaphors by which 'we' should live. Admittedly, Maitland is writing against Austin's sovereign (which the pluralists took to be an anglicized Hegel), but he is entirely Hegelian in his desire to press into service an alternative account of social life. However, there is a second important point and this does take us to something distinctive that Maitland brings to the articulation of a vision of *sittlichkeit*. If the articulation of the social bond is an invention and, in particular, if one is arguing for a 'counter hegemonic' metaphor as Maitland is doing, then one needs to adopt a certain style, a way of discriminating. One needs to produce a 'great work' – and, in this sense, Maitland's legal history rivals Hegel's philosophy of law. Style is authentic to an argument that must link together spirit and form and present itself in a public form to an audience who might be persuaded. Above all, the persona that animates the writing must summon a spirit that speaks through dogmas. Maitland seeks, in the words of T.S. Eliot, to give form to the desires of the tribe.

## DOGMA AND DESIRE

Our starting point is Maitland's pithy statement that '[a] dogma is of no importance unless and until there is some great desire within it.'[6] A dogma, a body of doctrine or ideas, conceals and gives form to something else:

---

5 G.W.F. Hegel, *Aesthetics, Lectures on Fine Art, Vol. 1*, tr. T.M. Knox (1975) 306.
6 Maitland, op. cit., n.1, p. 66.

'desire'. Maitland's 'desire' reaches towards something that needs to be captured and given form. Desire follows traces and echoes; memories of life buried in archived documents, medieval legal doctrines, the year books and court records. Whilst traces of ethical life might be recoverable from documents and records, ethical life is 'lived'. Maitland's desire to uncover this complex informs his practice as a historian.[7] Indeed, his quest for ethical life is motivated by the sense that all is not well with the contemporary social and political situation. The forms that law and government have taken 'shroud'[8] or distort more vital understandings that 'Englishmen' may recover by reflecting on their own history:

> When we speak of a body of law, we use a metaphor so apt that it is hardly a metaphor. We picture to ourselves a being that lives and grows, that preserves its identity while every atom of which it is composed is subject to a ceaseless process of change, decay, and renewal. At any given moment of time – for example, in the present year – it may, indeed, seem to us that our legislators have, and freely exercise, an almost boundless power of doing what they will with the laws under which we live; and yet we know that, do what they may, their work will become an organic part of an already existing system.[9]

The metaphor of organic growth is more than an example of figurative language. The figure is so 'apt' because it is true. Law is a living thing. The present is part of a historical pattern. If we have lost our common sense or our sense of our own history, we need to learn how to see things for what they are. This does not mean that one should abandon literal for figurative sense. To read metaphors is to understand how to translate or how to work from one thing to another. The voice that speaks in the passage above 'knows that' the organic pattern of the law will ultimately include into itself the work of those legislators who are unconscious of its greater power. But, who is it that knows? Maitland, of course. Maitland as 'knower' is the one who can read the pattern. Above all, he knows that the law is the 'external' or revealed form of an 'inner' or concealed spirit: a spirit that speaks through Maitland's knowledge. But this knowledge is not (despite appearances) mystical or metaphysical. It is the work of a historian who has studied the records. The knowledge is that of the institutions of the law and their material, historical development. The spirit (which remains hidden) is 'there' in law's empirical reality, provided that one can read its trace. To understand what Maitland is saying is to be able to distinguish between reality and metaphor and thus to share his vision. Dogmatic texts thus engage their reader's desires. Whilst, at the level of Maitland's text, one aspect of content may appear clear (the trust, for instance), it may also gesture beyond itself to

---

7 See M.B. Nolan, 'Metaphoric History: Narrative and New Science in the Work of F.W. Maitland' (2003) 18 *PMLA* 557.
8 Maitland, op. cit., n. 1, p. 305.
9 F.W. Maitland, 'Outlines of English Legal History' in Fisher (ed.), op. cit., n. 1, p. 417.

forms of life and social activity. To think of the spirit of the trust, for instance, we must grasp a complex sense of continuity and change, adaption and refinement rooted in the practices of social actors. We must also concern ourselves with dry, technical debates within jurisprudence. Our desire will discover the animating spirit of legal doctrine.

## CORPORATION, CONTRACT, FELLOWSHIP, TRUST

What, then, can we learn from the common law about 'our' spirit? In the introduction to von Gierke's *Political Theories of the Middle Age,* we find the following argument. Maitland asserts that lawyers outside the common law tradition struggled with the idea that individuals are 'real' and 'natural' persons. How, Maitland asks, can lawyers within the civilian tradition account for social aggregates; and, more specifically, in what way can they understand real political relationships such as that of the monarch, as a real person, to the office of the Crown and the body politic? In the terms of Roman law, the state becomes thought of as an 'artificial person.' This suggests that any form of group being as determined by law is ultimately a legal fiction. Maitland objects to this approach. The state is only one 'highly specific' expression of a more general phenomenon: 'permanently organized groups of men'[10] which are credited with will and intention. The state only becomes a template for this form of organization if we flatten out our understanding of the social world. Alternative forms of social and political organization will remain ill-understood if group being is coordinated with the 'unicellular' state. Struggling against these artificial constructions means rejecting the inheritances of Roman legal concepts, in particular, the legal fiction of the corporation.

Why should incorporation have such a hold over the legal imagination? Maitland writes that 'at the end of the middle ages ... a great change in men's thought about groups' took place. The catalysts for this transformation are the Roman law concepts of *corpora* and *universitates.* From the *Corpus Juris,* the legists and canonists exhumed a theory of the corporation that became the dominant way of articulating group being. Most importantly, this theory breaks the link between the corporation and the individual: the 'personality of the *universitas* ... is not natural – it is fictitious.'[11] Maitland credits this doctrine to Pope Innocent IV. The next link in the argument takes us from spiritual to temporal power and the adoption by the former of the latter's doctrine of the corporation. Theorists of temporal power pointed out that the fictitious corporation must rest on a power that, out of its beneficence, allows the group to assume its identity. This is the power of the

10  F.W. Maitland, 'Introduction' to O. von Gierke, *Political Theories of the Middle Ages* (1900) ix.
11  id., p. 65.

prince: '[o]nly the prince may create by fiction what does not exist in reality.'[12] Armed with the new doctrine of the fictitious personality of groups, the prince could challenge the federal structure of the medieval polity. It became more difficult to think of political community as '*communitas communitatum*' (the community of groups). The prince represents the political community and grants it corporate legal being in his name.[13] If the corporation is an alien fiction, how can group life authentically express its own legal and institutional form?

We can focus these questions on Maitland's analysis of the corporation sole. Motivating this scholarly engagement with the year books and the texts of Coke, Blackstone, and Littleton is a quest for the concepts that might replace the fiction of corporation. The problem of the corporation sole is the starting point of an 'English Law of Persons' that has been in existence since 'the days of Sir Edward Coke'.[14] Sir Frederick Pollock is credited with the observation that Roman jurisprudence contains the 'fiction' whereby momentary holders of office are turned into artificial persons who bear rights and duties. Roman law thus contains the mechanism or 'fictitious substance' that gives continuity and institutional longevity its form, albeit in a concept that creates as many problems as it solves.

For Blackstone, the roots of the corporation sole can be found in the work of Sir Richard Broke and the resolution of an issue in ecclesiastical law: the legal nature of the parson. It might seem somewhat strange that the jurisprudence of the corporation sole can be traced to such a lowly office of the church, but, the legal status of the parson takes us to the relationship of the office to church lands and thus to the issue of the church's control of the transmission of its wealth and its identity as an institution. One central debate was over the powers of the patron who could present to the office of parson. The church increasingly objected to this lay power. A papal doctrine allowed the 'right to present' to be seen not so much in terms of the patron's ownership but as based on the power of the church to reward a patron for his piety. Henry II managed to assert a counter-doctrine that gave the crown a far greater influence over the award of advowsons. Somewhat later, the need to resolve certain issues over tenure of land meant that those endowing chantries went to seek the licence of the king. This gave rise to the fiction that it was the crown itself that allowed the parson to have title to land and to pass land to successors. It would thus appear that the legal status of the parson was at the sufferance of the earthly power of the crown and did not rest on ecclesiastical foundations. Cases at law suggest a slightly different approach. There was resistance to the doctrine that the power of the king could determine the form of an office of the church.

---

12  id., citing von Gierke.
13  id., p. xxi.
14  F.W. Maitland, 'The Corporation Sole' in *State, Trust, Corporation,* ed. D. Runciman (2003) 13.

Let us try to follow what Maitland means by posing the following question: '[w]hy should not an advowson be vested in trustees upon trust to present such clerk as the parishioners should choose?'[15] The force of this question comes from the implicit assertion that people should define their own institutions. In explicitly religious terms, this means that parishioners should be able to define their faith, and the concrete forms that it takes as opposed to the Church of England or the crown. It only seems an obscure concern if we forget that religious affiliation is a potent source of identity. But note that the claim to religious 'self-determination' is a claim that the advowson can be held on trust. The trust makes the self-definition of the religious group possible. It does not need to refer to papal fiction or to the power of the sovereign state.

Early modern political theory inherited these debates. The crucial concern became the idea of the state as an artificial person. We can link the question of the nature of the state with the central theme of liberal political thinking: the social contract. The notion of the social contract returns to the idea of the *societas*. In the classical tradition, *societas* and agreement or contract were fundamentally linked. A term drawn from jurisprudence was thus pressed into service to present 'civil society [as a] partnership of citizens.'[16] Following von Gierke, Maitland pointed out that conceiving the nature of the social bond in terms of contract rather than incorporation is intriguing. The contract model becomes dominant because of the limits of the theory of corporation. The essentially artificial nature of corporation meant it never moved beyond private law. The possibility remains that (provided an adequate account of incorporation can be worked out) the private law of persons, focused upon the trust, could provide a way of thinking about group being without being dependent the social contract or sovereign power.

Why should this approach be necessary? An answer to this question can be found in the elaboration of themes from Maitland in the work of John Neville Figgis. Figgis gives us a very clear sense of how certain themes in Roman law terminate in modern positivist state theory:

> The great Leviathan of Hobbes, the plenitude potestatis of the canonists, the arcana Imperii, the sovereignty of Austin, are all names of the same thing – the unlimited and illimitable power of the law-giver in the State, deduced from the notion of its unity.[17]

The consequences of this meeting of Roman law and Austinian sovereignty are entirely negative:

> The theory of government which is at the root of all the trouble is briefly this. All and every right is the creation of the one and indivisible sovereign; whether the sovereign be a monarch or an assembly is not material. No

---

15  id., p. 57.
16  Maitland, op. cit., n. 10, p. xxiii.
17  J.N. Figgis, *Churches in the Modern State* (1913) 79.

113

prescription, no conscience, no corporate life can be pleaded against its authority, which is without legal limitation.[18]

Sovereign power squeezes out the diverse forms of associational life that constitute 'civil society' imposing a tyrannical government power on the network of rights and duties that have arisen organically in the community. Figgis saw this problem in terms of the freedom of conscience and the corporate life of the church. We might say, then, that for both Maitland and Figgis, sovereign power was a force that alienated social being from itself. In the place of life developing through its own plural patterns and complexity, the bogus 'one size fits all' of the modern state was imposed and justified by an artificial jurisprudence.

Against the theory of corporation, the common law treated aggregates of people as collections of individuals. This, for Maitland, is a thoroughly common-sense approach that understands the group as a collection of individual wills. The group may achieve an identity that goes beyond that of the individual, but, this is a matter for the individuals who compose the group. It is always necessary to begin with the reality of the single person, and, as far as possible, to see the nature of the group as the negotiation of these singular identities: '... we Englishmen expect that the organised group, whether it is called a corporation or not, will be treated as a person: that is, as a right-and-duty-bearing unit.'[19] For the common law, the 'primal' sense of associational being lies in the reciprocal relations of individuals, the rights and duties that all enjoy and owe to each other. Maitland seeks to denounce 'the absolute individual' as much as he criticizes the 'absolute state'[20] as rigid legalism. In *Trust and Corporation*, Maitland wrote that an 'English-man' would think seriously about 'appeal[ing]' a decision of a 'committee or the general meeting' that had inconvenienced him. This is because 'the thought of a "jurisdiction" inherent in the *Genossenschaft* is strong in us'[21] and, moreover, is 'strongest' where 'there is no formal corporation.' This point seems entirely coherent with the argument about rights and duties. Rights and duties are compelling to the Englishman because they come from forms of association that are part of the 'face-to-face' reality of civil society. This is a valorization of the quotidian, of daily life. It is as if the notion of an everyday Englishness is the touchstone for obligations rather than the 'petrifying action of juristic theory'.[22] We can read this as a resistance to theory; or rather, a resistance to any theory that cannot describe the genius of institutions created in such a spirit that the social life that they sustain and inform is not abstract but empirical. The unincorporated association or club is its figure.

18  id., p. 85.
19  Maitland, op. cit., n. 10, p. 63.
20  id., p. 67.
21  Maitland, op. cit., n. 14, p. 106.
22  id.

114

Long before Hart produced his metaphor of the external and internal point of view, Maitland imagined the tourist visiting London and asking questions about its great legal institutions. Maitland, the imaginary tour guide, replies:

> I believe that in the eyes of a large number of my fellow-countrymen the most important and august tribunal in England is not the House of Lords but the Jockey Club; and in this case we might see 'jurisdiction' – they would use that word – exercised by the Verein over those who stand outside it.[23]

Lincoln's Inn, with its 'ancient constitution'[24] is one of the great unincorporated bodies. Thus, if the Inn has to disbar one of its members for unprofessional conduct, an appeal may lie to the High Court, but the court's jurisdiction in this kind of case is as a 'visitor' or 'a second instance of the domestic forum'.[25] The problem should be sorted out by the members of the Inn themselves ordering the terms of their own association. It is certainly worth stressing that this is 'no purely legal phenomenon'.[26] Even though one may dismiss this argument as one of 'ethical sentiment', the real life of the group exists. Although the 'ethical philosopher' may have the task of explaining it in more detail, Maitland prefers to look at the way in which a concrete legal institution – the trust – provides a viable way of arranging social life.[27]

The problem is that the device seems so technical, so dryly legal that it appears 'unworthy of exploration'.[28] We can borrow from adventures in German jurisprudence and legal history. In Germany, the new account of group being labelled itself the theory of *Genossenschaft*. How should this word be translated? Neither 'company' nor 'society' is quite right. 'Fellowship', although not exactly right, may be the least inaccurate. We are concerned, then, with a law of friendship or fellowship. This theory does not see the fellowship as a 'fiction' or a 'symbol'; neither is it 'a piece of the State's machinery' or a 'collective name for individuals'. It is a 'living organism' with 'a will of its own'.[29] In short, it is a 'group person [with] a group will.' Why, though, does Maitland comment that a similar theory could never come out of English law? Why is it unlikely that we will ever see a volume entitled 'English Fellowship Law'? The forms of life, or the forms of group being are simply too wide to be described in a single theory, no matter how sophisticated. The problem of reconciling 'the manyness of the members' with 'the oneness of the body' can only be studied in specific instances across manifold fields of life. Philosophical speculation aside, the reason why such a law of fellowship has not taken root in England may also

---

23 id.
24 id.
25 id.
26 id., p. 68.
27 id., p. 69.
28 id., p. 70.
29 Maitland, op. cit., n. 10, p. xxvi.

be down to historical circumstance. There was no political need for a theory of fellowship to champion a notion of 'organic form'.[30] There was already an institution that performed a great many of the functions required by organicist theory of the fellowship: the trust. The trust provides a 'substitute for a law about personified institutions.'[31]

Maitland argues that the trust allowed English law to depart from the 'orthodox ... lore of the fictitious person'.[32] Through the device of the trust, English law arrives at the notion of the foundation or the institute 'without troubling the State to concede or deny the mysterious boon of personality.'[33] Most specifically, the trust allows a bypassing of the state's 'sovereign power'. What, though, is the point of this ancient jurisprudence? The pattern is there for those who want to read it: 'Now we in England have lived for a long while in an atmosphere of "trust", and the effects that it has had upon us have become *so* much part of ourselves that we ourselves are not likely to detect them.'[34]

What is it that is so close to us that we cannot see it; so close to us that it might be us? We need to go back to medieval jurisprudence in order to see ourselves. Let us, then, recount Maitland's story of the trust. The trust does not fit in to the divisions of Roman law. It is a creation of English equity lawyers – exemplary of their solutions to practical problems thrown up by the historical and political circumstances in which they were working. At the doctrinal level it brings together rights *in rem* and rights *in personam*. The trust is a 'dilemma'[35] as it belongs to two 'rubrics': the law of obligations and the law of things. Roman law kept separate and distinct the concept of rights against persons and rights over things. The beneficiary had certain rights against the trustee and over the property in trust. Perhaps the genius of the lawyers who devised the trust was to realize that social life is always lived within a network of rights and duties.

The development of the rights of the *cestui que trust* is inseparable from the history of the Court of Chancery for it was the Lord Chancellor who presided over the jurisprudence that transformed rights *in personam* into rights *in rem*. Thanks to the Court of Chancery, it became possible to speak of the existence of 'equitable estates in land'.[36] The notion of conscience was a central doctrinal development. Conscience underlies the concept of an equitable estate as the interest can be enforced against those whose 'conscience is affected' by the equitable estate.[37] Thus, a person obtaining

---

30 id., p. xxviii.
31 id., p. 57.
32 id., p. 58.
33 id., p. 59.
34 Maitland, op. cit., n. 1, p. 402.
35 Maitland, op. cit, n. 10, p. 53.
36 id., p. 55.
37 id.

title to trust property from a trustee is bound by the beneficial interest if he or she knew or should have known of them. The Court of Chancery also developed the doctrine that if the beneficiary could not recover the trust property itself, he or she could pursue the value of the fund into the other property into which it had been transformed.

Why should we concern ourselves with these technical issues? The answer is that they represent a peculiar form of 'theory'. Far from the abstractions of philosophy, they are the practical elaboration of the way in which reciprocal rights create viable forms of social life around property. Thus, unless we can grasp the precise way in which the trust becomes delineated, we will never appreciate the philosophy of social being in which it is embedded. To the extent that the law of trust is a law of friendship, it can be thought of as the emotional life of estates in land. The concepts of the friend and conscience are central to the historical structure of trust as a feoffment to uses. To repeat Maitland's own oft used metaphor – the trust is a shell in which life is both hidden and protected from the power of the lord or the crown.

To understand this point, we need to follow Maitland's technical analysis of the trust. In the fourteenth century, the 'feoffment for uses' became a common legal equitable device.[38] A fee is an inheritable estate in land. The feoffment, or transfer of land created a tenant who has 'seisin'.This term derives from the French/Norman verb '*saisire*' – to give or deliver into someone's hands; to render into someone's possession. The feoffment for uses would create a tenant who was seised of land, but, 'use' or enjoyment rested with another, the *cestui que* use. Equity lawyers exploited this struc-ture of ownership to provide a practical way of avoiding inheritance dues payable to the feudal lord at the point at which the fee passed to the tenant's heir or on the occurrence of other events such as wardship or marriage.[39] Land could be conveyed 'to use' to 'friends'.[40] This meant that the friend – or, more precisely, the friends – had possession of the land. If one of the seised friends died, then, provided that a number of friends had been seised as tenants in common, there was no change of ownership and the dues payable on death were avoided. Provided that the *cestui que trust* had confidence in the friends that held the property, the heir of the original tenants could 'enjoy' the benefits that title to property brought whilst avoiding the duties that were linked to seisin. The 'demand for personality'[41] is thus satisfied – the assets have an owner and the state has not had to 'bestow' personality.

After this examination of medieval jurisprudence, we can return to Maitland's main point:

38  id.
39  id.
40  id.
41  id., p. 58.

It has often struck me that morally there is most personality where legally there is none. A man thinks of his club as a living being, honourable as well as honest, while the joint-stock company is only a sort of machine into which he puts money and out of which he draws dividends.[42]

This passage uses a very interesting set of metaphors that contrasts the living and the dead, the honourable and the dishonourable. The reality of ethical personality is evoked through the metaphor of the club as a living body, the unincorporated association (holding its property in trust) whose identity comes from those real human beings who compose it. Their honesty and honour can be translated into the good name and reputation of the institution. The technical argument would be that the trust allows the unincorporated association to have a legal form that articulates its 'real' being. To understand this argument, one needs to know where metaphors begin and end. The figure of the club as 'living being' is apt. It expresses a doctrine that gives form to desire. Unless such doctrines and vehicles (such as the joint stock company) are reunited with honesty and honour, they express the mere instrumental utilitarianism of commercial life: contracts and dividends. Hinted at in such a sentiment is a critique of market relationships. Commerce might be necessary but without spirit, it is death in life.

If we allow that in the passages above we have been following Maitland's desire, we can see that his jurisprudence of the trust traces a path through medieval and early modern history to arrive at the present. In the passage quoted in the paragraph directly above, we can see that Maitland presents this vision as one of 'honour'. I now want to examine this theme a little further, moving away from doctrinal discussions of the history of equity and examining how Maitland's metaphors operate as part of his rhetoric, and how his work was received in Anglo-American jurisprudence. It is indeed intriguing that Maitland's work was a point of reference at the end of nineteenth and the beginning of the early twentieth centuries. The question of the relationship between law and society had become pressing for a jurisprudence that sought to distinguish itself from the rigid legalism of dominant formalist approaches. The issue – which brought together an engagement with the texts of Maitland and Hegel – was how to carry forward a new way of thinking about the form of the state and the nature of legal institutions. What language should jurisprudence use to speak of new realities?

## HOW TO TALK ABOUT ETHICAL LIFE

Metaphors are constructed through intellectual labour. It is the task of the historian who uses metaphor to articulate a compelling vision of the com-

---

42 id., p. 303.

118

munity as coherent and whole. Rather than an exercise in ideological mystification, this is the work of sensibility. The historian brings together themes drawn from philosophy, history, and law – not in indigestible lumps, but in a language that can be understood by English gentlemen. As a writer who concerns himself with what might seem obscure legal doctrines, the historian faces a particular problem in speaking to his audience. In *Trust and Corporation*, Maitland constantly returns to the peculiar distance between technical terms and the language of honest men with commercial sense. He acknowledges the differences between the lawyer, the businessman, and the professor. Despite their different concerns, these men are united in a culture that, whilst it might be organized around markets, is so much more than buying and selling:

> What the foreign observer should specially remember (if I may be bold enough to give advice) is that English law does not naturally fall into a number of independent pieces, one of which can be mastered while the others are ignored. It may be a clumsy whole; but it is a whole, and every part is closely connected with every other part ... let us [consider the legal form of] the Church of Rome (as seen by English law), the Wesleyan 'Connexion', Lincoln's Inn, the London Stock Exchange, the London Library, the Jockey Club, and a Trade Union. Also it is to be remembered that the making of grand theories is not and never has been our strong point. The theory that lies upon the surface is sometimes a borrowed theory which has never penetrated far, while the really vital principles must be sought for in out-of-the-way places.[43]

Law is a 'clumsy whole' – a complex set of interrelations. Now, however, we also 'have to remember' that 'grand theory' gets in the way of a proper sense of this 'whole'. Its 'vital principles' must be found in the study of specifics. These are really only 'out-of-the-way places' for the sweeping analysis of 'grand' theory that would prefer metaphysical abstraction. The 'out-of-the-way places' are actually not out of the way at all. They are those institutions that give form to our lives: 'the Wesleyan ... Lincoln's Inn, the London Stock Exchange, the London Library, the Jockey Club, and ... Trade Union[s].' This approach does not reject philosophical speculation. Rather, it is an exercise in what might be called 'rooted' speculation, or a questioning of the institutions that we define, and which define our lives. Maitland is elaborating a way of writing and thinking that captures the true spirit of English institutions (which, interestingly, includes Trade Unions as well as the London Stock Exchange).

So, conversations between professors, lawyers, and men of business reveal, in myriad different ways, that the spirit of ethical life is at work within English history. If history is animated by spirit, the past is never gone or forgotten. However, this concern with spirit or ethos may still seem like tilting at windmills. Why trouble oneself with such a perverse endeavour,

43 Maitland, op. cit., n. 1, p. 401.

reading against the grain of received wisdom that opposes the pluralist historian with the abstruse metaphysician? Our response to this question is that the very 'separation' of Hegel and Maitland has effectively prevented the development of a way of thinking that is alive to the fundamental problem with which we have been grappling. It has obscured the role that metaphors play in the creation and sustenance of ethical modes of life. Indeed, it has resulted in a jurisprudence where questions of metaphor and sensibility, of voice and style are seen as secondary – 'rhetorical trappings' – rather than central to the articulation of institutions in which we find ourselves. These are, of course, old themes, but reading Maitland and Hegel together directs our attention to something relatively new.

Given the complexity of this concern we can focus only on one particularly significant moment: the attempt to develop a sociological jurisprudence at the turn of the nineteenth century. The problem of a jurisprudence capable of addressing sociological and historical realities takes us to a particular set of questions about the 'spirit' of the institutions of the common law. We will follow these themes through some brief comments on the work of Holmes, Thayer, and Pound. Maitland was significant for these scholars because he had an instructive faith in the way in which institutions could develop organically to serve social ends. However, for all Holmes's concern with law in 'the lives of men',[44] a prejudice against metaphor (and Hegel)[45] narrowed the critical space in which Maitland could be understood. Perhaps there is another reason that meant that metaphor had to be downplayed and ignored. This takes us to ethics, but to deal with this point we need to go back to the fundamental reason why Maitland was misread.

Even those open to Maitland and alive to his organic vision of the common law tended to read his work in a somewhat narrow way. For Thayer, Maitland might be able to direct our attention to the detailed, historical study of sources, but any concern with metaphor was an irrelevance.[46] This theme emerges in a somewhat different but more pronounced way in Pound's criticisms of mechanical jurisprudence that were the leitmotif of his influential account of sociological jurisprudence. Sociological jurisprudence saw through mechanical jurisprudence. It presented itself as flexible, scientific, and pragmatic. Mechanical jurisprudence was something of a catch-all phrase. It covered the thinking of formalist and analytical schools, as well as philosophical jurisprudence. The latter was in some ways the most suspect. It dealt with abstractions and ingenuity, creating schemes of conceptual niceties that bore no relation to the pragmatics of law or a legal science.[47] It was also probably the case that mechanical

---

44 O. Holmes, 'The Path of the Law', reprinted in (1997) 110 *Harvard Law Rev.* 1005.
45 id.
46 J.B. Thayer, 'The Teaching of English Law at Universities' (1895) 9 *Harvard Law Rev.* 169.
47 R. Pound, 'Mechanical Jurisprudence' (1908) 8 *Columbia Law Rev.* 605.

jurisprudence was responsible for bringing about equity's 'decadence'.[48] Certainly, Maitland's careful, positivist work on the sources of English law was a vital resource, but broader concerns with questions of spirit could be dismissed as dangerous abstractions.

Why was Maitland so dramatically misread? The answer by now should be obvious. It was because Hegel was misread. Discounting Hegel's insights meant that Maitland's work was received in a most restricted way. If the task of sociological jurisprudence was to allow people to 'feel and see'[49] the spirit that animates the law, then these questions of affect would forever remain invisible to this most materialistic of sciences. In its most night-marish form, Hegelian jurisprudence was alien to the spirit of the common law. Hegel's philosophical jurisprudence represented a 'form of over-abstractness' which 'instead of resulting in a healthy critique of dogmas and institutions ... lead[s] to empty generalities.'[50] However, it was precisely through its refusal of ingenuity and sensibility that sociological juris-prudence failed to engage with the ethos of the institutions that it was studying and fell victim to the very mechanistic nature of thought that it denounced. At the same time, ignoring Hegel had a positive payoff. Any critical examination of law and society prompting difficult ethical and political questions could be left to one side. Policy scientists would be able to dispute technicalities with other policy scientists.

The point is not so much that jurisprudence stopped speaking to 'gentlemen' and became an increasingly specialist language, but that a way in which law could have been studied and talked about was shut down (whether or not critical legal studies picked up on these themes in a somewhat later period is a moot point). Sociological jurisprudence might have been constituted as a study of law and metaphor. The emergent field at least had the potential to deal with the 'structuring' of legal subjectivity through modes of recognition linked to nascent market forms. In the end, perhaps the institutional and disciplinary spaces were simply not available and the intellectual and political prejudices of the protagonists ill-suited to ethical enquiry. After all, to read Maitland and Hegel properly is to see jurisprudence (sociological, philosophical or otherwise) as animated by a set of ethical questions: how should we live; what do we want to become? These are necessarily speculative concerns, but, for this line of thought, such questions of social being cannot be separated from normative concerns. As Maitland and Hegel showed, this does not mean that we must accept the form of the state, nor the seemingly autonomous rules of the market. Social and economic life is not defined by rules that are somehow 'there' or immanent in the phenomena observed. Institutions are creations. Behind

---

48 R. Pound, 'The Decadence of Equity' (1905) 5 *Columbia Law Rev.* 20.
49 Pound, op. cit., n. 47, p. 608, quoting Sir George Jessel.
50 R. Pound, 'The Scope and Purpose of Sociological Jurisprudence' (1911) 24 *Harvard Law Rev.* 610.

them are the metaphors that fashion the expression of our inner lives. Anything made can be remade.

Indeed, reflecting on the art of writing history, Maitland asserted that '[s]omething not unworthy of philosophic discussion' is necessary in thinking about law and ethics.[51] In *Ethical Personality and Legal Personality*, Maitland went on to argue that 'ethical philosophy' and the 'English' concern with 'ethics' is 'a byproduct of the specifically English history of English law.'[52] Rather than following Pound and Holmes and criticizing the 'empty generalities' in such thinking, we can read it as an application of 'Hegelian' critique where metaphor, ethics, and history are fused together. This, then, is the key to ethical life. Ethical life is an invention, a cultural creation; a club or class; a way of belonging; something that can be passed from father to son, teacher to pupil. Ethical life is a way of writing history, of talking to an audience. It is the way in which men relate to each other and get things done. Ethical life is an English version of *sittlichkeit*. Maitland's 'Englishmen' reflecting on themselves and their history are versions of Hegel's notion of the thinking/doing subject rooted in a culture of mutual recognition.

So, where does this leave us? Where does a metaphor begin and end? The ideas that travel under the names of Hegel and Maitland are themselves perhaps metaphors and can be animated by different desires. It may be that a more authentic account of an ethics of law must take us beyond Hegel and Maitland's rather limited critique of the market and further interrogate the voices, concepts, and texts that define 'us'. However, even were we to press ahead with such a critique, it may be that we must also carry forward the fundamental insights of philosophical jurisprudence. Ethics are about living well. And writing well.

51 Maitland, op. cit., n. 10, p. xii.
52 id.

122

JOURNAL OF LAW AND SOCIETY
VOLUME 43, NUMBER 1, MARCH 2016
ISSN: 0263-323X, pp. 123–43

# Debating Rape: To Whom does the Uncanny 'Myth' Metaphor Belong?

## David Gurnham*

*This article focuses on the language and metaphors used in debating rape myths, arguing that it is their uncanny aesthetic and affective qualities that accounts for the debate's fractious nature but also brings the possibility of a more productive politics. For much feminist-informed rape myth acceptance scholarship (FRMAS), 'myths' in this context are more than merely mistaken beliefs: rather, they comprise a world made up of illusions or spectres that must be laid to rest. Critics of this view, too, while critical of feminists' reliance on 'myths' as a way of stifling open discussion, likewise tend to use a discourse of myths explicitly or implicitly and with a similarly disorienting effect. For both sides of the debate then, 'myth' serves as a disquieting, uncanny metaphor that displaces and substitutes whatever else apparently erroneous beliefs, attitudes, and knowledges about rape might signify.*

## INTRODUCTION

In a recent publication I argued that the adolescent female victims at the centre of the English sexual exploitation trials of 2011 and 2012 significantly came to be associated in the public imagination with the cheap consumables that were used to win their trust. The most conspicuous example of this was the metaphor 'white meat' that identified the victims' bodies as objects for the satisfaction of appetite and distinguished them racially from their

* School of Law, University of Southampton, University Road, Southampton SO17 1BJ, England
d.gurnham@soton.ac.uk

Grateful thanks to Andreas Philippopoulos-Mihalopoulos, Ian Ward, Alex Dymock, Sue Chaplin, Robin Lister, and Mark Thomas for feedback and advice on previous drafts; also to Oren Ben-Dor, Ummni Khan, and Helen Reece for arranging for this article to be double-blind peer-reviewed and to the anonymous reviewers who provided those reviews.

123

predominantly Asian abusers.[1] Focusing here on debates about 'rape myths', this article builds on the basic insight of that previous work – namely, that we can learn something important about our political and cultural discourses on sexuality and violence by attending to such metaphoric substitutions – and takes it in a new direction.

It hardly needs to be said that the political stakes involved here are very high. The topic of rape myth acceptance has garnered a degree of convergence, but at the same time has also generated debate that is sometimes fraught with discord. On the one hand, a broad consensus of legal scholarship from various feminist positions insists that a 'mountain of evidence' supports the view that the public's understanding of rape is widely and seriously distorted by the acceptance of myths: widely held stereotypical beliefs that either have no basis in fact or else are ethically wrong inasmuch as they serve to deny or trivialize male sexual violence against women.[2] For present purposes only, and without seeking in any way to deny the various differences and nuances of positioning, methodology, and genealogy, I hope I can be forgiven for referring to this consensus as Feminist-informed Rape Myth Acceptance Scholarship (hereafter FRMAS). On the other hand, a comparatively much smaller body of scholarship critical of FRMAS has always existed, though generally occupying a more marginal space. This latter body of work has questioned the methods FRMAS uses for ascertaining rape myth acceptance,[3] the significance of its findings,[4] and even the very label of 'rape myth' for the beliefs so determined.[5]

Without claiming to occupy a neutral or disinterested position, this article argues that it may be both possible and desirable to take a step back from the question of the *truth* of rape and rape myth acceptance, and to focus instead on the hitherto unexplored aesthetic and affective dimensions of this debate. It argues first that, being characterized as a dispute about beliefs, attitudes, and claims that somehow exist in a world of unreal and insubstantial

1 D. Gurnham, *Crime, Desire and Law's Unconscious: Law, Literature and Culture* (2014) ch. 4.
2 This is the currently authoritative formulation as given in H. Gerger, H. Kley, G. Bohner, and F. Siebler, 'The Acceptance of Modern Myths About Sexual Aggression Scale: Development and Validation in German and English' (2007) 33 *Aggressive Behaviour* 422. The reference to a 'mountain of evidence' comes from J. Conaghan and Y. Russell, 'Rape Myths, Law, and Feminist Research: "Myths About Myths"?' (2014) 22 *Feminist Legal Studies* 25, at 26.
3 K.A. Lonsway and L.F. Fitzgerald, 'Rape Myths: In Review' (1994) 18 *Psychology of Women Q.* 133; D. Gurnham, 'A critique of carceral feminist arguments on rape myths and sexual scripts' *New Crim. Law Rev.* doi:10.1525/nclr.2015.150001.
4 W.A. Kerstetter, 'Gateway to Justice: Police and prosecutorial response to sexual assaults against women' (1990) 81 *J. of Criminal Law and Criminology* 267; D. Gurnham, 'Victim-blame as a symptom of rape myth acceptance?: another look at how young people in England understand sexual consent' (2016) 36 *Legal Studies* 1.
5 H. Reece, 'Rape Myths: Is Elite Opinion Right and Popular Opinion Wrong?' (2013) 33 *Oxford J. of Legal Studies* 445.

imaginings, debating rape in terms of myths amounts to using a metaphor that substitutes whatever other meaning, usefulness or nuance that those beliefs may otherwise have; secondly, that this use of metaphor has an important *uncanny* effect. FRMAS's critics, too, while sceptical of this understanding of myth, likewise tend to use the same sort of strategy, albeit for them the myth metaphor is applied to feminists' own claims to tell the truth about myths.

In approaching this debate by focusing on the aesthetic quality of the language used in debating the 'mythic' status of certain beliefs about rape, I will try also to give an account of the uncanny itself, a concept which, although not unknown within legal scholarship, has not to date been used to frame rape myth discourse as such. In very brief terms, 'the uncanny' is an imperfect English translation of the German word *unheimlich* and tends to be associated with the sense of unease, uncertainty, creepiness, and disorientation produced by the sinister and supernatural inventions of gothic literature and film.[6] In these respects the word may to be understood as being opposed to *heimlich*, which in German conveys a sense of the homely or familiar. As a concept for intellectual study, the uncanny is most familiar in disciplines such as literary, film, and cultural studies, and with intellectual movements and positions such as psychoanalysis and deconstruction.[7] This article draws on Freud's association of the uncanny with repression, and uses this to emphasize the tendency for opposing factions in the rape myths debate to try to show that the other side subdues and obscures (that is, *represses*) the truth about rape.[8]

I should make it clear at this point that I do not try to argue that Freud had anything to say about rape myths as such (indeed, the term was unknown to him), and nor am I concerned here with Freud's claim to be able to trace the origin of the uncanny to childhood sexual repressions. Instead, my approach in this regard is pragmatically political (in seeking to use theory to reconfigure rape myth debate in a way that is productive and enabling) and opportunistically disloyal (in presenting the uncanny as cut off from Freud's larger psychoanalytical framework and alongside a theorization that Freud rejected). It is an effect of the use of myth as a metaphor by both FRMAS and its critics that means that the uncanny figure of the 'double' or 'doppelgänger' can be found lurking there. This article thus proposes some ways in which the uncanny might account for the particular difficulties associated with creating space for a more productive political debate about rape and its 'myths'.

---

6 S.S. Prawer, *Cajigari's children: the film as tale of terror* (1980) 112. On what English law owes to and shares with gothic literature, see S. Chaplin, 'Written in the Black Letter: The Gothic and/in the Rule of Law' (2005) 17 *Law and Literature* 47.

7 See N. Royale, *The Uncanny* (2003) 23; A. Masschelein, *The Unconcept: the Freudian Uncanny in Late-Twentieth-Century Theory* (2011) 13–14.

8 Freud's 1919 essay 'The Uncanny', in S. Freud, *The Uncanny* (2003).

In very general terms, FRMAS uses the metaphor of the rape myth to construct rape-as-popularly-understood in terms of a ghost that must be
exorcised and laid to rest. In one way or another, FRMAS seeks to expose
the unreality and insubstantiality of popular beliefs about rape, and the
failure of those beliefs to withstand cold, hard scrutiny in light of the facts.
The designation of these beliefs as myths aims to show that, despite their
regrettable prevalence and durability, there is something ghost-like about
them, and as such they may be dispelled by being exposed to the 'daylight'
of informed opinion. Following this metaphor further, FRMAS also
demonstrates why people are not generally willing to 'give up their ghosts'
since, qua myths, they serve a useful social purpose. Ernst Jentsch
characterized the uncanny (*unheimlich*) by associating it with resistance to
ideas that challenge received wisdom. He describes the bewildering sense of
a 'lack of orientation', the 'mistrust, unease and even hostility' that tends to
greet new ideas that seem to undermine 'the power of the habitual'.[9] It is this
sense of security and familiarity in a corpus of received wisdom or
orthodoxy that Freud finds in the meaning of *heimlich*:[10] a sense that may be
disrupted when we encounter its opposite (*unheimlich*). However, unlike
Jenstch, Freud describes *unheimlich* as a symptom of the return of buried
knowledge, or as he puts it himself, 'that species of the frightening that goes
back to *what was once well known* and had long been familiar.'[11] The
uncanny is thus a disruption of what we generally take to be real or natural,
as a result of the return of something which, for whatever reason, had long
ago been banished, suppressed or otherwise kept out of sight. The troubling
influence of the 'repressed' that gives rise to a sense of the uncanny
represents what this article seeks to bring out in analysing the texts of
FRMAS and its critics, as we shall see.[12]

A strange quality of the German words *heimlich* and *unheimlich* as
highlighted by Freud and by subsequent commentators, is that in fact they
are not merely opposites: they oppose each other in the sense that the former
means 'homely' and the latter '*un*homely' as I have said already, but at the
same time both words can mean *hidden*.[13] In other words, the 'un' of
uncanny (or *unheimlich*) does not necessarily negate or cancel out its sup-

---

9 E. Jentsch, 'On the psychology of the uncanny (1906)' (1997) 2 *Angelaki: J. of the Theoretical Humanities* 7, at 8–9.
10 Freud, op. cit., n. 8, p. 126.
11 id., p. 124, emphasis added.
12 Royale, op. cit., n. 7, p. 1.
13 Freud, op. cit., n. 8, p. 132. In English too, canny and uncanny are rarely used in opposition to one another, and indeed may be more likely to be used to convey a complementary meaning, for example: 'As a spy, Bond was a canny operator, and had an uncanny ability to turn an apparent dead-end into an opportunity.'

posed opposite, but merely 'hides', 'covers' or 'denies' it. It is not difficult to appreciate therefore why Freud came to insist that the prefix 'un' is the 'token of repression',[14] or the broader implication that 'denying something at the same time conjures it up'; that what is repressed is 'always too near'.[15] These observations arguably carry a normative implication for critical scholarship and one that I propose to apply in the context of rape myths: that we ought to sceptical about claims that a certain belief may be negated by exposure to 'the facts'; that we ought to remain open to the possibility that such a claim merely represses that belief and doing so does not kill it but merely keeps it at bay. On the one hand, therefore, for FRMAS the truth of acquaintance and partner rape is repressed in favour of false beliefs and stereotypes about 'natural' male sexual aggression and 'blitz' or 'stranger' rape its other. On the other side of the argument, FRMAS's designation of certain beliefs as *fundamentally* wrong or unacceptable and hence beyond any further debate, is itself claimed to be repressive.[16]

## 1. 'Miscommunication' as a repressive myth

One argument commonly made within FRMAS is that to excuse rape and sexual assault as innocent miscommunication and misunderstanding constitutes a *knowing denial of deliberate coercion* that serves dominant male interests. To this end, and in a manner not dissimilar to a psycho-analyst's identification of unconscious knowledge and intentions in a language-user's unintended slips, Kitzinger and Frith's exposé of mis-communication works on the basis that 'even the finest levels of con-versational detail, every speech error, pause, overlap or lexical correction may be a "designed" or consequential feature of social action.'[17] Their analysis of non-sexual conversations in which people are heard to make – and to understand – refusals without explicitly saying 'no' (and instead using techniques such as 'pausing, hedging, producing a palliative ...') leads Kitzinger and Frith to surmise that:

> young women are communicating in ways which are usually understood to mean refusal in other contexts and it is not the adequacy of their communication that should be questioned, but rather their male partners' claims not to understand that these women are refusing sex.[18]

---

14  id., p. 151.
15  Masschelein, op. cit., n. 7, p. 8; H. Cixous, 'Fiction and its Phantoms: a reading of Freud's *Das Unheimliche* (The "uncanny")' (1976) 7 *New Literary History* 525, at 537.
16  Reece, op. cit., n. 5.
17  C. Kitzinger and H. Frith, 'Just say no? The use of conversation analysis in developing a feminist perspective on sexual refusal' (1999) 10 *Discourse & Society* 293, at 299.
18  id., p. 310.

In other words, the claim that responses like 'um, I'm not sure ...', 'maybe later', and 'I'd love to *but* ...' are inadequate as expressions of refusal is a dishonest one that may be facilitating and covering up acts of sexual coercion by men.

O'Byrne, Rapely, and Hansen followed this up with a study that analysed responses given by men in two focus groups, finding that the men were fully competent to comprehend the idea of refusing sex indirectly as well as non-verbally.[19] The researchers note how, when asked about how women might signal refusal, the young male participants responded with examples involving 'a complete absence not only of ... the word "no", but of verbal refusals of *any* kind'.[20] Then Jozkowski and Peterson's questioning of college students uncovered a host of imaginative strategies amongst young men for deploying miscommunication cynically to ensure they get the kind of sex they want, irrespective of their partner's wishes.[21] For example, a theme that the researchers discovered 'unexpected[ly]' was the use of deception by some men (11.8 per cent) to gain consent to anal sex:

> 'Most women hate it, so I would slip it in the back door and pretend like I had done it by mistake.' Similarly, other men wrote, 'I would pretend like I did not know I was putting it in her ass', 'I would flip her over and pretend like I was going to do it doggy style [rear-entry sex], but then I would stick it in her butt' ...[22]

What all these studies seem to agree on is that the figure of the innocently misunderstanding man, although apparently real for many people, on closer inspection turns out to be a fictive creation of male-dominated culture that serves as 'a self-interested justification for coercive behaviour'.[23] This creation – this spectral double for 'real' man – tends not to be directly invoked as such, but his haunting presence in the language of FRMAS is (I suggest) an effect of constituting one thing (whatever it is that actually happens when D claims that V's complaint can be explained as 'miscommunication') in the terms of another (a belief that is so fundamentally wrong that it amounts to a myth).

At the same time however, FRMAS seeks to supress the metaphorical character of construing miscommunication as a myth by expounding on the cultural basis for the false beliefs in question. By showing that those beliefs serve a broader ideology that prioritizes the interests of one group (men) over

19 M. O'Byrne, M. Rapely, and S. Hansen, '"You couldn't say 'No', could you?" Young men's understandings of sexual refusal' (2006) 16 *Feminism and Psychology* 133, at 9–10, 13–15, and 16–17 respectively.
20 id., p. 147: 'Mike: "... [if] she doesn't respond in the same way then you know it's a pretty good sign and you're not on the same level."'
21 K.N. Jozkowski and Z.D. Peterson, 'College Students and Sexual Consent: Unique Insights' (2013) 50 *J. of Sex Research* 517.
22 id., p. 520.
23 Kitzinger and Frith, op. cit., n. 17, p. 295.

another (women) they implicitly claim that the label of myth is a literal truth, rather than a metaphor.[24] Hence the three studies referred to above all agree that, to the extent that miscommunication is popularly believed to be real, this is explicable in terms of the strength of that ideology and the incentives it offers both men and women to try sustain it. Imbuing 'miscommunication' with explanatory power, for example, arguably allows women to avoid the 'negative ramifications of being a rape victim',[25] keeps at bay 'the possibility that men are abusing their power in heterosexual relationships', and offers women a sense of control over their future by 'learn[ing] to communicate more effectively'.[26] For men, meanwhile, it serves to 'rationalize and justify' coercive behaviour,[27] and to 'delete the accountability of men for rape [and] to preserve a positive shared masculine identity.'[28] For society as a whole it fosters and sustains a sense of a just world (the belief that rape does not happen to those who communicate 'properly')[29] and draws attention away from structural inequalities and injustices that might otherwise threaten social solidarity and cohesion.

Therefore, although I characterize these claims as an effort to supress the metaphorical character of myth, they are made in order to establish that our culture itself supresses the truth that men are routinely excused when they subject women to sexual coercion, and to combat that suppression. For FRMAS, heterosexual culture enlists a broad coalition of interests to sustain its repressive ideology. For those individuals who buy into that ideology, it should not be surprising if the *encounter* with the repressed truth (if truth it be) might be experienced as unpleasant, disorienting, or as a 'species of the frightening [that] ... should have remained hidden and has come into the open.'[30]

## 2. What's sauce for the goose ... turning the uncanny tables on FRMAS

But if the production of an uncanny effect can be described as any kind of rhetorical strategy, it is one that is also available to and discernible in scholarship that is critical of FRMAS. For example, replying to critics of her

---

24  See Lonsway and Fitzgerald, op. cit., n. 3, p. 134.

25  K.M. Ryan, 'The Relationship between Rape Myths and Sexual Scripts: The Social Construction of Rape' (2011) 65 *Sex Roles* 774, at 777.

26  H. Frith and C. Kitzinger, 'Talk about sexual miscommunication' (1997) 20 *Women's Studies International Forum*, 517, at 524, 525.

27  Ryan, op. cit., n. 25, p. 775; see, also, M. Duran, M. Moya, J. L. Megías, and G.T. Viki, 'Social Perceptions of Rape Victims in Dating and Married Relationships: The Role of Perpetrator's Benevolent Sexism' (2010) 62 *Sex Roles* 505.

28  O'Byrne et al., op. cit., n. 19, p. 46.

29  T. Stahl, D. Eek, and A. Kazemi, 'Rape Victim Blaming as System Justification: The Role of Gender and Activation of Complementary Stereotypes' (2010) 23 *Social Justice Research* 239, at 241–2.

30  Freud, op. cit., n. 8, p. 148.

argument that feminists have systematically exaggerated the prevalence and impact of rape myths,[31] Helen Reece argues that it is FRMAS, not the myths themselves, that silences honest and open discussion.[32] Her calling into question the designation of certain beliefs about rape as myths – on the basis that some myths are factually true, that others are not in fact widely believed, and others still are not myths about rape at all – does two important things. First, it draws attention to the fact that the term 'rape myth' is not necessarily meaningful in any literal sense but is, in fact, a figure of speech designed to group together a number of different matters under one banner, and to deflect from potentially troubling factual distinctions. Secondly, it draws attention to the repressive nature of the metaphor itself, both because of this substitution of those different matters (factual truths, falsities not widely believed, and sex myths) for one thing (rape myths) and the repressive use to which it is put by FRMAS.[33] An example of this repressive use is the campaign led by *Feminists@Law* (a group of feminist legal scholars based at Kent Law School) condemning both Reece's arguments and the LSE for providing her with a platform from which to advance them.[34] It made no difference that LSE was Reece's own employer, that her paper had been peer reviewed and deemed fit for publication by the eminently respectable *Oxford Journal of Legal Studies*, or that she shared that platform with Professor Jennifer Temkin (whose book *Rape and the Legal Process* is something of a classic[35]) and Chief Crown Prosecutor for North West England, Nazir Afzal to contest her position. In a telling passage, the editors of *Feminists@Law* declared that they:

> deplore LSE Law's decision to give a platform to Reece and Hewson's *dangerous and unsupported* views and its failure to engage responsibly with the public on such an important and sensitive issue as rape. Stating that there is a distinction between blame and responsibility *cynically elides the appeal to rape myths embedded in the argument itself.*[36]

The claim made in the passage above is that to call into question the truth about rape myths as understood within FRMAS is a practice that is necessarily and inseparably intertwined with rape myth acceptance itself, and thus endorses beliefs that are fundamentally either false or unethical. Reece reframes the distinction, crucial to the intellectual and moral integrity of FRMAS, between right and the absolutely wrong as a *mere difference of*

---

31 As presented in her 2013 article (Reece, op. cit., n. 5).
32 H. Reece, 'Debating Rape Myths', LSE Law, Society and Economy Working Papers 21/2014 (2014), at <http://papers.ssrn.com/sol3/papers.cfm?abstract_id=2497844>. For relevant criticism of Reece, see Conaghan and Russell, op. cit., n. 2, p. 27.
33 On this last point see Reece, id., p. 20.
34 'A Response to the LSE Event "Is Rape Different?"' (2013) 3 *Feminists@Law*. See, also, Reece, id., p. 22.
35 J. Temkin, *Rape and the Legal Process* (2002).
36 Editors, op. cit., n. 34, p. 3, emphasis added.

*opinion*. For Reece, the idea that having the 'wrong' belief about rape amounts to a myth is to create *myths about myths*. In appropriating talk of myths in this way, Reece not only exposes the metaphoric quality of myth discourse, she also makes a bid actually to steal it from FRMAS and claim it for its critics!

We can readily appreciate the uncanny effect of this attempt to prise the myth metaphor away from FRMAS and to use it to undermine feminist scholarship. In this move, FRMAS find themselves in the sort of position that Freud describes in *The Uncanny*: that of a staunchly rational person who despises superstition being one day 'caught' indulging in super-stitious thinking.[37] Similarly, the hostility within FRMAS to the *myths about myths* claim cannot be surprising, given that FRMAS fundamentally relies upon being able to separate truth from myth and facts from fictions. We saw above that the studies seeking to establish that miscommunication is a myth evokes the sense that the man who *genuinely* misunderstands the cues is a largely fictional character. In the same way, Reece's argument implies that FRMAS's image of the feminist researcher as a reliable guide shining an authentic light of truth and ethical correctness on the dark landscape of ignorant prejudice – is similarly fictional. In both cases, the character of the 'double' is invoked as a result of talking about rape in terms of myths.

To the extent that FRMAS finds its own status undermined in this way, it is not far-fetched to imagine its proponents experiencing that same discomforting and disorienting feeling of the 'unhomely' (*unheimlich*) that they are more used to producing in others. As if to confirm this, Conaghan and Russell's rebuke to Reece takes the phrase 'Myths about myths' as its title and hence as *the* central problem for positioning FRMAS. If it is correct to say that the myth metaphor as deployed in FRMAS is repressive, then this move by Conaghan and Russell arguably evokes Cixous's characterization of the repressed as 'always too near'.[38] In this light we may understand more clearly the insistence by the *Feminists@Law* editorial that Reece's arguments 'appeal to existing rape myths in society'. Only by positioning her criticism as *itself* a symptom of rape myth acceptance can FRMAS re-establish its claim to control the myth metaphor it relies so heavily upon, thereby re-establishing the reality of its own claim to truth, and its own footing.


## THE DOUBLE IN THE JURY ROOM: RAPISTS AND NORMAL MEN

Let us now delve a little further into how the metaphor of the rape myth evokes an uncanny effect by implying the presence of the fictional or imagined character of the 'double'. Such an effect is sometimes invoked

37 Freud, op. cit., n. 8, pp. 154–5.
38 Conaghan and Russell, op. cit., n. 2; Cixous, op. cit., n. 15, p. 537.

directly as an integral part of the myth metaphor, for example, in Kathryn Ryan's description of rape myths in general as 'a projection ... of fears and desires'[39] or by Michelle Anderson in conceiving rape myths as visions 'conjure[d] up' in the mind.[40] But if we are to find in FRMAS evidence of the uncanny double whose defining feature is seeming to be *identical* to a real person, we must dig slightly deeper into the metaphorical allusions in FRMAS and their (sometimes intended, sometimes not intended) implications.[41] In literature and film, the encounter with one's own 'double' is uncanny in the sense I have described above because it is associated with experiencing the hitherto familiar (that is, one's own identity) as unfamiliar.[42] In Dostoevsky's short story *The Double*, for example, the protagonist Mr. Goliadkin is initially 'confused, and even frightened', when he first perceives that 'this stranger [whom he passes in the street on a miserable night in St Petersburg] now seemed somehow familiar to him.'[43] When this stranger then turns up at Mr. Goliadkin's place of work as a new clerk (the same job as Goliakin), the protagonist perceives with 'horror' that he is:

> a different Mr. Goliadkin, *completely different*, but at the same time *completely identical* to the first [such that it might be impossible to] determine precisely which was the real Goliadkin and which was the counterfeit.[44]

What makes the story of Mr. Goliadkin uncanny for the reader is the uncertainty it sustains about the status of his double: are we supposed to think of the 'other Mr Goliadkin' as real, as a ghost, or an illusion produced by Goliadkin having a nervous breakdown? What makes this 'counterfeit' Goliakin ultimately so dangerous for the protagonist of Dostoevsky's story is that, not unlike a metaphor, the double quickly begins to substitute and marginalize the real. This process of doubling and substitution is key to understanding how FRMAS uses the rape-myth metaphor and in so doing achieves an uncanny effect. The remainder of this section analyses four examples of this challenge. In each case, FRMAS moves to strip away a normalizing disguise for rape and in doing so invokes the metaphor of the double. We will focus here on intimacy, seduction, kink, and social drinking.

39 Ryan, op. cit., n. 25, p. 274.
40 M. Anderson, 'Diminishing the Legal Impact of Negative Social Attitudes toward Acquaintance Rape Victims' (2010) 13 *New Crim. Law Rev.* 644, at 645.
41 Freud, op. cit., n. 8, p. 142; J. Fletcher, 'Freud, Hoffman and the Death-Work' (2002) 7 *Angelaki: J. of the Theoretical Humanities* 125, at 126; Royale, op. cit., n. 7, p. 6.
42 See, for example, *The Double Life of Veronique* (Sideral Productions, 1991) and *The Double* (Alcove Entertainment, 2013). The device is arguably also used, though in a different way, in *Fight Club* (Fox 2000 Pictures, 1999) and in *The Devil's Double* (Staccato Films, 2011).
43 F. Dostoevsky, *The Double and the Gambler*, trs. R. Pevear and L. Volokhonsky (2005) 48.
44 id., p. 55, my emphasis.

## 1. *Intimacy*

Louise Ellison and Vanessa Munro describe, across a number of publications, how participants in their empirical research (recreating the conditions of a rape trial in order to study jury deliberations) betray reliance on mythical thinking. They report, for example, that mock jurors try to explain away a counter-stereotypical rape – alleged to have been committed by the complainant's former lover after having shared a glass of wine at her invitation – as a mutual and spontaneous rekindling of sexual passion.[45] In the case put before a panel of mock jurors, the 'defendant' was designed so as to challenge stereotypical assumptions by being apparently *completely identical* to the stereotypically 'normal' man in every respect except that he seems to have raped a woman (that is, *completely different* from a normal man).[46] For the researchers, jurors' reluctance to convict in this case of disputed consent indicates that acquaintance rape 'remains peculiarly problematic' in the popular imagination.[47] Despite being 'receptive, in principle' to the idea of rape between former and current sexual partners, jurors felt moved to reconstruct the event as one of consensual sex – even filling in the facts with speculation about the parties' internally conflicted emotional and sexual desires.[48] The degree of detail with which jurors perform this extra-factual thinking would seem to imply that they are, in effect, *seeing double*: by identifying so closely with a potential rapist, jurors are moved to conjure a new and different character in order to save him from conviction.

A very interesting double-doubling is happening here, because while the implication of Ellison and Munro's research is that it is the *jurors* who are projecting a fictional double to substitute the defendant on trial, this is itself an implication that can only be drawn by first accepting that a plethora of beliefs, attitudes, and perceptions about rape can be substituted for the metaphor of the rape *myth*. The researchers' language testifies to a courtroom full of ghosts: to the '*spectre* of sexual miscommunication [that] *loomed large*' in jurors' imaginations, creating a murky 'grey area' in their moral reasoning.[49] Of another of Ellison and Munro's jury studies, Carline and Easteal observe that a 'culture of scepticism continues to *haunt* the jury room.'[50] The language carries obvious overtones of spectral, other-worldly

---

45 L. Ellison and V. Munro, 'Better the devil you know? "Real rape" stereotypes and the relevance of a previous relationship in (mock) juror deliberations' (2013) 17 *International J. of Evidence & Proof* 299.

46 On the stereotypical belief that 'normal men' do not rape, see Temkin, op. cit., n. 35, pp. 95–6.

47 Ellison and Munro, op. cit., n. 45, pp. 304, 302.

48 id., pp. 309, 312–14.

49 id., pp. 314 (emphasis added), 310.

50 A. Carline and P. Easteal, *Shades of Grey–Domestic and Sexual Violence Against Women* (2014) 184.

133

presences in the minds of jurors and in the legal process. In this respect, we can build on Sue Chaplin's appeal to the gothic in her critique of the 'marginal, mercurial quality' of law that acts 'as a point of passage between one order [namely the real world] and another [i.e. the supernatural].'[51] I would suggest that Chaplin's description could also apply to the function of the myth metaphor, transferring or carrying over the meaning of a disputed incident: from whatever might *literally* be going on to an uncanny *figurative* language.

The language used in FRMAS to describe these spectral presences is very appropriate, since the jurors' apparent motivations for projecting this 'double' strikingly reflect the motivations described by both Freud and Otto Rank respectively: as 'a means of protection' and as a 'paranoid awareness of oneself as an object of someone else's observation'.[52] Participants in studies such as those of Ellison and Munro would be quite right to perceive themselves as the objects of someone else's observation, and if we assume that their responses are accurately represented in the published articles, they would furthermore have reason to feel it necessary to protect themselves somehow against the implications of being provoked to identify with a rapist (or victim). Like the initially sceptical Hamlet confronted with the 'questionable shape' of his father's ghost,[53] Ellison and Munro's jurors are invited to question the basis in reality for their beliefs. Indeed, the title that Ellison and Munro give to their article – 'Better the devil you know' – signifies much more than a facile idiom. It also alludes to the devil's traditionally infamous expertise in exploiting people's susceptibility to seduction and disguise, misleading them with potentially disastrous consequences.

## 2. *Seduction*

A review of other studies provides further examples of how this imaginative appeal to the double comes about when a potential rapist appears in the guise of normality. These studies all achieve an unsettling effect by framing apparently common and popular attitudes about aspects of 'ordinary' sexual life in terms of rape myth acceptance. A classic example is the ostensibly sociable and pleasurable practise of sharing a bottle of wine during which a woman and a man chat and flirt. For Ellison and Munro, these activities take on the far darker quality of being 'grooming' behaviours if they are engaged in with the intention of having sex with the other.[54] For Ryan, similarly,

---

51 Chaplin, op. cit., n. 6, pp. 54–5.
52 S. Meckled, 'The Theme of the Double: An Essential Element throughout García Márquez Works' (1982) 6(2) *The Crane Bag* 108, at 108.
53 W. Shakespeare, *Hamlet*, Act I, scene IV, line 43.
54 L. Ellison and V. Munro, 'Of "Normal Sex" and "Real Rape": Exploring the Use of Socio-Sexual Scripts in (Mock) Jury Deliberation' (2009) 18 *Social & Legal Studies* 291, at 301.

'[t]he socially skilled *predator* may be able to con himself and potential victims because he does not resemble the myth of the obviously different rapist.'[55] In this passage of Ryan's, any doubt about the truth of the defendant's nature is entirely erased, but access to this truth is so compellingly and seductively disguised by rape myth that it even convinces the rapist himself. At the same time, however, Ryan insists that such men are not unaware that they are committing rape, but that they simply 'believe it is acceptable to coerce sex.'[56] Certain empirical studies of sexual behaviour and attitudes confirm the existence of this double-faced perpetrator, for example, Jozkowski and Peterson's young college men who self-identify as masculine seducers or lovers rather than rapists, but who (as noted above) also openly advocate the use of various forms of deception or coercion.[57] For Ryan, not only is 'sexual foreplay' a 'precondition' for men to get away with rape, but she further identifies the date rapist as he who will 'frequently profess love, promise to further the relationship, and threaten to terminate the relationship.'[58] The meaning of all of these words and actions, which we might traditionally think of as part of ordinary sexual negotiations or scripts, can thus be swallowed up by the myth metaphor.

## 3. *Kink*

This is a technique that is given something of a twist by Alex Dymock, analysing the trial of *R* v. *Lock* (unreported) in England in 2013. Steven Lock was acquitted on charges of assault occasioning actual bodily harm to his female partner, whom he chained up and beat 14 times with a rope, in accordance with a 'master/slave' contract they had drawn up together.[59] The contract stated that her body was to become his sexual property (a fact further emphasized by a tattoo around her genitals stating as much) and, furthermore, that he would be entitled to punish her if she failed to fulfil her obligations.[60] Although according to the authorities of *R* v. *Brown* and *R* v. *Donovan*[61] consent is not available to violence that inflicts bodily harm for sado-masochistic sexual motives, the judge did leave the defence to the jury, and the jury duly acquitted him. Dymock describes Lock's defence – that they were acting out a *Fifty Shades of Grey*-type scenario – as 'ingenious'. Notwithstanding the extremity of the behaviour and the complainant's resolute insistence that she did not consent at the time, Lock apparently

---

55 Ryan, op. cit., n. 25, p. 779 (emphasis added).
56 id., p. 778. Presumably such a belief would be held unreflectively.
57 Jozkowski and Peterson, op. cit., n. 21.
58 Ryan, op. cit., n. 25, p. 778.
59 s. 47 of the Offences Against the Person Act 1861.
60 'Gardener cleared of assault after Fifty Shades of Grey-inspired sadomasochistic sex session' *Independent*, 22 January 2013.
61 *R* v. *Brown* [1994] 1 A.C. 212; *R* v. *Donovan* [1934] 25 Cr. App. R. 1 CCA.

succeeded in positioning himself in jurors' minds within familiar normative bounds, and hence what had happened as 'harmless' consensual kinky sex rather than abuse.[62] Importantly it is not the improbable figure of the billionaire dom, Christian Grey, who was summoned in the imaginations of the jurors to acquit Mr Lock but, rather, that of the ordinary consumer of popular fiction, whose sexual behaviours are likewise deemed to be within tolerable bounds. For Dymock, however, *Lock* is a case of a woman's 'subjective experience of non-consent' being 'silenced' by society's readiness to find ways to normalize and hence overlook male sexual violence.[63]

4. *Social drinking*

In studies on attitudes towards alcohol consumption and its relevance for rape, we find a similar sense in which criminal activity is overlooked and excused as a consequence of the widespread normalizing of coercive strategies. FRMAS will often seek to refute beliefs such as that many alleged rapes can be explained as mere regrets about drunken sex, that alcohol merely reduces a woman's sexual inhibitions, and that a woman who alleges she was raped whilst too intoxicated to consent is likely to be lying. For FRMAS, these are all myths that serve to excuse male sexual coercion and to blame women.[64] This designation of prevalent beliefs as myths is a move to force people to confront the uncomfortable implication that practices (and beliefs) commonly accepted as normal are not necessarily distinct from rape (and rape-approval). As Shlomit Wallerstein warns, this does imply that 'the conduct of [normal] people in many cases [constitutes] a criminal offence, and [thus that they are] rapists and sexual assaulterers.'[65] Finch and Munro similarly refer with strong disapproval to the 'normalization' of the cultural intermingling of drink and sex that explains the strong resistance they find in their mock jurors to seeing alcohol-assisted sex as rape, despite those same jurors acknowledging that this could constitute 'taking advantage'.[66] Once again, we can see that the affective force of FRMAS lies in its defamiliarizing of apparently 'normal' behaviours, and thereby collapsing the distinction between rapists (or potential rapists) and non-rapists.

The argument is emphasized by undercutting the popularly assumed distinction between *normal* and *culpable* uses of intoxicating substances to

62 A. Dymock, 'Abject Intimacies: Sexual Perversion in the Criminal-Legal Imaginary', unpublished PhD thesis, University of Reading (2015) 228.
63 id., p. 229.
64 S. Wallerstein, '"A Drunken Consent is Still Consent" – Or is it? A Critical Analysis of the Law on a Drunken Consent to Sex Following Bree' (2009) 73 *J. of Crim. Law* 318, at 329–33; Temkin, op. cit., n. 35, pp. 4–8; Carline and Easteal, op. cit., n. 50, p. 163.
65 Wallerstein, id., p. 329.
66 E. Finch and V. Munro, 'The Demon Drink and the Demonised Woman: Socio-sexual Stereotypes and Responsibility Attribution in Rape Trials Involving Intoxicants' (2007) 16 *Social & Legal Studies* 591, at 593–4, 603.

gain consent. On this point, Finch and Munro are critical of their jurors' apparent belief that (say) the buying of double measures in order to get a woman drunk is normal, whilst the use of rohypnol would be compelling evidence of malicious intent.[67] The stereotypical thinking that jurors are engaged in here, claim Finch and Munro, relies on the mythical distinction between criminally devious rapists and the natural sexual opportunism of social drinkers. Challenging this stereotype, Gunby, Carline, and Beynon suggest that a man who uses socially normalized ways to 'cause' a woman to take alcohol (that is, by 'encouragement, social pressure, and the intentional buying of double measures') ought to be caught by s.75(2)(f) of the Sexual Offences Act 2003, triggering a rebuttable presumption that the complainant did not consent.[68] Despite the statutory provision seeming broadly enough worded to be applied in this way, barristers interviewed by Gunby et al. seemed to think that this presumption could apply only in a drink-*spiking* scenario. Even for legal experts for whom challenging the stereotype might be professionally advantageous therefore, there seemed to be some unarticulated and yet potent reason why the practice of merely buying alcoholic drinks needed to be kept separate from deceitful drink spiking.[69] Gunby et al. furthermore find it 'disappointing' that their interviewees seemed reluctant to treat a complainant's lack of memory as evidence of a lack of consent and thus for a prosecution to proceed.[70] But are such apparent failures not entirely predictable within the critical framework that Gunby et al. assume, in which myths about alcohol and sex constitute a part of a '*supposed reality*' in the popular mindset about rape and sexual assault?[71] If nothing else, then this research further demonstrates ways in which we might view the affirmation of stereotypes as another example of a self-defensive reaction against the troubling implications of being too closely associated with the perpetrator of rape.


## FRMAS AND THE CARCERAL STATE

This article has argued so far that the feminist-informed criticisms about the insubstantiality of popular beliefs about rape ('myths') as well as counter-criticisms about how FRMAS construes those beliefs ('myths about myths') can be understood in terms of a struggle for control over the myth metaphor. Freed from its fuller Freudian foundation in castration anxiety, the uncanny offers a valuable tool for understanding the particular toxicity of debates

---

67  id., p. 604.
68  C. Gunby, A. Carline, and C. Beynon, 'Alcohol-related Rape Cases: Barristers' Perspectives on the Sexual Offences Act 2003 and its Impact on Practice' (2010) 74 *J. of Crim. Law* 579, at 591.
69  id., pp. 594–5.
70  id., p. 591.
71  id.

such as this in which opposing sides accuse the other of using repressive strategies in this way. But it is helpful also for guiding us towards a potentially more politically enabling engagement with FRMAS's broader theoretical underpinnings.

Janet Halley has argued that at the root of feminism from its second wave to postmodernizing strands, is a sense that injury (and sexual injury in particular) is only really intelligible or important when it can be articulated through the formula of 'm/f, m>f and carrying a brief for f'.[72] The feminist 'politics of injury' carries the implication that, for example, an increased proportion of accused men who are finally convicted and punished for committing rape and sexual assault against women may be thought of as a political victory (so long as the numbers of reported rapes also do not drop for any reason), notwithstanding any possible costs that might also thereby fall 'on myriad social interests that can't be spelled in the alphabet of m/f.'[73] Such costs might be, for example, an erosion of defendants' rights to due process or the potentially harmful effects of incarceration itself that most often falls upon men who are already those most socially marginalized and disadvantaged.[74]

Halley's formula can seem provocatively reductive and she has been criticized on this basis elsewhere.[75] Whether or not we agree with Conaghan's assessment of Halley's argument as merely 'a series of glib equations', it seems clear that what gives her critique bite is a quality that she shares with all the other commentators (FRMAS or otherwise) considered above, namely, her recourse to wresting control over a particular metaphor that allows her to command her own terms of reference. Halley asserts that feminism has a secret 'Will to power'[76] in allying itself with the aims of the carceral state to inflict punishment: an alliance and a Will that (Halley claims) is denied by feminists, who in maintaining a critical distance from the state need instead to be seen as identifying with the power*lessness* of women subordinated by men (hence the 'politics of injury'). Relevantly for our own analysis of FRMAS and its critics, we might observe that a frequently alleged consequence of rape myth acceptance is that too many men go unpunished when they commit rape or sexual assault and that too many victims are left without justice as a consequence of allegedly low rates of reporting, investigating, prosecuting, and convicting rape.[77]

---

72 J. Halley, *Split Decisions: How and Why to Take a Break From Feminism* (2008) 289, 342.

73 id., p. 343.

74 U. Khan, *Vicarious Kinks: s/m in the socio-legal imaginary* (2014) 265–6.

75 J. Conaghan, 'The Making of a Field or the Building of a Wall? Feminist Legal Studies and Law, Gender and Sexuality' (2009) 17 *Feminist Legal Studies* 303.

76 Halley, op. cit., n. 72, pp. 22, 32, 342.

77 See J.M. Brown, C. Hamilton, and D. O'Neill, 'Characteristics associated with rape attrition and the role played by scepticism or legal rationality by investigators and prosecutors' (2007) 13 *Psychology, Crime and Law* 355; also, Carline and Easteal, op. cit., n. 50.

Subjecting more men to carceral punishment arguably represents a shared aim, at least in principle, but in practice, law's apparent failure to rid itself of patriarchal bias blocks any formal alliance and legitimizes feminists' refusal to acknowledge one. There is an uncanny evocation of the 'doubling' between truth and illusion here too, since the perspective that Halley advocates is one in which feminist theorizing (and consequently, by implication, FRMAS) involves the projection of the myth of a powerless, subordinated, and injured group (or 'class' if we follow MacKinnon's Marxist terminology) that, in being popularly believed, masks the reality that feminism in alliance with the carceral state is an empowered, influential, and furthermore *dangerous* political force.

Halley certainly does not paint her picture (of feminism as secretly allied with the state) in terms of repression, nor the exposure of this alliance in terms of an uncanny return; however, her argument leads us nicely to what I contend is the broader political significance of the uncanny. Halley writes of her desire to cause 'disorientation' in her readers: 'Above all I hope this disorientation – however painful it might also be – will be pleasurable, erotically animating, and politically enabling.'[78] But *for whom* could this disorientation be 'pleasurable' and 'politically enabling'? Halley's account of the benefits of 'Taking a Break From Feminism' repeatedly returns to the point that it is only *certain people* who are capable of (even temporarily) putting aside feminism's presuppositions – 'm/f, m>f and carrying a brief for f' – who can 'see around the corners' of these notions and treat them simply as working hypotheses that may be laid aside when other, potentially contradictory hypotheses may be more useful.[79] Halley does not specify what hypotheses may actually be 'around the corners', but that is really the point since for her: '*Not knowing* ... is an erotic event – risky, pleasurable, obliterating, full of promise.'[80] Those too dogmatic or unimaginative to embrace such a laying aside will prefer to 'wrap [themselves] tightly in [their] secure and familiar social theory.'[81] If this point of Halley's carries any whiff of intellectual elitism, then, in this respect too, there is a point of contact between her 'erotic' politics and Freud's uncanny. As Brian McCuskey has pointed out, in the romantic tradition of the nineteenth century, the uncanny is not *merely* unpleasant for those equipped to appreciate it properly, but is, rather, an affect in part to be desired by intellectuals and artists seeking to distinguish themselves from soulless rationalists, capitalists, and the working classes prosaically occupied by more mundane concerns.[82]

78  Halley, op. cit., n. 72, p. 285.
79  id., p. 321.
80  id., p. 236.
81  id., p. 304.
82  B. McCuskey, 'Not at home: Servants, scholars, and the uncanny' (2006) 121 *PLMA* 421.

What this suggests to me, however, is that (for example) Reece's disorientating critique of FRMAS and its theoretical commitments – that the editors of *Feminists@Law* and those who supported their campaign were able only to understand as 'deplorable' and 'dangerous' – also carries productive and enabling potential. Inasmuch as this disorientation is identifiable with the 'uncanny' affect described here, it may not be very surprising to find the sort of invocations of the gothic in Halley's writing as we earlier noted in Ellison and Munro's mock jury research. For example, describing feminists' privileging of harms that are expressible in terms of m/f and m>f, Halley invokes the metaphor of superstition ('our precommitments ensure that we'll "see it because we believe it"')[83] and of death (the 'death-like pall of sexual injury').[84] Describing feminists' defensiveness about 'prodigal' theorists who abandon feminism in favour of other possibly more exciting arenas, she refers to feminists experiencing a sense of being 'pushed into the grave'[85] and to being 'buried alive' by such betrayals.[86] Reinforcing this imagery of the grave, Halley imagines feminism as a kind of coffin that traps its proponents with fixed and unbending conditions that fail to 'create *living* space' for the intellectual and emotional growth necessary for a living, breathing movement.[87] Feminism is furthermore conceived as an executioner who, wielding the power that it does and with the consequences that this inevitably has, 'must find itself occasionally looking down at its own bloody hands.'[88]

We can follow the implications of Halley's use of such noticeably marked metaphors to situate a *carceral* form of feminism, which is to say: a feminism with hidden teeth and claws that are capable of inflicting real injuries. Halley imagines this creature, first, as an:

> old ... dog ... roaring that ominous roar and baring its teeth [and because he was blind] I could not communicate to him by mutual gaze his success [at controlling me] or the possible harm I could do to him.[89]

Secondly, she presents a re-reading of the Texas Supreme Court ruling of *Twyman* v. *Twyman*,[90] which found a husband (William) liable for the tort of negligent emotional distress after he tried to insist that his wife (Sheila) engage in bondage, despite it reminding her of being raped. Reading the facts against the grain so as to reverse the order of (male) injurer and

---

83  Halley, op. cit., n. 72, p. 344.
84  id., p. 354.
85  id., p. 32.
86  id., pp. 12, 31, 32, 253, 255, 273, 275.
87  id. p. 341, emphasis added. Halley's morbid metaphors may betray the influence of Leo Bersani's 'Is the rectum a grave?' (1987) 43 *AIDS: Cultural Analysis/Cultural Activism* 197.
88  Halley, id., p. 33.
89  id., p. 343.
90  *Twyman* v. *Twyman* 855 S.W.2d 619 (1993).

140

(female) injured, Halley exhorts her readers to imagine Sheila '*pursuing William like a Valkyrie* for breaking [the moral law of the couple's sex life], and *her alliance with the state against him*.'[91] The Valkyrie is of course invoked by analogy rather than metaphor, but the allusions to pursuit and to a wartime alliance are powerfully metaphoric. Halley's reading provokes a sense of disorientation by defamiliarizing the predictable order of m>f. The point is to bring about the possibility for a creative 'opening up' of political discourse that we noted in Reece's complaint about the censorious implications of labelling certain beliefs as 'myths'. Like Reece, Halley seeks to trouble feminist readings in order to free questions of what a given account about sexual injury *means* from the 'monolithic'[92] narrative of male entitlement and female oppression presupposed by dominance feminism and thereby to bring them within 'our political reach'.[93] We might think of the idea of rape myths as part of such a monolith ripe for breaking up.

In order to regard either of these projects as potentially productive as opposed merely to disarming and diminishing, we need to be prepared to invest political capital in suspending commitments to presuppositions about gender and harm and thereby risk losing that which makes the diverse intellectual coalition that I have described collectively here as FRMAS as distinctive and effective as it is. The question of whether or not Reece's and/ or Halley's re-appropriations of myth metaphors are indeed a positive contribution is brought into focus by the critical storm that blew up briefly around *Gone Girl* – the popular thriller novel[94] and Hollywood film[95] – which begins with the disappearance of a woman (Amy Dunne). The meaning of Amy's disappearance for the police and for the public watching the case unfold in the media gradually emerges thanks to a trail of clues that she leaves behind that ingeniously frame her unfaithful husband for murder as well as for various acts of domestic abuse and rape. In this way she exploits – *apparently from beyond the grave* – the susceptibility of the police, public, and friends to being thus manipulated.

The key point of contention in *Gone Girl* that forced reviewers of both the novel and the film to take sides, is that it seems to imply that the reason why the police and public fall into error is that they do *not* operate on the assumption that women who suffer domestic abuse (including murder) 'ask for it' or that women 'cry rape'. Some reviews condemned the story for this reason as 'dangerous', 'a gift to rape culture', the 'wet dream of every misogynistic men's "rights" activist', 'the justification to misogyny', and as affirming 'rape myths' such as that 'women are liars who will accuse you of

91 Halley, op. cit., n. 72, p. 356, emphasis added.
92 id., p. 178.
93 id., p. 301.
94 G. Flynn, *Gone Girl* (2013).
95 *Gone Girl*, Dir. David Fincher (Twentieth Century Fox, 2014).

rape if and when they want'.[96] Others celebrated it for challenging female stereotypes such as 'women [as] innately good, innately nurturing', incapable of callous and terrible deceit about rape, and as inevitable 'victims'.[97] The reception of *Gone Girl*'s audacious undermining of some key principles underpinning FRMAS serves as a case study of the disorientating, uncanny affect produced in rape myth debate. For some this affect may be experienced as 'pleasurable, erotically animating [or] politically enabling', but for others, merely as a deplorable appeal to sexist stereotypes and prejudice.

## CONCLUSION

This article has not sought to make any claims about the 'truth' of rape itself or about the culture in which beliefs about rape are formed. At the same time it has not pretended to take a disinterested or objective perspective on the relevant debates. It has instead offered some thoughts on the affective aspect of engaging in debate about rape myths, whether from the position of designating certain popular beliefs to be 'myths' on account of their being widely held despite being factually or ethically wrong, or else from that of criticizing such a designation as just another form of myth making. The article has looked to texts of FRMAS and also of scholarship that is critical of FRMAS and its broader feminist commitments. It has suggested that we can gain a clearer perspective on this point of contestation if we are prepared to recognize, first of all, that the term 'rape myth' is not (and indeed cannot be) a literal explanation for the beliefs in question, but a metaphor. Secondly, that there is profit in attending to the uncanny effect that myth-talk can have, again from and for both sides of the argument. For, advancing a 'myth' argument with respect to rape and sexual assault seems to involve drawing attention to the insubstantial, spectral qualities of beliefs that the 'other side' takes to be real and true. So the texts of FRMAS are populated with ghostly apparitions such as men who innocently misunderstand refusal cues, and who are merely the invented and imagined 'doubles' for men who in truth knowingly coerce and assault women. Conversely, the texts of FRMAS's critics are populated with similarly insubstantial figures: feminist theorists

---

96 J. Smith, '*Gone Girl*'s recycling of rape myths is a disgusting distortion' *Guardian*, 6 October 2014; Reel Girl, '*Gone Girl*' makes violence against women a punchline', 4 October 2014, at <http://reelgirl.com/2014/10/gone-girl-makes-violence-against-women-a-punchline/>; L. Brookshier, 'The Misogynistic Portrayal of Villainy in Gone Girl' *GBDH Sadiron*, 2 December 2013, at <http://www.gbdh.sadiron.com/archives/13093>; M. Lovan, '*Gone Girl* undermines rape' (2014), at <http://www.imnotamotivationalspeaker.com/gone-girl-undermines-rape/>.

97 E. Saner, 'The Gone Girl backlash: what women don't want' *Guardian*, 7 October 2014; R.L. Cosslett, 'Gone Girl is not anti-feminist. True equality is admitting that women can be evil too' *New Statesman*, 7 October 2014.

who *in truth* can show us how to separate fact from myth (Reece) and who are themselves disempowered, unheard, without any powerful friends, and incapable of harming men (Halley). All of these are examples of deployment of the same substituting metaphor, and consequently all are vulnerable to being criticized for strategically narrowing the terms of the debate to a certain extent. In highlighting this point, however, I have tried to emphasize not only the political dimension of the uncanny as a concept that has traditionally been marginalized in legal studies as being 'merely' aesthetic, but also some important continuities between conflicting perspectives on sexual violence. The juxtapositions of 'reality' and 'myth' in this debate invite us to consider the relationship between the seen and the unseen, and the implications and consequences of dedicating one's efforts to bringing the latter to light.

143

JOURNAL OF LAW AND SOCIETY
VOLUME 43, NUMBER 1, MARCH 2016
ISSN: 0263-323X, pp. 144–65

# Is the Blush off the Rose? Legal Education Metaphors in a Changing World

MICHELLE LeBARON*

*Seismic shifts in legal practice associated with globalization, rapid technological and economic change, and shifting client expectations have yet to spur concomitant changes in legal education. While governing bodies and scholars study trends, pressures, and shrinking markets, legal educators in many countries have resisted effective curricular, pedagogical, and programmatic changes. Positing metaphors as powerful cues about the effectiveness of reform efforts, I use examples from conflict analysis to illustrate how so-called 'unmarked' metaphors are often more powerful than marked ones. Exploring metaphors used by scholars and professional bodies in advocating reform, I scan linkages between proposed metaphors and change, highlighting metaphors in the American Carnegie report as particularly generative. While crisis metaphors have increased in use, they do not seem to have stimulated significant changes. I suggest this may be because of powerful unmarked metaphors. The article concludes with recommendations on discursive and dialogic ways of guiding legal education reform.*

'The future is a foreign country', writes Graham Ferris about the impossibility of relying on traditional legal education practices.[1] This metaphor launches us into an unfamiliar world where old maps don't work and previously reliable practices must be re-examined. We face transforming contexts where shifting conditions, complexities, and the increasing velocity

\* *Peter A. Allard School of Law, University of British Columbia, Vancouver V6T 1Z1, British Columbia, Canada*
*lebaron@allard.ubc.ca*

The author acknowledges with thanks the able research and editing assistance of Ashli Akins, Carrie MacLeod, Tannis Baradziej, and Yael Efron.

1 G. Ferris, 'The Legal Educational Continuum that is Visible through a Glass Dewey' (2009) 43 *Law Teacher* 102, at 102.

of change put pressure on already-stretched systems. Technology has made globalization a fact of life, generating the need for adaptation and resilience. The legal world is no exception; indeed, given that law is a service industry intimately intertwined with economy, policy, and social relations, it may be more vulnerable than other professions.

Law as a discipline has undergone significant change in the recent past as scholars, practitioners, and educators strive to stay current.[2] New areas within legal studies have emerged; the field of critical legal studies has underlined social justice concerns and the imperative of interdisciplinary scholarship has grown. Empirical perspectives, once minimized in importance, have become far more salient as DNA and neuroscientific findings offer new avenues of proof. Technology has affected virtually every aspect of legal practice from initial communication to resolution, as did the global financial crisis that dramatically changed corporate legal practice in the United States and elsewhere. Systems theory has spawned new ways of thinking about social and organizational dynamics, including legal issues in their interrelation with social dynamics. Lawyers of the future will enter an increasingly competitive world requiring expert competencies to navigate mounting complexity. Legal education must change dramatically to meet these challenges; it cannot remain what has become a traditional course in Canada and the United States.

Law students themselves have changed substantially in the twenty-first century. Incoming class numbers in the United States have fallen dramatically, while those in other countries have remained steady or experienced smaller declines amidst the Bologna reforms in the EU and significant shifts in Asia-Pacific legal education.[3] Increased gender, social class, ethnic, and national differences characterize incoming classes.[4] With diversity has come a widening aperture of reasons to study law, and also an increased emphasis on vocational needs and away from liberal or critical thinking.[5] Students bring 'instant gratification' expectations that, along with multiple competing time demands, lead them to seek efficient ways of studying and evaluation-

---

2 C. Menkel-Meadow, 'Megatrends in Law' (2006), at <http://www.mediate.com//articles/Megatrends_Menkel-Meadow.cfm>.

3 M. Nisen, 'US Students are fleeing Law Schools and Pouring into Engineering' (2015), at <http://qz.com/358929/law-school-enrollment-decline/>. See, also, D. Hasselback, 'Fewer Students Apply to Law School this Year' *Financial Post*, 12 February 2013, at <http://business.financialpost.com/legal-post/fewer-students-apply-to-law-school-this-year>; H.M. Kritzer, 'It's the Law Schools Stupid! Explaining the Continuing Increase in the Number of Lawyers' (2013) 19 *International J. of the Legal Profession* 209, at <http://scholarshi p.law.umn.edu/faculty_articles/4/>; S.P. Sarker (ed.), *Legal Education in Asia* (2014).

4 A. Bone, 'The Twenty-first Century Law Student' (2009) 43 *Law Teacher* 222, at 222, 224–6.

5 A. Kronman, *Education's End: Why Our Colleges and Universities have given up on the Meaning of Life* (2007).

145

relevant material. They tend to multitask and look to technology to support their learning needs.[6] Law schools cannot reach these students by doing things the way they have always been done.

How can legal education prepare students to live in the foreign country of the future, when emerging conditions cannot be anticipated easily from our present vantage point? I explore this question by examining metaphors as discursive frames, considering their potency that is often beneath conscious awareness. Then, I offer an approach to metaphor analysis, illustrating the usefulness of peering beneath the surface of ubiquitous associations. From this foundation, I survey the current landscape of American and other writing about legal education reform, exploring which metaphors or spheres of understanding shape and reflect this discourse at present. I then examine an alternative metaphor for legal education and explore how imaginative discursive choices could catalyse substantive shifts. Finally, I argue that dialogic engagement amongst stakeholders in legal education is needed, along with thoughtful metaphor choices to shape reform efforts.

## WHY METAPHORS?

Metaphors are sensory images that relate one world of things or ideas to another. Because they resonate with sound, visual imagery, and sensations, they are more likely to lodge in consciousness and physical felt/sensed awareness than more abstract vocabulary. Metaphors are rich in information; they are tightly wrapped buds that convey textures of perceptions, experience, emotional tenor and intensity. Not only are they powerful in reflecting attitudes and understandings, they are also influential in shaping and framing them. They give a window into whole worlds of understandings, reflecting and shaping ontology, epistemology, and theories of change. They also yield clues about how people see themselves and situations, revealing perceptions, assumptions, and blind spots. Metaphors are a hidden grammar of being, subtly framing what is possible and impossible, what is likely and far-fetched. They interweave with agency, analysis, and ethics. Without awareness of the pervasive shaping power of metaphors, we see through a glass darkly.

Once a metaphor has been identified, we can inquire into its pervasive effects, all the more potent when out of conscious awareness. Lakoff and Johnson write about the significance of marked and unmarked metaphors.[7] Marked metaphors are explicitly named, as in 'law is a blunt instrument'.

---

6 G. Joughin, 'Assessment, Learning and Judgement in Higher Education: A Critical Review' in *Assessment, Learning and Judgment in Higher Education,* ed. G. Joughin (2009) 13, at <http://www.springerlink.com/content/j565566gjl77666m/>.
7 G. Lakoff and M. Johnson, *Metaphors We Live By* (2003, 2nd edn.).

146

The more unusual or novel a metaphor is, the more likely it is to be noticed, that is, marked. Unmarked metaphors are those that we no longer consciously recognize because they have become conventional or idiomatic. The term 'bear market' no longer conjures a literal bear, for example. Nor do we think of the term 'bullets' connoting point form in writing as connected to ammunition. Notice these phrases in common use in relation to peace:

It was a hard-won peace.
Neither side would allow the other to score points at their expense, so the treaty was elusive.
Their demands were part of a dangerous game.

Which discursive worlds are invoked in the above statements? All three of these 'opening salvos' come from war or games and are frequently encountered in popular accounts. These unmarked metaphors, replete with imagery of attack and aggression, prime readers for opposition, resistance, and struggle, if not utter decimation. Writers who use war or games metaphors in relation to peace are framing it as necessarily interwoven with battle or contest and related adversarial processes and outcomes. Sleeping within written accounts, these unmarked metaphors shape understandings of reality, suggesting that if conflict is war or ritualized battle (games), peace is a part of the same discursive field. As unquestioned parts of our lexicon, war and game metaphors function as self-fulfilling prophecies. Whether stated explicitly or not, they have become so ubiquitous that they blend into language and are not ordinarily questioned. But these unmarked metaphors limit the scope and possibilities of peace. What might gardening, geographic or climatic metaphors have to contribute as alternatives? Lakoff and Johnson observe that journey metaphors are more generative than war metaphors in relation to conflict because the former signal mutuality, forward momentum toward a desired endpoint, pleasure, and aesthetic appreciation.

Metaphors, then, powerfully influence how we pay attention, shaping a range of perceptual choices about situations and the people in them, as well as possible actions and outcomes. Ubiquitous and often unquestioned, they are part of nearly every verbal or written exchange including scholarly papers, all the more powerful for their frequently cloaked nature. Before examining metaphors in American writing about legal education reform, I offer thoughts on how to analyse and work with metaphors.

## METAPHOR ANALYSIS

Metaphors carry a wide range of discursive influences. Like a picture frame, they direct attention inside their borders. Metaphors communicate what is important, inviting the viewer within and simultaneously turning her attention away from what is outside the frame. Thus, surrounding context and other associations are muted as a subject is paired with something disparate

147

for purposes of communicating aspects of the subject's essence. When this is done through unmarked metaphors, it may go completely unnoticed, yet it can still have a profound influence. Examples from conflict engagement are illustrative. If a writer successfully pairs a particular conflict with battle imagery, it is likely to influence readers to see the conflict as dangerous. The reader may similarly expect combative tactics to be used and be less attuned to collaborative potentialities than to eventual winners and losers. Given its framing role, metaphor's potency is apparent; effective negotiators know that they need to suggest alternative metaphors to foster change. To leave unmarked framing metaphors like war and battle undisturbed and unnamed is to invite conflict escalation; we know from complex systems theory that the course of interactions is very strongly influenced by initial conditions.

One of the functions of metaphors that become more apparent when studied is their capacity to continually shape communication. Thus, not only do metaphors frame narratives initially, their potency increases over time. When a conflict is framed using war imagery, parties tend to use words that come from the same discursive menu of battle, strategy, and weaponry. Thus, the embedded association becomes reified. Alternative frames may be offered and – when accepted – can reveal whole ranges of nuanced and different possibilities. In a deliberate choice of metaphor, my latest book is titled *The Choreography of Resolution*.[8] Invoking dance as a way of thinking about and engaging conflict draws attention to rhythm, physical ways of expressing and navigating difference, somatic sensations associated with emotions, stress, and intuition, and aesthetic dimensions of relations. It also implicitly takes combative images out of the frame, replacing their ubiquitous presence with an alternative expressive language.

Dancers with whom we collaborated spoke about conflict using tactile imagery and developed physical exercises to reveal patterns of engagement and choice points in conflict. For example, mediators in training learned to move across a floor with attention to being everywhere their counterpart was not. Given that parties in conflict are frequently vying for the same terrain or scarce resources, physical experiences of spaciousness, complementarity, and sensitivity to others' movements gave learners constructive sensory anchors for working with actual conflicts. Dance literally became a moving metaphor, a vehicle for learning how to uncover possibilities for common understandings from different vantage points.

One of the things revealed when working on dance and conflict was the importance of negative space. In the West, we tend to fill up space, over-relying on words to convey meanings. Mediators use talk to convene, structure, order and identify issues, and uncover common ground. Designer Alan Fletcher explores why space is important. He writes:

---

8 M. LeBaron et al., *The Choreography of Resolution: Conflict, Movement and Neuroscience* (2013).

Space is substance. Cézanne painted and modelled space. Giacometti sculpted by '*taking the fat off space*'. Mallarmé conceived poems with absences as well as words. Ralph Richardson asserted that acting lay in pauses ... Isaac Stern described music as '*that little bit between each note – silences which give the form.*' The Japanese have a word (*ma*) for this interval which gives shape to the whole. In the West we have neither word nor term. A serious omission.[9]

Metaphor analysis involves excavating language for unmarked and marked images; it is literally to look for what inhabits the space between an idea and the metaphors associated with it. It can reveal unnoticed similarities, important divergences, and collaborative possibilities. It can also reveal power dynamics – very important both in conflict engagement and in relation to legal education reform, as we will see. For example, in a multi-party conflict over a forested watershed, industry, government, labour, and local community representatives shared a farming metaphor for the forest, though it was never announced or negotiated. Thus, it seemed natural to them to talk of seeding, harvesting, eliminating weed species, and replanting. The conservation representative at the table was the only stakeholder who did not share this discursive frame, and thus faced an extra hurdle to effective participation. Imagine what would have happened if the conservationist had suggested an alternative metaphor: the forest as the hair of mother earth. All heads at the table would have turned in the conservationist's direction. Why? Because she would have used a marked metaphor in stark contrast to the unmarked metaphor shared by many powerful representatives.

In this negotiation, the unmarked metaphor was unchallenged by parties including the conservationist for whom it was dissonant, because it was not explicit and therefore not offered as negotiable. Perceiving this barrier to effective participation, the mediator might have asked questions about the diverse ways people at the table perceive the forest. By not doing so, she risked unconsciously aligning with an unmarked metaphor, imperilling the impartiality of the process as well as full and meaningful participation of all parties.

For effective engagement, metaphors to bridge different discursive terrains are needed. Understanding this, a mediator could pose a question at the outset, such as: 'What can we do to invite a range of views about the nature of the forest and human relations to it in our conversations?' All parties in the conversation might be able to find a common or shared frame about the forest. For example, they might agree on seeing the forest as a garden. While different people may have various associations with the word *garden* – from a wild, untended country area outside a cottage to a manicured, heavily-managed urban plot – the ambiguity within the metaphor 'garden' may be helpful. Its very spaciousness may give parties a sense of a shared frame. When people have even a thin experience of commonality, they engage with less defensiveness and more openness to possibility. When they sense little or no common starting points, discussions are much harder

9 A. Fletcher, *The Art of Looking Sideways* (2001) 370.

to engage and advance. Metaphor analysis, then, means paying attention to the discursive grammar of underlying conversations. Listening closely to language choices allows the analyst to uncover unmarked metaphors that may otherwise operate in hegemonic ways. Hidden in plain sight, a whole world of possibilities follow once a common metaphoric frame is agreed. This is true not only in conflict engagement, but in human communication in general. Families who hold similar metaphors about relationships, hierarchy, communication of love and respect, and appropriate intergenerational behaviour are more likely to experience harmonious relations. A community who shares common metaphors for progress, development, and social justice will have an easier time making decisions about new projects than one in which widely divergent images operate. Metaphor analysis goes hand-in-hand with dialogue to uncover shared images; when parties listen deeply to each other, communication effectiveness improves.

Of course, in many contentious situations, metaphoric frames are starkly different and finding shared terrain is challenging. Common metaphors may surface through listening for unmarked metaphors in stories. Dialogue, a mutual exchange centred on metaphor-rich narratives, is thus a helpful path to uncovering commonality. Later in this article, I examine how dialogue might be useful in assisting with the design of needed curricular and pedagogical change in legal education. I also consider commonly-used metaphors for legal education reform and why they may have aroused defensive resistance to change.

In the next section, I explore metaphors about legal education to see what discursive possibilities are embedded within them.

## METAPHORS IN LEGAL EDUCATION REFORM EFFORTS

A literature survey yields wide-ranging metaphors about legal education and practice, almost all of them situated in dire predictions about lawyering or major reform campaigns. Diverse global commissions, studies, task forces, and conventions have made the case for change.[10] In Europe, the Bologna Convention calls for extensive overhaul of legal education.[11] East Asia, notably Japan and Korea, have both undergone substantial shifts in their philosophy and practice in the past several years. The United States and Canada have had parades of reports from national bar associations and special task forces.[12] Given myriad materials, I primarily trace reform-associated metaphors in the United States, with some references to

---

10 T.M. Fine, 'Reflections on U.S. Law Curricular Reform' (2009) 10 *German Law J.* (Special Issue: *Transnationalizing Legal Education*) 717.
11 Bologna Declaration of 19 June 1999, see <http://ec.europa.eu/education/policies/bologna/bologna_en.html> and <www.ond.vlaanderen.be/hogeronderwijs/bologna/>.
12 Fine, op. cit., n. 10, p. 717.

Australian, Canadian, and British scholars. Later, I discuss applications of this exploration to the United States and Canadian contexts in particular.

T.M. Fine summarizes some of the major work done in the United States between 1979 and 2007. The Cramton report arrived first during this period, commissioned by the American Bar Association (ABA).[13] This report was heralded as a 'watershed' in thinking about legal education, and recommended changes to curricula to shift the accent onto critical thinking and problem solving. Little major change followed, notwithstanding the use of the watershed metaphor.

Resistance to change might be expected from a legal profession that has traditionally valued stability and resisted rapid change. When the rule of law is metaphorically described as the backbone of social and economic prosperity, associations are not easily altered,[14] nor is the education of those whose job it is to uphold legal institutions. When proponents of critical legal studies and other movements have pushed for more social justice perspectives and skills training in legal education, they have run into powerful opposition. For example, following the release of the Cramton report, the ABA added requirements for all schools to offer rigorous training in legal writing, and instruction in professional skills like counselling, negotiation, advocacy, and drafting in order to maintain accreditation. Some schools embraced the idea, but the Dean of Harvard Law at the time, Albert M. Sacks, employed a powerfully trivializing metaphor when he wrote, 'One is tempted to treat the new proposal as a flyspeck to be ignored ... I hope it will be strongly resisted.' It was.[15]

The same body commissioned the MacCrate report over a decade later.[16] Responding to critiques that legal education did too little to prepare lawyers for practice, the report's authors focused on skills and clinical competencies. They wrote:

> Surprisingly, throughout the course of extensive, decades-long debates about what law schools should do to educate students for the practice of law, there has been no in-depth study of the full range of skills and values that are necessary in order for a lawyer to assume the professional responsibility of handling a legal matter.[17]

---

13 American Bar Association (ABA) Section of Legal Education and Admissions to the Bar, *Report and Recommendations of the Task Force on Lawyer Competency: The Role of Law Schools* (1979) (Cramton report).

14 D. Doyle, 'Rule of Law: The Backbone of Economic Growth' (2014), at <https://www.gov.im/lib/docs/courtservice/Lectures/ruleoflawoxfordlecture.pdf>.

15 R.B. Stevens, *Law School: Legal Education in America from the 1850s to the 1980s* (1983) 257.

16 ABA Section of Legal Education and Admissions to the Bar, *Legal Education and Professional Development – An Educational Continuum: Report of the Task Force on Law Schools and the Profession: Narrowing the Gap* (1992) (MacCrate report), at <http://www.abanet.org/legaled/publications/online pubs/maccrate.html>.

17 id.

151

The report's authors draw on the metaphor of the 'gap' that is featured in its title, concluding that it is not possible to narrow the distance between practising lawyers and the legal academy without 'first identifying the fundamental skills and values' needed by every lawyer.[18] They go on to list ten 'fundamental lawyering skills' needed for competent representation.[19] Taking their cue from the earlier Cramton report and going even further, they include the following as essential: problem solving, communication, counselling, negotiation, litigation, alternative dispute resolution, and a range of legal analytical, ethical problem-solving, and research skills. More than its predecessor, the MacCrate report stimulated extensive discussion amongst legal academics, the bar, and the bench. While it is sometimes credited with catalysing an increase in clinical law school courses, the identified gap between the profession and the academy remained.

In 2009, the Carnegie report was issued. This report was one of a series of in-depth looks into curriculum and pedagogy in education for professionals in the United States, and featured five key observations. The Carnegie report draws on markedly different metaphors from those of the ABA, and will be discussed in more detail below. More recently, in 2014, the ABA Task Force on Legal Education again issued a scathing report on legal education.[20] The report's authors opined that it was necessary to rush their work and hasten publication because of 'the urgency of the problem and the serious threats to public confidence [that] demanded rapid action.'[21] In the report itself and in explaining its early release, the ABA Task Force drew on metaphors of crisis and precipitous risks of falling and failure. The arc from the Cramton report through the MacCrate report culminates in the use of even more emergency-based metaphors in the 2014 report. Was the same arc evident in what American legal scholars were writing on the subject over the previous thirty years?

## 1. Gluts, curses, and journey metaphors

In discussing challenges facing American legal educators in 1987, Pye refers to the excess of lawyers being trained as the 'lawyer glut'.[22] Jerry, writing five years later, situates his comments in a journey frame quoting Robert F. Kennedy:

---

18  id.
19  id.
20  ABA, *Report and Recommendations: American Bar Association Task Force on the Future of Legal Education* (2014), at <http://www.americanbar.org/content/dam/aba/administrative/professional_responsibility/report_and_recommendations_of_aba_task_force.authcheckdam.pdf>.
21  E. Chemerinsky and C. Menkel-Meadow, 'Don't Skimp on Legal Training' *New York Times,* 14 April 2014.
22  A.K. Pye, *Legal Education in an Era of Change: The Challenge* (1987) 202.

Just because we cannot see clearly the end of the road, that is no reason for not setting out on the essential journey. On the contrary, great change dominates the world, and unless we move with change we will become its victims.

While initially using Kennedy's journey image to argue that the legal profession and professoriate have actually exacerbated challenges facing them rather than ameliorating them, Jerry later devolves into combative metaphors claiming 'assaults' on the profession arising from the 'rich vein' of public resentment that has undermined broad support for lawyers.[23]

In a more recent piece, University of Hawai'i scholar Matsuda argues for fundamental changes to legal education.[24] In writing full of marked metaphors, Matsuda echoes Jerry in assigning blame for the current crisis to lawyers themselves, not 'an Old Testament curse'.[25] She suggests that legal education move away from mechanical instructions, for example, how to take a deposition, and reclaim the terrain of social sciences and liberal arts as the best preparation for practice. Future lawyers will need understandings of philosophy, history, economics, and politics more than any technical training, to be able to embrace roles. Thus, a central function of legal education is to help students understand social contexts to inform and anchor leadership roles. Matsuda's work fits well with the Carnegie report, to be explored later.

## 2. Nature and climate metaphors

Interestingly, authors from outside the United States have used metaphors from nature to make points about legal education. Watson begins her work with a Dylan poem:

> Come gather 'round people
> Wherever you roam
> And admit that the waters
> Around you have grown
> And accept it that soon
> You'll be drenched to the bone
> If your time to you
> Is worth savin'
> Then you better start swimmin'
> Or you'll sink like a stone
> For the times they are a-changin'.[26]

---

23 R.H. Jerry, 'The Legal Profession, Legal Education and Change' (1992) 41 *University of Kansas Law Rev.* 1.

24 M.J. Matsuda, 'Admit that the Waters Around you have Grown: Change and Legal Education' (2014) 89 *Indiana Law J.* 1381.

25 id., p. 1399.

26 P. Watson, *Leading Change in Legal Education: Interesting Ideas for Interesting Times* (2012), quoting song by Bob Dylan, 'The Times They Are A-Changin'' (1963), at <http://www.ler.edu.au/website%20docs%20vol%2022%20and%2023/2012-9.pdf>.

Advocating for broad curricular and cultural change in Australian legal education, Watson emphasizes the importance of awareness about beliefs and attitudes and how these make change more or less possible. She writes that legal educators can choose to see mounting pressures as a 'curse' or an impetus to 'harness our creative energy'.[27] Interestingly, Watson uses explicit metaphors from environmental law to illustrate that legal education is embedded in an organic and dynamic process of renewal. This device gives her work a positive cast and leaves readers with a modicum of encouragement about future prospects even in the midst of large-scale change.

Climate metaphors are employed by James O'Connell to describe the changing roles of paralegals in the legal landscape.[28] For lawyers to continue their historic indifference to the roles of paralegals, he contends, is a form of egregious denial leading to the same kind of disastrous end as denying climate change. Citing the work of the United Kingdom Institute for Paralegals, he urges legal educators to see paralegals as legitimate providers of legal services, and to coordinate and collaborate in changing existing hierarchies. Interestingly, he uses the metaphor of midwifery to argue that the Institute for Paralegals and law schools should work together as 'midwives' to bridge current gaps between academically trained law graduates and vocationally trained paralegals.[29] Casting reform efforts in terms of midwifery pairs a marked gendered image with legal training and practice. Given the many unmarked masculine metaphors that pervade Western legal education discourses, O'Connell's choice of a marked feminine metaphor is a clear challenge to traditional ways of thinking about navigating change.[30]

## 3. Metaphors of revolution, crisis, and vanishing lawyers

American scholar Kevin Lee, in a comprehensive work arguing for humanistic legal education, summarizes the work of a number of writers with dire future predictions including fellow Americans Campos and Katz, and British scholar Susskind.[31] Acknowledging that legal education is in

---

27  id., p. 200.
28  J. O'Connell, 'Climate Change: It's happening in the legal profession too' (2008) 42 *Law Teacher* 219.
29  id., pp. 222–3.
30  See D.M. Kolb, 'Negotiations through a Gender Lens', Center for Gender Relations Working Paper 15 (2002) 31.
31  K.P. Lee, 'The Citizen Lawyer in the Coming Era: Technology is Changing the Practice of Law, but Legal Education Must Remain Committed to Humanistic Learning' (2013) 40 *Ohio Northern University Law Rev.* 1. See R. Susskind, *Tomorrow's Lawyer: An Introduction To Your Future* (2013); P. Campos, *Don't Go to School (Unless): A Law Professor's Inside Guide to Maximizing Opportunity and Minimizing Risk* (2012); D.M. Katz, 'Quantitative Legal Prediction – or – How I Learned to Stop Worrying and Start Preparing for the Data Driven Future of the Legal Services Industry' (2013) 62 *Emory Law J.* 909.

crisis, he relates 'changes on the horizon'[32] to rapid technological advances which he describes using images of revolution. Concluding that 'the middle-class lawyer is vanishing',[33] Lee argues that legal practice in the future will be 'more like engineering than statesmanship'.[34] Yet, rather than suggesting a shift to engineering-like education as appropriate, he foreshadows Matsuda's work, emphasizing humanistic learning in law school to shape lawyers who can function as 'artisans of democratic citizenship'.[35] Lee ends his article by invoking Plato's work, *The Statesman*, to underline his thesis.[36]

Ward and Zahorsky, discussing needed changes in the *ABA Journal*, invoke the language of rebellion and revolution.[37] Showing how legal inno-vators are doing things differently, they argue that creativity in education and practice is needed to find new ways of responding to client needs. While their metaphors are evocative and powerful, rebellion and revolution connote violent upheaval – not the most generative way to invite colleagues into contemplating change. Legal educators, like the profession of law itself, have shown themselves resistant to revolution.

In *Failing Law Schools*, Brian Tamanaha continues the trend of dire predictions. Looking at the situation faced by United States law students today including 'crushing debt-loads' and disappearing jobs, he draws a number of conclusions including the necessity of reducing law school to two years and abolishing tenure.[38] Predictably, many scholars have been critical of his work, with one terming the book a 'misguided missile'.[39] Author Michael Olivas decries the way Tamanaha 'lays this dire assessment at the feet of the requisite ABA accreditation process', which he feels forces law schools to meet higher (and more expensive) standards.[40] Scholar Richard Lempert uses a telling metaphor in his critique of the book, opining that Tamanaha's 'suggestion that legal education be reduced to two years to cut costs puts the cost horse before the educational cart and has little to commend it.'[41]

Only a few voices deviate from those predicting a plummet off a steep cliff for legal education if massive change is not initiated. In a recent *New*

---

32 Lee, id., p. 6.
33 id., p. 14.
34 id., p. 6.
35 id.
36 id. See Plato, *Statesman*, trs. E. Brann et al. (2012).
37 S.F. Ward and R.M. Zahorsky, 'Legal Rebels: Remaking the Profession' (2009) 95 *ABA J.* 35.
38 B. Tamanaha, *Failing Law Schools* (2012) 22.
39 P. Schrag, 'Failing Law Schools – Brian Tamanaha's Misguided Missile' (2013) 26 *Georgetown J. of Legal Ethics* 387, at 388.
40 M.A. Olivas, '*Failing Law Schools* by Brian Z. Tamanaha (review)' (2013) 84 *J. of Higher Education* 739, at 739.
41 R.O. Lempert, '*Failing Law Schools* by Brian Z. Tamanaha: A Review' (2014) 43 *Contemporary Sociology* 269.

*York Times* op-ed, Americans Chemerinsky and Menkel-Meadow revisit the 'crisis' motif, arguing that claims of dire straits are exaggerated and unfounded.[42] They submit that claims of imminent catastrophe always focus on three things: a tight job market, waning law school applications, and the increasing cost of legal education. Presenting data that contradicts crises in each of these areas, they maintain that the negative potency of the crisis metaphor may lead to reforms that will do more harm than good. They worry, for example, about President Obama adopting Tamanha's suggestion and suggesting that law school be reduced from three to two years. In their words, 'this is a terrible idea.'[43]

Chemerinsky and Menkel-Meadow assert that the profession needs to train lawyers who are better prepared to practice law, not less well trained. They recommend following the lead of other professional schools including architecture, business, and planning where increased emphasis has been put on leadership, corporate governance, negotiation, and finance skills. Further, they suggest a wider range of problem-based courses be taught to prepare students for dealing with the challenges of our time.

Their op-ed attracted many dissenting voices, including a piece the following day in the *Washington Post* from George Washington University Professor, Orin Kerr.[44] Dismissing their 'very sunny perspective', Kerr argues in favour of reduced law degree duration and major curricular change. He counters the wider range of courses suggested, indicating that these are already offered in many schools and emphasizing the need for legal training to prepare students practically for their careers.

Without treating the validity of these rival claims, Chemerinsky and Menkel-Meadow's concern about the crisis metaphor itself is significant. In a crisis, there is little time to make thoughtful, reasoned decisions that take a range of interests into account. Crises are moments to take quick and decisive action, even though these actions will almost certainly lead to unintended and unforeseen consequences. Chemerinsky and Menkel-Meadow point out that the rush of the ABA Task Force on Legal Education to release its report early (in January 2014), attributed as it was to serious and imminent threats to the profession, lent an air of catastrophe to their work. This crisis tone is surprising, given decades of similar criticism about legal education. Whether it is justified by the rapid rate of change in legal practice and the changing marketplace affecting both legal services and education remains to be seen. The crisis metaphor, however, is troubling for the associations it brings into the conversation, and may not foster the change desired.

Our earlier discussion about metaphors for mediation and problem solving helps to illustrate the perils of crisis and revolution metaphors. Sometimes, a

---

42 Chemerinsky and Menkel-Meadow, op. cit., n. 21.
43 id.
44 O. Kerr, 'Chemerinsky and Menkel-Meadow on Curricular Reform' *Washington Post*, 15 April 2014.

firefighter image is helpful to inform conflict intervention: quick action may be needed to avoid a calamity. More often, the immediate action of the adrenalin-fuelled firefighter metaphor may be counterproductive. Many issues require the patience of a gardener coupled with the practical intelligence of a chef to achieve lasting resolution. In relation to legal education, a spectrum of consciously chosen metaphors as well as effective processes for decision making may similarly be needed to foster necessary reform.

Looking beneath the surface of the varied metaphors described above, it is reasonable to ask whether there are unmarked metaphors shaping resistance to change that remain more powerful than efforts to dislodge them. Law and legal practice associated with core professional values have long garnered considerable social power. Prominent amongst these values are independence, confidentiality, and integrity.[45] These and other values buttress legal monopolies (including legal education) currently under challenge in many areas of the world. It may be that the very independence that defines lawyers' and tenured professors' identities, combined with vocational security, reinforce a complacence that is difficult to unsettle. The story of the metaphors chronicled above is also a story of disconnected discourses, intractable relations, and decision-making structures that have been ineffective in responding to rapid change. If it is not also to be a story of a sleeping giant who awakes to find himself sidelined, a different approach to legal education reform is needed.

What should this different approach entail? Proactive national dialogues in both Canada and the United States amongst those with the power to change legal curricula and pedagogy and those with an interest in how it is changed, are essential.[46] If the profession is to be transformed, legal education must be transformed too. A chorus of law deans, scholars, and other stakeholders suggest that legal practice and education needs to accent problem solving and feature higher-quality, more experiential teaching. As Calgary Law Dean Holloway points out, 'law school is hard because we keep shovelling stuff at our students', yet equating volume with rigour is not a sound way forward.[47] The Carnegie report offers a useful suite of metaphors to guide this change.

---

45 J. Goldsmith, 'The Core Values of the Legal Profession for Lawyers Today and Tomorrow' (2008) 28 *Northwestern J. of International Law & Business* 441, at 451.
46 Canadian Bar Association Legal Futures Initiative, August 2014, at <http://www.cbafutures.org/>.
47 H. Gardiner, 'Time for Law Schools to Rethink Teaching Law' *Canadian Lawyering Magazine*, October 2013, at <http://www.canadianlawyermag.com/4848/Time-for-law-schools-to-rethink-teaching-law.html>.

## 4. *The three apprenticeship metaphor*

The Carnegie report on legal education reform reaches into the past for its inspiration.[48] The metaphors used by the report's authors contrast markedly with many of those discussed above. They expound on 'the three apprenticeships of professional education': intellectual, expert practice, and identity and purpose.[49] By situating their discussion within an apprenticeship frame, they point to shared terrain across law, medicine, divinity, and engineering education in connection with contemporary learning theory. Apprenticeship as a metaphor suggests the imperative of preparing students for the complex demands of professional work with its analytic, skill-based, and judgement dimensions. It also evokes a sense of dawning identification with a profession and others with whom it is shared, bringing identity and purpose into a conversation that is often more technical than human.

The apprenticeship frame also orients readers to the powerful effect of unmarked or hidden messages within legal curricula. Shining a light on the tacit socialization that operates below clear awareness, the Carnegie report authors advocate redesigning the legal curriculum in ways that align change with the qualities, competencies, and social relations important for future lawyers.[50] Observing the corrosive effect of public assaults on the 'guild-like structures of esoteric knowledge' that characterize professions, the authors argue that it is essential that the formative dimension of professionalism be rekindled.[51] The apprenticeship metaphor serves well to raise the diffuse question of how legal education can provide a 'powerful experience of the best sense of what it means to take up a profession.'[52] This metaphor is expansive enough, yet also precise enough, to foster discussion of the importance of moral and ethical development of professionals, development that 'requires a holistic approach to the educational experience that can grasp its formative effects as a whole.'[53]

Legal education, if it is to respond successfully to vast changes in the world, must engage these three dimensions. If law schools across the Western world were to do so, their attempts at reform could surmount the tinkering and bickering that often attends such efforts, and begin to grapple more seriously with needed fundamental change. The apprenticeship frame may also be useful in places like Japan where reform efforts are running into serious challenges, though recent wholesale changes to legal education there have also created a host of different issues to those faced in the West.[54]

---

48 W.M. Sullivan et al., *Educating Lawyers: Preparation for the Profession of Law* (2007) (Carnegie report).
49 id., pp. 27–8.
50 id., p. 29.
51 id.
52 id., p. 30.
53 id., p. 31.
54 S. Matsui, 'Turbulence Ahead: The Future of Law Schools in Japan' (2012) 62 *J. of Legal Education* 3.

Surely, the three dimensions of intellectual learning, expert practice, and identity development have resonance for the globalizing world where there is no singular intellectual tradition that is accepted universally, where expert practice varies with context, and where identity is increasingly salient.

Another particular strength of the Carnegie report is its emphasis on pedagogy as well as curriculum. As its authors point out, there is 'striking conformity in outlook and habits of thought among law school graduates',[55] not only across the United States but even further afield. This conformity arises from a widely used signature pedagogy, the case-dialogue method that emphasizes 'the priority of analytical thinking in which students learn to categorize and discuss persons and events in highly generalized terms'.[56] In turn, this approach:

> conveys at a deep, largely uncritical level an understanding of the law as a formal and rational system, however much its systems and rules may diverge from the commonsense understandings of the layperson.[57]

The connection between curricular and pedagogical methods that carry unmarked metaphors of order and structure is vitally significant. Not only should these unmarked, value-laden messages be unpacked, but the way they are conveyed must be examined in the light of recent scholarship on teaching and learning. Multiple empirical studies have shed light on optimal ways to teach, underlining the importance of double-loop learning and integrating contemplative practices.[58]

How do embedded metaphors of order and structure conveyed to students affect learning? They privilege the procedural and the systematic, often at the expense of a focus on substantive fairness, innovation or diversity. They also give rise to a number of unintended consequences, including a habit of reductionist thought that may lead students, and the lawyers they become, to see clients as other than multi-dimensional human beings, and clients' stories primarily as distillable into legal categories. Thus, uneven and unjust applications of law to those whose metaphors for social or economic relations are alternative and 'marked' are perpetuated.

This accent on order and structure may give way to the malaise that many students report after beginning legal studies. Lawrence Krieger writes that the negative toll law school exacts on many is pervasive and potentially

---

55 Sullivan et al., op. cit., n. 48, p. 186.
56 id.
57 id.
58 M. LeBaron and M. Patera, 'Reflective Practice in the New Millennium' in *Rethinking Negotiation Teaching: Innovations for Context and Culture*, eds. C. Honeyman et al. (2009) 50, at <http://digitalcommons.hamline.edu/dri_press/2/>. See, also, D.S. Austin, 'Killing Them Softly: Neuroscience Reveals How Brain Cells Die From Law School Stress and How Neural Self-Hacking Can Optimize Cognitive Performance' (2014) 59 *Loyola Law Rev.* 791, at 838.

debilitating.[59] Some of the experiences he warns about include 'dis-connection from yourself' and 'losing faith in the law'.[60] He goes on to admonish that learning to think like a lawyer is '*a legal skill but not a life skill*'.[61] Krieger likens skills of legal analysis to 'learning to weld or use some other powerful tool'.[62]

Metaphors about trades and tools may appear to sit well alongside the Carnegie report's focus on apprenticeship, but they actually go in another direction. Comparing legal analysis to welding invokes an image of a technical, severable skill that can be used and set down at will. It suggests a linear relationship between the application of the skill and a desired out-come. Further, it contemplates an approach where step-by-step application of procedures will bring things together, and where it is possible to leave work on the work site. But legal analysis requires a diffuse orientation as well as a specific one. It means thinking abstractly, and across categories, in under-standing multiple aspects of an issue with reference to the social context. Legal analysis is not easily left at the work site, but becomes intertwined with a new lawyer's way of seeing the world. Metaphors like welding actually frame legal education as a trade school, and – if used to guide curricular and pedagogical reform – risk leaving students even more bereft.

Why is this a risk? Because, as the Carnegie report makes clear, a vital component of legal training relates to identity. Legal analysis is not only a way of thinking or a set of technical skills. It is an indivisible part of a *Weltanschauung*, a worldview. Cognizant of this, law schools should do more to connect meaning and purpose to legal education, not surgically separate them. Using a welding metaphor as an analogy for legal analysis does nothing to assist students in the critically important task of linking these skills to their professional identity and purpose. Indeed, there is a widening chasm now that the cognitive aspects of legal education are separated from practical internships and socialization into the profession. As the Carnegie report says:

> School-like settings are very good environments for learning [cognitive and intellectual aspects of law]. At the same time . . . professionals must be able to integrate, or re-integrate, this kind of knowledge within ongoing practical contexts. But in this area, students learn mostly by living transmission, through pedagogies of modeling and coaching. For law schools . . . re-integration of the now-separated parts is the greatest challenge.[63]

Later in the report the authors reiterate the inseparability of these components:

---

59 L.S. Krieger, 'The Hidden Sources of Law School Stress: Avoiding Mistakes that Create Unhappy and Unprofessional Lawyers' (undated), at <http://services.unimelb.edu.au/counsel>.
60 id., p. 8.
61 id., p. 9, italics in original.
62 id.
63 Sullivan et al., op. cit., n. 48, p. 79.

[a]lthough some people believe that law school cannot affect students' values or ethical perspectives, in our view law school cannot *help* but affect them. For better or worse, the law school years constitute a powerful moral apprenticeship, whether or not this is intentional.[64]

The challenge of integration of clinical, theoretical, and attitudinal aspects of legal training has been taken up by a number of scholars, including Peggy Cooper Davis of NYU Law School who suggests that as the cognitive, practical, and ethical-social aspects of an apprenticeship approach become more intertwined, students' understandings of fundamental concepts improve. She points out that integrating the curriculum in the way the Carnegie report recommends can be mutually enhancing, and need not be seen as a zero-sum game.[65]

Lande and Sternlight argue that the recommended reforms of the Cramton, MacCrate, and other committees have fallen prey to those who resist centrally situating skills like dispute resolution or negotiation in law school curricula.[66] Competitive metaphors that so often characterize legal education reform debates function as unmarked metaphors, and are thus key parts of the problem, they argue. Integrating these skills into the curriculum does not mean replacing an emphasis on litigation; rather, it involves teaching students to integrate broader, complementary, and more robust repertoires for handling clients' problems. While Lande and Sternlight do not explicitly use geometric metaphors, their work is redolent of a more rounded, multi-dimensional approach to supplant the static, linear methods that are still too characteristic of legal education. In countering the competitive metaphor shaping much of the discussion over the past three decades, they offer new possibilities for consensual ways forward.

As the Carnegie report makes clear and others have realized, linear metaphors that accent structure and the status quo are unlikely to be responsive to the scale of change needed. Because curriculum and pedagogy are closely interrelated, substantial reform in one could – and must – help catalyse a shift in the other. To inspire this, a new metaphor is needed, or a variety of new metaphors, to guide dynamic, context-sensitive reform.

---

64  id., p. 139.
65  P.C. Davis, 'Experiential Legal Education in the United States' in *Can Justice be Taught? Social Responsibility and Legal Education* (2006), report by the Publications Committee of the results of the First International Symposium, Kwansei Gakuin University Law School Support Program for Professional Graduate School.
66  J. Lande and J.R. Sternlight, 'The Potential Contribution of ADR to an Integrated Curriculum: Preparing Law Students for Real World Lawyering' (2010) 25 *Ohio J. of Dispute Resolution* 247.

Several scholars have responded to the challenge of fundamental and multi-dimensional change in legal curriculum and pedagogy, suggesting that a paradigm shift is needed. In a particularly innovative piece, Israeli legal scholar Dr. Yael Efron poses the metaphor of a pentalectic sphere as a way of thinking about reform.[67] As described by Efron, the 'sphere encompasses five elements of legal education [and perhaps of legal scholarship as well] that are ... essential to the process: knowledge, skills, values, capacity building and cultural fluency.'[68] The sphere is surrounded by a membrane representing technology, which touches pervasively on each of the nodes. This pentalectic sphere, illustrated in Figure 1, is a compelling image for legal education reform – consciously chosen, dynamic, and evocative.

The sphere has multiple dimensions and any of them can have primacy at any given time, while still remaining related to the others.[69] As the figure shows, each node is connected to each other node, emphasizing that reform of one aspect of legal education affects all other aspects. The sphere is not flat but multi-dimensional, dynamic, and always interacting in complex ways with its environment. Based as it is on systems principles, the pentalectic sphere nudges reform in non-hierarchical, synchronistic, and non-sequential ways that match ways that students in the current generation learn.

A striking feature of the sphere as conceptualized by Efron is its basis in inquiry. Not a prescriptive tool, it is instead meant to serve as a focal point for curiosity and dialogue informed by contemporary learning theory. Existing as it does in a multi-dimensional spatial setting, the pentalectic sphere also accents the socio-political context in which legal education is always operating. In its textured, changeable form, the sphere constellates an alternative to more linear ways of conceiving reform. As Efron writes, a pentalectic sphere-inspired curriculum would be asymmetrical, dynamic, and flexible, with considerable variation across law schools. Because it envisions a dialectic process of ongoing questions and answers specific to contexts, the sphere could spawn and anchor diverse approaches to legal curricular reform.

As the Carnegie report authors emphasize, pedagogical innovation is an essential accompaniment to curricular reform. Experiential activities, embodied exploration, and dialogue using the figure as a focus could bring it to life in spacious and inspiring ways. The salience, potency, and impact of the metaphor itself are integrally interconnected with how it is applied

---

67 Y. Efron, 'The Pentalectic Sphere as a Means for Questioning Legal Education' (2015) IX *Arizona Summit Law Rev.* (forthcoming).

68 id., p. 3.

69 Y. Efron, 'The Legal Education Pentalectic Sphere as Inquiry: Towards a Paradigm Shift', Faculty colloquium, Allard School of Law, University of British Columbia, April 2015.

**Figure 1. Efron's pentalectic sphere**

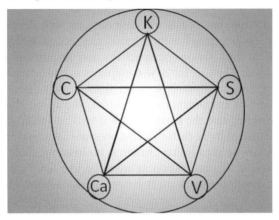

pedagogically. If scholars encountering the pentalectic sphere use it to foster creative, dynamic engagement with students, new spaces for reflection and innovation may further inform curricular changes. As a metaphor for pedagogical and curricular reform, the pentalectic sphere is not only a marked one; it seeks to inspire metacognitive reflection on the unmarked assumptions that keep outmoded metaphors securely anchored even as the whole world changes.

More remains to be done to examine the utility of new metaphors like the pentalectic sphere for spurring change in legal education. What appears clear from my review is that metaphors posing crisis have not catalysed substantial change. Perhaps lawyers and their counterparts in the academy have become inured to dire predictions. Perhaps legal scholars are too comfortable to be aroused from their somnolence. Or perhaps, as discussed earlier, legal identities and the structure of the legal profession itself form powerful unmarked metaphors that resist external pressures. Perhaps only more dramatic changes in legal practice will drive curricular change, like a tail wagging a dog. For change to happen, new conversations amongst legal professionals, scholars, governing bodies, policy-makers, and members of civil society are needed to uncover shared discursive frames rather than reproducing unrelenting dialogues of the deaf.

Signs of change are accelerating everywhere. In Canada, for example, two new firms have recently appeared, calling themselves matchmakers for prospective clients and lawyers. LawyerLinx and Kabuk Law use web-based directories and algorithms to make matches, taking into account clients' budgets and preferences for fee-per-hour or per-job billing.[70] The legal landscape is changing, and legal education must too.

70 J. Gray, 'Like Match.com, but for Lawyers' *Globe and Mail*, 8 June 2015, B3.

163

To guide this change, new kinds of conversations with deliberately chosen metaphors that signal urgency without crisis are needed. Kinetic images that invite engagement from various perspectives may inspire collaborative ways of moving forward. The call for new metaphors is widespread, though most often it is expressed in substantive rather than process-oriented arguments. Richard Susskind, a prominent legal futurist, draws on the metaphor of adaptation. Predicting that the legal landscape will be unrecognizable in only a few years because of three factors – cost pressures, disruptive technologies, and liberalization – he argues that change is no longer a choice.[71] If lawyers are going to survive as a profession in anything like the forms and numbers of the present, legal curricula must be reformed in ways that respond to current realities.

Already behind the change curve, legal scholars must find ways to think differently about law: its boundaries, its adaptation to technological shifts, and the pressure to do more for less. Susskind's challenge suggests nothing short of a multi-faceted sea change in how lawyers see lawyering and themselves in it, analogous to the Carnegie report's focus on needed identity shifts. All of this points to the urgent need for new metaphors to scaffold a large-scale change programme, metaphors that not only positively guide changes to legal curriculum and pedagogy, but also inform meaningful engagement processes that foster positive changes.

If, as Robert J. Lifton wrote, we live in a 'protean' age, legal education must mirror the humans we are coming to be.[72] Lifton contends that modern life is drawing us into developing fluid, many-sided personalities, restless yet comfortable with continuous exploration, dynamism, and experimentation. He envisions a society that increasingly disregards previously established traditions, one in which the continuities of previous times are no longer taken for granted. Does this mean discarding old identity attachments as lawyers and legal scholars? With which identity metaphors do we replace them? In the foreign country of the future, legal education and institutions alike will have to find ways of answering this question.

If law and legal education are to be part of the solution to the wide range of social ills we face, from alienation and violent conflict to potential economic, social, and environmental collapse, reform is imperative. Given the preponderance of voices that insist that change is urgently needed, legal scholars would do well to take a long step back and rethink the 'givens' of legal education, in terms of both pedagogy and curriculum. We can and should ask many questions, including whether black-letter law courses are still the most important staple of a legal education and how most effectively to communicate lawyering identities, values, and purpose.

71 R. Susskind, 'Tomorrow's Lawyers' (2014) 81 *Defense Counsel J.* 327.
72 R.J. Lifton, *The Protean Self: Human Resilience in an Age of Fragmentation* (1999).

Which social values will future lawyers best fulfill? Arguably, if lawyers are to be 'healers of conflict', then law schools need to meet the major contextual challenges that are radically altering practice.[73] They also need to model effective dialogue, engaging in data-rich, thoughtful exchanges that draw on best practices from process design and dispute resolution. Seeding dialogues with generative metaphors including innovative images like the pentalectic sphere may advance these much needed conversations.

## NEXT STEPS

There is little doubt that there is much time-sensitive work to be done. We are overdue to replace the tired metaphors of combat and revolution that shape conflict over curricular reform. Instead, we need to find collaborative ways to engage the change happening all around us. Dispute resolution scholarship has yielded numerous tools to design effective conversations, complete with careful attention to metaphors, marked and unmarked. The field of dispute process design remains disconnected from legal education reform efforts, but its insights into effective engagement and decision-making processes are urgently needed.[74]

At the same time, no single reform effort or process expertise will foster the lasting change needed. Change can and should arise from top-down policy change, from multi-sectoral consultations to imagine new ways forward, and from the bottom up as faculty members re-examine and re-adjust their metaphors and approaches to legal education. It should involve seamless interfaces amongst these three levels. Metaphors that connote spaciousness, context mindfulness, interconnectedness, and accountability are essential. Consciously chosen metaphors and sound dialogic processes are important steps toward embracing the transformation of legal education. As this is done, the petals of the rose that is legal education may be revitalized.

---

73 Chief Justice W.E. Burger's address to the American Bar Association Winter Convention, Las Vegas, February 1984.
74 A. Acland et al., *Dialogue by Design. A Handbook for Public and Stakeholder Engagement* (2012), at <http://designer.dialoguebydesign.net/Docs/Dialogue_by_Design_Handbook.pdf>.